DAFFODIL DAYS
Glamorgan's Glorious Summer

DAFFODIL DAYS

Glamorgan's Glorious Summer

Grahame Lloyd

Preface by H.R.H. The Prince of Wales
Patron, Glamorgan CCC

First impression – April 1998

ISBN 1 85902 593 5

Printed in Wales by
Gomer Press, Llandysul, Ceredigion

For the other 'team' in my life . . .
Nicola, Tom, Becca and Alys

ACKNOWLEDGEMENTS

My grateful thanks must go to everyone at Glamorgan CCC and, in particular, to the players and secretary Mike Fatkin. As well as editing the county's Year Book, Mike found the time to read the manuscript of *Daffodil Days* and then suggest appropriate amendments.

I am indebted to Matthew Engel for his Foreword, John Hardy and Phil Blanche for helping with the research of the book and David Irving and John Spencer for their part in tracing the missing 1948 championship-winner Jimmy Eaglestone.

My next door neighbour Peter Walker, from the Cricket Board of Wales, is well-known throughout the game for his keen eye and extremely safe pair of hands. They were as reliable as ever as he meticulously read the manuscript before returning it, complete with alterations, chapter by chapter, either at dawn or the dead of night, through my front door. I am most grateful.

The support and encouragement of my editor Dyfed Elis-Gruffydd at Gomer Press has been invaluable and, finally, I would like to thank the Somerset farmer and his wife who, quite inadvertently, provided the inspiration for the whole project. With half of Wales having apparently emigrated to Taunton for the championship-decider, accommodation was at a premium. My 12-year-old son Tom and I eventually managed to book bed and breakfast for the Saturday night at the couple's farmhouse on the outskirts of the town. We were to sleep in the snooker room – on a couple of camp beds rather than the table!

Glamorgan's three-day victory led to an unfortunate mis-understanding over the telephone and we arrived at the farm to find that our luxury accommodation had been double-booked. Tom and I spent the night in a small, four-berth caravan in the middle of the farmyard and it was there, as I reflected on such an incongruous end to such an extraordinary day, that the idea of *Daffodil Days* was born. I hope you will enjoy reading the result as much as I have enjoyed writing it.

G.L.
Cardiff, April 1998

CONTENTS

CONTENTS

ST. JAMES'S PALACE

As the Patron of Glamorgan County Cricket Club, I began to realise, as I followed the progress of Matthew Maynard's team during the season, that 1997 could prove to be one of the most memorable years in the Club's history. The achievement of winning the Britannic Assurance County Championship ranks alongside those of the sides led by Wilfred Wooller in 1948 and Tony Lewis in 1969 - the year of my Investiture!

The timing of the team's success could not have been better in view of Glamorgan's exciting plans to develop its headquarters ground at Sophia Gardens in Cardiff into a national cricketing centre of excellence.

It also brought a renewed pride to Wales and to the thousands of loyal supporters who have followed the fortunes of Glamorgan over the years. Congratulations to everyone involved in what I know was a real team effort.

FOREWORD

In rugby, the English and Welsh are mortal enemies. The clubs play in different leagues and the national teams engage in fierce annual combat. The Severn bridges could easily be hostile frontiers, with armed guards in the toll booths. There are even rumours that the Welsh regularly used to win these skirmishes. So my great-grandfather told me, anyway.

In football, the national teams are also separate, but it's different; nothing like as fierce, unless you happen to be on the terraces at a Cardiff-Swansea match. The three top clubs do weekly battle against the English, but used to find their pride only when they represented Wales against continental teams.

And in cricket it's different again. (Life is very complicated in the United Kingdom, you know. It is devilish hard to understand where nationhood begins and ends, never mind try and explain it.) Anyway, in cricket, the highest ambition of a Welsh cricketer is to play for . . . England.

But the second-highest ambition is to bash all 17 English counties on the head and make Glamorgan county champions. And that's what happened in 1997, for the third time in the past half-century. The funny thing is that many Englishmen were actually rather pleased. That would never happen in rugby.

The Welsh have an extraordinary record in the County Championship. It is almost as though they are trying to make some kind of subconscious point: that deep down they would rather not be taking part in this alien competition, but conducting their own Championship, with Pembrokeshire, Carmarthenshire and Merionethshire.

So they lurk round the bottom of the table, giving the English a false sense of security. Then, every couple of decades or so, they stage a ferocious ambush. Glamorgan's overall record in the Championship is not something to shout about too loudly. But only half a dozen English counties have won more titles since the war.

And when they win, the Welsh win delightfully. Glamorgan were a beautifully-balanced cricket team in 1997. Yes, the presence of Waqar Younis gave them the confidence that they could be champions again. But that confidence spread itself to every member of a small, happy, settled first-team squad. It was the perfect recipe for success.

The English didn't mind, really we didn't. Of course, we all want our own county to be champions. Failing that, most of us would settle for a team that plays on fresh, green fields rather than inside big-city concrete canyons; a team that draws strength from its supporters who both cheer from afar and come along to watch; and a team that draws enjoyment from its cricket, and spreads that enjoyment. Glamorgan fulfilled these criteria. And, at a time when the very concept of the Championship is under attack, this was good news for . . . well, English cricket.

Glamorgan's situation remains decidely confused. In 1998 there is apparently some new-fangled 38-county competition to do with amateurs and second teams. Glamorgan aren't in it, but Wales are instead. This is an idea from the England and Wales Cricket Board, which is known for short as the ECB.

But what if it happens again? If James has another season like the last one, if young Powell slots himself into the space vacated by Morris, if Crofty and Watty keep going, if Cosker and Thomas maintain their promise, and if Maynard holds them all together the way he did last year?

Why, they might have to take the sign down at Lord's and put up another one: The Wales and England Cricket Board. Known for short as the WCB.

Matthew Engel is a columnist on
The Guardian and editor of
Wisden Cricketers' Almanack

In Memory

Wilfred Wooller was standing on the summit on the three occasions Glamorgan have scaled cricket's Everest by winning the County Championship.

Twice in the flesh, once in spirit.

As captain of the 1948 team, the first Glamorgan side to win the blue riband event of professional cricket, Wilf had led by personal example. Fearless in the field and in his approach to opponents, abrasive in the use of the spoken word, Wilf implanted fear and drew grudging respect from all who took him on.

As a survivor of the Changi prisoner of war camp in Singapore, he left an indelible impression on all who came into contact with this most remarkable of Welsh sportsmen.

Arguably the finest all-round athlete ever produced by Wales, Wilf was a top-class tennis and squash player, good enough too to turn out at centre forward for Cardiff City and a living legend as a schoolboy rugby centre three-quarter for Cardiff and Wales. Tragically, the Second World War took 6 years of his sporting prime while capture by the Japanese in Java reduced the high stepping, powerful runner to a shambling shadow.

Wilf, or Skipper as everyone close to the game called him – to his face at least – returned to Wales in 1946 weighing a shade over nine stone, his sporting career a fading memory. But in typical Wooller style, there was much more to come. So very, very much more.

Together with fellow ex-POW and Cardiff RFC stalwart Les Spence, Wilf rebuilt his first love, Glamorgan County Cricket Club through a mixture of cajoling, pig-headedness, supplication and sheer determination. At that moment in 1948 in Bournemouth when 50-year-old Johnny Clay took the last Hampshire wicket to win the County championship for the first time since they'd become first class in 1921, it was Wilf, eyeball to eyeball with the batsman at forward short leg who joined pre-war Glamorgan batsman-turned-umpire Dai Davies in a yell that has become part of sporting folklore . . . 'That's out and we've won!'

Twenty-one years later, this time as secretary of the club, Wilf stood on the pavilion balcony at Sophia Gardens as Glamorgan swept Worcestershire aside to secure their second championship and said, with a magnanimity given to few sporting elder statesmen . . . 'This side is better than mine in '48.'

In 1997 and now President of the club he had served for nearly 60 years, even indestructible Wilf found the light fading. His death in March of that year separated Wales from its most dominating sportsman. But even without his physical presence, Matthew Maynard, Glamorgan's winning captain, in the last match of the season at Taunton, acknowledged Wilf as the man to whom he had regularly turned to for advice and who had loyally stood by him as a staunch supporter of the kind of adventuresome, combative approach to the game Maynard personifies.

Wilf left many cricketing legacies in the minds and memories of the generation of cricketers who played with and against him. Those who, like me, fell under his powerful influence, marvelled at his physical courage on the field, his all-round cricketing skills and, although fiercely disagreeing with him on many issues, particularly in the political arena, still respected his many and vigorously expressed opinions on the game and the society he lived in and often dominated.

Friend and foe, all have extraordinary personal memories of Wilfred Wooller, cricket's Colossus.

If Wilf had one quality above all others it was his ability to forget. Irrespective of how fierce the arguments on the field or in the bar that evening, the slate was wiped clean next day. No malice, no vitriol, always a new beginning.

As a 17-year-old, I had climbed the brown linoleum-covered stairs to the club's 2nd floor offices in High Street, Cardiff to agree a contract to become a junior professional on Glamorgan's books. Two years previously, I'd been spotted and coached at my school in Johannesburg, South Africa, by Allan Watkins, a leading all-rounder in the 1948 championship side. A quick bat and bowl in the depressing dark and dismal indoor nets, high in the old North rugby stand at Cardiff Arms Park, persuaded Wilf and an onlooking Johnny Clay that I might have the makings of a cricketer.

However, pausing on the steps, my confidence seeped away and I turned to go back into the street and another life when the office door opened and Wilf gruffly said, 'You're late. Where have you been? Come on in and let's get on with it!'

Eighteen years later, when my playing career came to an end, it was Wilf, still acting *in loco parentis* who found me a job reporting on Welsh club rugby for *The Sunday Telegraph* and encouraged me to broaden my business and commercial interests. He never stopped being a supportive father figure even when I was nearing pensionable age!

I learnt the art of close catching between two of its finest exponents, Allan Watkins, he of the dumpy build and prehensile fingers, and Wilf, all bristling aggression and self confidence – few who knew him well can ever remember him admitting he might be wrong on an issue close to his heart! From Wilf too came recognition that to succeed one had to be prepared to live with pain. I was at the backing up end when Frank Tyson, surely the fastest bowler who ever lived, hit him under the heart with a fearsome bouncer. Fifty-year-old Wilf, looked up from the bat handle he was crouched over in agony and, as Tyson and the other Northampton players crowded around to see if he'd been badly injured, dismissed the England fast bowler with . . . 'Bugger off, Frank, you're not quick enough to hurt me!'

Wilf once threatened me with the sack if I did not remain on the mark he'd scratched on the ground some six feet from one of the game's most fearsome hitters, the late Arthur Jepson of Nottingham.

Remember, these were the pre-helmet and body padding days. As the ball regularly flew past my head with 'instant death' printed on each shot, I'd gradually inched backwards at short square leg until a rare defensive prod by Arthur ballooned the ball in a gentle arc to where I should have been. I failed to make ground to the catch, hence the scratch mark and the threat. I have no doubt Wilf meant it. Typically, during the onslaught, he himself had not budged from his position right in front of the batsman at forward short leg.

So many moments, so many memories of a man who shaped the destiny of Glamorgan's fortunes and my own career for over half a century.

At Taunton on 20th September 1997, Don Shepherd, another of Wilf's adopted 'sons' and I stood on the television gantry trying to make ourselves heard over Robert Croft leading in song the crowd of Welsh supporters as they celebrated the team's magnificent performance in winning the game and the championship. They had proved themselves worthy successors to Don, myself and the others who formed the last winning team in 1969.

During the bedlam, I looked towards the distant Bristol Channel and Wales and thought . . . 'You should have been here, Skipper. They're out – and we've won!'

Whether Wilf is looking 'up' or 'down' on us from the hereafter, his friendship, his strength of purpose, his dedication to the cause of Glamorgan CCC will endure for as long as cricket is played in Wales.

Peter Walker

PART 1

Leading from the Front

A CAPTAIN'S INNINGS

GLAMORGAN won the 1997 Britannic Assurance County Championship because they were, quite simply, the best. Look in the book, or more importantly, at the final table. Therein lies the proof, in black and white. They finished four points clear of Kent to bring the title back to Wales after 28 years.

What you will not find hidden away among the minutiae of the scoresheets is any record or even hint of what might have been, so gossamer-thin is the difference between success and failure. Any season is littered with collections of the ones that got away – the spilled skyer in the deep, the agonisingly close run-out, the thick-and-thin edges put down in the slips. They are all part and parcel of cricket.

But there was one missed chance during the summer of 1997 which, in retrospect, perhaps provided more than a helping hand to Glamorgan as they lifted the game's premier prize for the third time in their 76-year first-class history. Catches win matches – they can also lose championships.

It is Saturday, September 13th, the fourth day of Glamorgan's penultimate game against Essex in Cardiff. Everything is going along swimmingly. In one of the wettest seasons on record, the weather has behaved and Paul Prichard's men have been forced to follow on. Steve Watkin's second five-wicket haul of the summer has restricted Glamorgan's Nat West Trophy conquerors to 340 and the team, not to mention the locals, scent victory.

To some supporters, the sweet smell is dangerously over-powering. 149 to win? No problem. How can it be with such a formidable and in-form batting line-up of James, Morris, Dale and Maynard? Three of them have already made runs in the first innings and hasn't Cottey, the vice-captain, showed signs of emerging from a nightmare season with a near half-century? Very timely, Tony. Pleased you're feeling better. Good to have you back.

Twenty minutes later, a packed Sophia Gardens is starting to fidget. Glamorgan are struggling at 13 for 2. Runs, rather than chickens, are suddenly being counted. Thoughts of a championship-clinching finale at Taunton are rapidly being replaced by memories of 31 all out against Middlesex in sixteen overs in June. It couldn't happen again – could it? Lightning may not strike twice but who said anything about fast bowlers?

For once, the run machine has broken down. James and Morris are back in the pavilion – courtesy of the new kid on the block, Ashley Cowan. It isn't looking good. All eyes focus on the Glamorgan balcony as Matthew Maynard prepares to make his way to the middle. As he strides over the boundary rope and heads for the square, sporadic cries of nervous tension punctuate the air – 'C'mon, Matt!' the most frequent, more a form of release than a shout of encouragement. Everyone is agreed that what is needed now is a captain's innings.

Cowan is in the process of earning his England call-up with a blistering spell from the Taff End. James has been bowled for his first championship duck of the season and Morris caught behind for four. It is a former Test bowler, Mark Illot, who is making the captain look unusually uncomfortable. Ill at ease at the crease, he would have been strangely out of sorts with a nought after such a magnificent season as both skipper and middle-order batsman. So far, Maynard has amassed nearly a thousand runs as his imaginative leadership has brought Glamorgan to the brink of the championship.

As Illot runs in from the Cathedral Road End, Maynard prepares himself before tentatively playing at a good length delivery. The ball flies straight into the welcoming glove of reserve wicket-keeper Barry Hyam. A definite nick and a definite chance. Neither difficult nor straightforward but certainly one you would expect to be taken. The ball drops from Hyam's right hand – it might have stuck in two. In and out. Maynard out, then in. Sophia Gardens gulps and heaves a collective sigh of relief.

Thirteen runs later, Adrian Dale is bowled by Peter Such and Tony Cottey joins Maynard at the crease. On the balcony, new coach Duncan Fletcher is unperturbed – 'someone else will get them if these two don't' – but around the ground, the crowd has slightly changed its tune. What is also needed now is a vice-captain's innings. Cometh the hour, cometh the men. In the event, neither main man nor right-hand man fail to deliver but it could all have been so different. Had Maynard been dismissed without putting a run on the board, who knows what might have happened? The scorer would not have been troubled – not so

Glamorgan's hopes of seeing a new name added to the roll of honour alongside Wooller and Lewis.

What followed represented the final evidence, if any were needed, that Maynard the Maverick had matured. In previous seasons, a quick dart to fifty or two-thirds of the way to a ton, would have often been ended by a flamboyant but injudicious stroke. The most naturally-gifted Glamorgan batsman of recent times had been capable of both infuriating and enthralling spectators in equal measure with his enormous talent.

Matthew's reprieve appeared to concentrate his mind on the job in hand. Aided and abetted by the man he had dropped and then courageously recalled, the captain led by example. From 34 for 3 at lunch, Maynard and Cottey saw Glamorgan home to a seven-wicket victory which took them one point clear at the top of the table and on to their date with destiny at Taunton. Having curbed his natural instincts, Maynard settled down to play one of his best innings for the county. Less spectacular than usual, it still contained enough derring-do to prompt one spineless spectator to implore him 'to hit 'em on the ground!' as, with the winning post in sight, the captain took control. By mid-afternoon, he and his deputy both remained unbeaten having put on 124 invaluable runs. Victory at Taunton and the title would be theirs.

'My innings against Essex was crucial,' is Matthew's modest memory of that Saturday in September. 'It was just a case of "can I bat?" Obviously, the session before lunch was pretty intense. The wicket had quickened up a little bit but it had become uneven – quick in some places and slow in others. It was more difficult to bat on than at any other stage in the game. The wicket dictated that you couldn't hit the ball on the up. If that's the case, then you don't try. It was turning quite prodigiously for Peter Such and the ball he bowled Adrian Dale with spun back a lot.

'When Cotts came in we said we'd stick it out until lunch. Essex were really gunning for us but the lunch break came at just the right time. If that first session had continued, then maybe they might have got a couple more wickets but in the first afternoon session, it was less intense – as it often is after lunch. They were still fired up but Cowan didn't quite put it in the same place, Illot's slower balls moved a bit but he didn't quite put them on the right line and Such began bowling a little bit too full.

'All these things played their part and once we got over the hundred, it was our game and it was up to me and Cotts to see us

5

through. We had done the hard work and we didn't want to throw it all away. It was a very big win for us and a very rewarding knock for me personally.'

According to Peter Walker, the commentator and former Glamorgan and England all-rounder who now runs the Cricket Board of Wales, the importance of Matthew's performance against Essex cannot be overestimated.

'I think it was the best innings of his career and, I suspect, of any Glamorgan player in the last 30 years,' says Peter. 'If we had lost that game, we would have lost the championship. Matthew played a wholly out-of-character innings – he hardly ever hit the ball off the ground. It was a majestic knock which, in terms of pure skill and temperament, had everything.'

Another member of Glamorgan's 1969 championship side, Alan Jones, the county's director of coaching, agrees with his former team-mate's assessment. 'People have often said Matthew is a great player who lacks the temperament for the big occasion. Against Essex, he came up trumps by batting absolutely brilliantly.

'In this game, you need a little bit of luck. He had it by being dropped and then he took on the responsibility. He knew that Tony hadn't been in very good form during the season and he realised that he had to see it through. He led from the front and showed the boys in the dressing room that they were good enough as a team to win the championship. It was a big partnership in a very big game which ended up as a hiding for the opposition.'

When the championship campaign began, Matthew Maynard was hoping to hand out hidings to quite a few counties following two crucial close season signings. In 41 Test matches for Pakistan, Waqar Younis had taken 216 wickets at a strike rate of just over 40 – way ahead of all-time greats like Marshall, Trueman, Hadlee and Holding. 'Waqar can win us four games,' the captain declared and he wasn't far wrong. Another important new face was coach Duncan Fletcher who'd arrived hot-foot from Western Province in South Africa with glowing references and a growing reputation.

'After finishing tenth and winning six of our seventeen games in 1996,' recalls Matthew, 'we started to believe in ourselves again. With the addition of Waqar, we felt we could actually do some-thing. We targeted our first three games to see how good we were. We had to look at results positively.

'After the weather had produced a draw against Warwickshire in the first game, I told the boys that we'd just outplayed the team of the Nineties. It was a good start, we took eleven points out of the game and we had to look forward. In Waqar's debut, we drew with Yorkshire after losing two sessions to rain on the final day but again it was a positive performance. I urged the lads to keep it up for the next game which we did in beating Kent, and our rewards then started to come.'

Matthew Maynard and Duncan Fletcher are the two members of a mutual appreciation society. Blood brothers as captain and coach, they were united from first ball to last, creating a special relationship based on the twin values of trust and respect. Together they meticulously mapped out a game plan to win the championship.

'We felt that if we scored as many runs as we did in 1996, we would have a good year,' says Matthew. 'We did occasionally go for six batsmen but more often than not we played five with Crofty at six because it gave me a full complement of five bowlers to try to win the game. Robert's a good batsman and there's no reason why he shouldn't get runs. To my mind, if our top five can't make runs, how is a youngster coming in at six going to get on? We went with that theory and it served us well.

'We had the added bonus of both Waqar and a left-arm spinner, Dean Cosker, which gave us an overall better balance. We went for Adrian Shaw behind the stumps because of his batting – he wasn't as good a keeper as Colin Metson but Adrian's a fine cricketer who was great in the dressing room. Having a happy dressing room was vital to me.'

The creation of a unique team spirit based on the side's Welsh roots proved the cornerstone of Glamorgan's success. The chain of command was clear: the team would be run by the captain with the help of the coach and a management committee made up of senior players. Duncan Fletcher would organise pre- and post-match sessions and undertake individual coaching.

'I got on well with Matt from the word go,' says Duncan. 'I had this rapport with him and I really enjoyed his outlook on life. We had a great working relationship right through to the end – it was brilliant.

'The captain is in charge, he's the general manager and I'm just a consultant so I said to Matthew: "You run the shop". A lot of other coaches want to be more involved and that's when you have clashes. When the pressure is on, the players must look to one person, one leader – the captain. I just think that Matt's a tremendous leader and individual. He captains with a gut feeling, he can read the game, and has this amazing ability to have a bit of an argument and then walk away as if nothing has ever happened.

'The management team was something I did want to introduce so I said to Matt that he should be general manager. We had a middle management of three senior players – Tony Cottey, Hugh Morris and Steve Watkin – and we sat and discussed strategies – whatever we were going to do. Everything came out of those meetings. I told Matt that he had to use the management team but, at the end of the day, he had to walk away and make a decision. Whatever it was, he would always have my support. That's what was great – we never undermined each other, we had this trust.

'For example, sometimes when a player was dropped, he would approach me for an explanation. "What did Matt say?" was always my first question and then I would expand on the selection. There are certain instances that no one knows about when Matt would come into my room and ask my advice. He appreciated that. We didn't always agree – that would have been crazy – but there was always support for each other.'

The two men were as one in their response to the disquiet generated by Glamorgan's collapse against Middlesex at Cardiff in the middle of June. A workmanlike victory over Durham by an innings earlier in the month had lifted the county to the top of the championship table for the first time in four years. Such heady heights appeared not to suit Maynard's men as they were dismissed for 31 by Middlesex, with James Hewitt producing a career-best 6 for 14 and Angus Fraser picking up the rest. Six of the wickets were leg-before and Middlesex won by an innings. While many supporters threw up their hands in horror, the captain and his coach threw back their heads and roared with laughter.

'The Middlesex result was a freak,' recalls Matthew, 'an amazing incident that wouldn't happen again. It was quite comical on the balcony. I was laughing and talking to Fletch as one wicket after another went down. It was just one of those things. For some reason, the wicket had just started to go up and down a little bit. There may have been a questionable lbw early on but, to be fair, Middlesex bowled straight and a lot of the time we played and missed, so the ball hit our pads or bowled us. It was one of those days – it was just a blip.'

'It didn't worry me at all,' says Duncan Fletcher, 'and I wasn't concerned about the effect it would have on the team. I had seen it happen before in our Sunday League defeat by Kent and I was then warned about such infamous Glamorgan collapses. That defeat by Kent worried me because we should never have lost – that was the most disappointing game all season for me because we played very badly that day.

'But through our meetings, we managed to instill confidence in the players and I think we made progress as the season went on. We got mentally stronger, the players became tougher as we showed against Essex in the Nat West semi-final. We weren't prepared to be bullied by the so-called big boys but the Middlesex collapse just happened.'

Four days later, Lancashire were on the receiving end of a remarkable backlash as Maynard's intuitive approach to captaincy influenced both the result and any doubting Thomas, Cottey, Watkin, or indeed Fletcher, in the Glamorgan dressing room. Having made 173 for 1 on the first day, the side kicked their heels because of rain until being fed them some easy runs on the final day to make a game of it. Maynard declared on 272 for 1 and then both sides forfeited an innings.

'The lads weren't too happy that I'd set Lancashire that size of target,' recalls Matthew. 'They thought it wasn't enough. I said, "If anyone goes out there with the belief that we're not going to win this game, then I don't want you on the field."

'We went out and Waqar and Watty did the damage. A career-best 7 for 25 for Waqar – including his first ever hat-trick – and 3 for 21 for Steve. All over in 14 overs. The wicket had been under cover for two days, Lancashire had a couple of guys away on Test duty and I fancied beating them.'

'Matt insisted that we set Lancashire a target of 273 to win,' recalls the coach. 'Even the management team didn't agree but, after we'd bowled them out for 51, everyone complimented Matt on such a brave decision. That's what was so good about this management team. Matthew had this amazing gut feeling and it was right.'

With the championship train back on track, Glamorgan arrived in Swansea to record two comprehensive victories. As he steamed into Sussex, Waqar re-wrote the record books with 8 for 17 as Glamorgan won again by more than 200 runs. Then a Morris-Maynard partnership of 223 set up the defeat of Gloucestershire as Dean Cosker finished with match figures of 7 for 146.

'We took full advantage of the poor season Sussex were having by beating them by 234 runs and then had a big win over Gloucestershire by 10 wickets,' says Matthew. 'They were up near the top of the table at the time and that thrashing showed just how good a side we were.'

Rain helped to produce two disappointing draws against Derbyshire and Nottinghamshire, and then Glamorgan lost at Worcester in what turned out to be only their second championship defeat of the summer. It was a mixed match for Maynard who scored a magnificent 161 not out, followed by a first-ball duck. His hundred, made off just 81 balls and including 20 sumptuous fours, prompted the former England and Worcester-shire batsman Tom Graveney to describe the innings as the best he had ever seen at New Road. For once though, the captain's instinct let him down.

'We had drawn with Nottinghamshire at Colwyn Bay which was very frustrating because we were playing some very good cricket,' recalls Matthew. 'The fact we had to play Northamptonshire next at Abergavenny on a flat wicket, which meant it would be difficult to get a result, was all the more reason to go for it at Worcester. We needed to win after the frustration of Colwyn Bay.

'Worcestershire batted quite well in the first innings, making 476 with Tim Curtis getting 160. We had a bit of a collapse, with me and Waqar seeing us past the follow-on. In their second innings, we missed a couple of opportunities to bowl them out for less than 295 – Weston made 114 – and, in the end, it was a very stiff target – 373 to win. Worcestershire didn't really have a specialist spinner – although Graeme Hick was playing – the wicket wasn't really turning anyway, it was a beauty – a real corker – and there was a short boundary on the leg side so I decided we'd go for it – all the way – but we lost by 54 runs.

'Having made my highest score of the season in the first innings, I got a golden duck in the second! That's the beauty of cricket.'

Without a win for a month, doubts were starting to surface about Glamorgan's chances of staying in the championship race. Some supporters and seasoned commentators were quietly questioning Maynard's judgement.

'I was very impressed with Matthew's captaincy,' says Don Shepherd, a member of the 1969 championship-winning side, who now covers cricket for BBC Wales radio and television. 'But I thought he went too far against Worcestershire when he went for the win and they lost. At the end of the season, those three points could have been vital. That win sent Worcester off on a run and they finished third with an outside chance of the championship at the end.'

'That said, Matthew has always been adventurous as a cricketer and it was thought that captaincy might stifle his natural ability but it didn't. He never ignored the chance of a win and he was backed to the hilt by all the players.'

After the abortive run-chase at Worcester, Glamorgan moved south to play Northamptonshire at Abergavenny where they were hit by injury before and during the game. In a pre-match touch-rugby session, Hugh Morris twisted his ankle and had to withdraw. Maynard then dislocated a finger while dropping a difficult chance in the slips. But Steve James decided it was time to make some personal history by scoring centuries in both innings as Glamorgan reached their target of 196 to win by 6 wickets.

'That win took us back to the top of the table,' recalls Matthew. 'We were building up quite a head of steam and playing some good cricket – as we had done all year.'

The momentum was immediately lost in a bizarre rain-affected draw against Leicestershire at Grace Road. The first day had been wiped out by the weather and then Glamorgan made 180 for 7 before being bowled out for 226 on the third. An inspired 7 for 41 by Steve Watkin saw Leicestershire skittled out for 175 and on the eve of the final day, Glamorgan were 118 ahead and confident of victory.

'For some reason, Leicestershire then made a decision to cut the outfield instead of covering a couple of wickets which had been damp before. The weather forecast was good but we had overnight rain and as soon as those wickets got wet again, there was no chance of playing. It was an absurd decision because you can play with the grass long but you can't play on a surface where you can't stand up. There was nothing sinister in it – just a breakdown in communication between the chief executive, coach Jack Birkenshaw and the groundsman.

'Their captain James Whitaker is a good friend of mine and he was very apologetic about what happened. He was disappointed as well because he felt they still had a chance of winning the game. I felt it was 60-40 maybe even 65-35 in our favour.'

There was more controversy in Glamorgan's next game against close rivals Surrey at the Oval. Maynard's 76 and one run less from Darren Thomas helped produce a first innings lead of 234 but after Graham Thorpe had made a career-best 222, Glamorgan were left

11

needing 254 to win. At 65 for 3, the captain decided that discretion was the better part of valour and settled for a draw. Once bitten, twice shy? Perhaps, though surely more a case of sound cricketing sense. Glamorgan collected eleven points and Surrey only eight. At a stroke, it became a three rather than a seven horse race for the title.

'Even if we had lost the championship,' insists Matthew, 'I was still right. We took 20 wickets in the game, Surrey didn't declare, Steve James had dislocated his finger, Adrian Dale had injured his back and I just didn't think there was any chance of us winning the game – we finished on 107 for 3. At the end of the day, I made a cricketing judgement. We could not have won that game and I made the right decision.'

Surrey were so incensed by Maynard's refusal to play ball that coach Dave Gilbert was unable to contain himself. As Kent beat Gloucestershire to move 12 points clear with two games to go, Gilbert laid his cards on the table by promising that Glamorgan could expect no favours from Surrey in the run-in.

'If there's any justice,' he declared, 'Kent will win the title because they are the best all-round side. They are prepared to lose games to win them.'

His words, as well as his club's debatable decision to 'rest' key players for their final match against Kent, only stiffened Glamorgan's resolve. In the event, Glamorgan scored at 3.8 runs an over compared with Kent's 3.3 and took a wicket every eight overs – one better than the championship runners-up.

'Some foolish comments were made by some people,' says Maynard, 'but nobody in the Glamorgan camp said anything publicly. Not me, nor Fletch or the players. It wasn't a case of us speaking to the lads about it – their reaction just showed we had that bit more determination to succeed. At the end of the season, Fletch said it all: "Glamorgan play with their hearts. Sadly, there is another team in the competition who seem to play with their mouths."'

As the championship race moved into the finishing straight, Glamorgan demonstrated that they, rather than Kent, had what it took to take the title. There would be no last-minute stumbles as the finishing line beckoned. Essex were beaten by six wickets at Cardiff, Somerset by ten at Taunton. From his vantage point of the commentary box, Don Shepherd sat back and admired the captain's handling of his side.

'Matthew seemed to have learnt the lesson of the Worcester-shire defeat by not opting for the run-chase against Surrey. He read the game correctly because, again, it was a very very long odds chance of winning and he didn't throw away the three points. Knowing that they had to get maximum points from their last two games was a huge burden which they came through exceptionally well.

'Matthew had only one year's full-time captaincy under his belt but leading the side gave his batting more stability and we saw some stunning innings. I don't think anyone will ever forget the one at Taunton. Hugh Morris provided the backbone but it was Matthew's brilliance and speed of scoring which gave Glamorgan the time to bowl Somerset out.'

Maynard's 142 which set up the championship-clinching victory over Somerset will rightly be remembered as one of the greatest innings in the county's history. With Matthew at his majestic best, it will rank alongside any produced in the 1948 and 1969 seasons. When the chips were down, he battered the ball in the direction of every advertising hoarding in the ground.

'We knew that if we had four days of cricket,' recalls Matthew, 'then we could beat anyone. I wasn't sure how much the wicket would do. It looked like it might seam around a bit so I spoke to the bowlers and they fancied it, so I gave them the ball. Waqar rose from his sick bed – he'd been suffering from a stomach bug – to pick up 4 for 41 and Steve Watkin chipped in with three as Somerset were all out for 252.'

When Steve James and Adrian Dale were both dismissed for 8, the county's two most senior professionals joined forces for what turned out to be the final time. Former rivals for the captaincy, the pair dovetailed perfectly. Hugh Morris provided the platform while his successor began his assault on the Somerset attack. By close of play, Glamorgan had reached 159 for 2. Maynard had raced to 76 off just 72 balls while Morris was a run short of his half-century.

In the summer of 1997, it was perhaps inevitable that the weather would continue to dog Glamorgan right up to the end. More than 2,000 championship overs had been lost to the elements and rain on the second day at Taunton meant play couldn't resume until 3.50 p.m. Having lost so much time, there was now none to lose. The immediate target was 200 and the first of four available batting bonus points.

'When Hugh and I went out to continue,' says Matthew, 'it was dark and getting darker. Remarkably, I know I didn't score a single in reaching a hundred but I didn't go out there with the intention of smacking every ball for four. As soon as you try to do that, you tend to get out. As soon as I got in, it turned out to be a nice batting wicket. I could hit the ball at the top of the bounce, it was a quick outfield and it was just one of those days when I hit the gaps.'

It was a masterful exhibition of attacking batting at its finest. The deteriorating light served only to inspire the Glamorgan captain. Four after four – twenty in all – fizzed to the boundary as he unleashed an awesome array of shots on his way to his third championship century of the season off just 89 balls. Poor Graham Rose could only watch in wonder as his good length off-stump delivery was turned nonchalently into an unstoppable on-drive for the milestone boundary.

The celebrations were brief and to the point. Off came the helmet – revealing the near-shaven hairstyle created by mistake in New Zealand in the winter, a symbol of the skipper's fierce determination. Short waves of his flashing blade acknowledged applause from supporters and team-mates alike and, after a brief handshake with his partner, it was back on with the helmet and back to business.

As Hugh Morris helped himself to four boundaries in an over from Andy Caddick, a top edge over the slips secured the first bonus point which edged Glamorgan to the top of the table above Kent. By the time Matthew had bludgeoned another 42 runs, the five lights on the scoreboard – as well as his team's championship hopes – were burning brightly. The end came immediately after umpire George Sharp had donned a pair of light-enhancing glasses. Matthew was caught at first slip off a Kevin Shine away-swinger with Glamorgan on 227 for 3.

'There was a lot of pressure on Matthew at Taunton,' recalls Alan Jones. 'We needed a big knock from him and from the first over, when he went back in on the second day, he just middled everything. Nobody could match him. Hugh Morris played a brilliant innings at the other end because he just let Matthew carry on in his own way while he dabbed it here and pushed it there. You can't compete with Matthew when he's going like that and Hugh knew that. Significantly, most of Matthew's runs came along the floor, he wasn't hitting the ball in the air very much.'

It was fitting that on the ground where one of his idols, Viv

Richards, had established his reputation, Matthew Maynard should graduate to matching greatness. Recklessness had been replaced by responsibility, the cavalier tempered by caution. Batting was made to look ridiculously easy. Head and heart in harmony. As the innings unfolded, Duncan Fletcher watched in awe from the Glamorgan balcony.

'As far as Matthew's reputation for being a bit of a maverick is concerned,' says the coach, 'I hadn't been told anything before I came. And, anyway, I wouldn't have listened. I'm a great believer in making up my own mind. I used to joke sarcastically with Matthew and pull his leg in an attempt to get him to realise his responsibilities. I'd say, "Oh – you're just a waste of talent!" but I was just trying to get to him. Maybe it worked, I don't know. I don't know if Matt would know. He's an incredible batsman – one of the best I've seen. His hundred in the dark at Taunton was unbelievably brilliant.'

The partnership of 235 with his predecessor had set the standard which his team-mates were keen to follow. In Matthew's absence, Hugh Morris took control before eventually being bowled for 165.

'On the third day,' recalls the captain, 'I decided to carry on batting and Crofty and Adrian Shaw chipped in with useful scores as we ended up with 527 all out. Somerset were 265 behind and made a solid start as they tried to avoid an innings defeat. They put on 60 for the first wicket on a track that was a belter for batting but Darren Thomas turned in a wonderful performance – 5 for 38 from 15 overs. I particularly remember the two balls he bowled to get rid of Rob Turner and Mark Lathwell. One did Rob for pace and nipped back, the other did Mark for pace and left him a little bit. Watty picked up three with Crofty and Dean Cosker taking one each. Once again, it was a good team effort but Darren especially bowled well.

'We needed eleven to clinch the title and it was nice that Steve James should hit the winning runs, after not being selected for the senior England tour.'

Victory at Taunton crowned a wonderful season for Matthew Maynard. Three times the captain had played truly memorable innings – against Worcester, Essex and Somerset; in every game he had skippered the side with brio, verve and imagination. After nearly three decades, Glamorgan were county champions again and his fellow professionals – past and present – were quick to pay tribute.

'Matthew is one of those extraordinary characters who, when he comes in to bat, makes you sit on the edge of your seat,' says Peter Walker, a co-opted member of Glamorgan's cricket committee as well as Director of Development at the Cricket Board of Wales. 'In the past, he was either going to blast you a quick 60 or something like that – or hit one straight up in the air just when his side needed him to stay in.

'The captaincy has transformed him and I'm delighted to see this has happened. On the cricket committee, all the people who played the game professionally – the substantial minority – had pushed for Matthew to succeed Alan Butcher as captain but had initially been outvoted. When Hugh Morris decided to step down in 1995, Matthew took over and took a season to find his feet. In 1997, he matured not only as a captain, because he would take chances where no chances existed, but also as a batsman.'

'Matthew is an excellent captain,' says Alan Jones, 'because he's not afraid to make mistakes. The game's never dead with him – there's always something happening. Over the last two years, I think the responsibility of captaincy has made him a better player than he's ever been. He's a brilliant fielder and I think England should give him another chance.'

According to Tony Lewis, former England and Glamorgan captain and club chairman, Matthew Maynard stands comparison with Ray Illingworth. 'As a kid, Ray always knew which way the wind was blowing, which way the grass was lying, he could feel it. He could make it very uncomfortable for batsmen, he was much more animal-like, more fox-like. Like Ray, Matthew's got what's become a natural cricketing intelligence. There's just something about him.'

'I shall never forget, when he was standing in as captain for Alan Butcher, Matthew tearing into Viv Richards who'd turned up late for practice. He was very positive about that sort of thing and you could see that, as long as the wheels didn't fall off, he would make an outstanding captain. I take nothing away from Hugh because he won us the Sunday League but Matthew definitely had it.'

'The great tragedy,' says Peter Walker, 'is that to date Matthew has been unable to translate his talent into the next rung up – at international level. Underneath a very positive exterior – it's not brash or arrogant, more supremely confident and articulate – I suspect lies a very nervous human being. When you take him up that one extra rung, he hasn't yet been able to deliver high quality innings when it matters, as he is able to now and I suspect as he

Magnificent Maynard . . . leading his side to victory over Essex.

(Doug Danter)

Former chairman David Morgan with the 1993 AXA Equity and Law Sunday League Trophy – a winner from start to finish.

Davis and Davies . . . Roger and Hugh in committee – setting the agenda.

Secretary Mike Fatkin . . . a baptism of fire, rain, wind and falling trees.

Director of Marketing Tony Dilloway with the coveted trophy . . . 'Now this is something I can *really* sell!'

Victoria, Joan and Caryl . . . the friendly faces of Glamorgan CCC.

In the nets . . . the director of coaching and the new recruit.

John Derrick looks into the future with Tony Cottey . . .
'Congratulations on your promotion, JD – what are you having to drink?'

Steve James making personal history . . . two hundreds against Northants at Abergavenny but still no England call-up.

The ECB's new Technical Director demonstrates just how he got the job.

'Any sign of an England selector yet?'

will do for the next five years or more. Had he been given a longer run in the England team, I think they would be talking about Matthew as they do about Graham Thorpe at the moment.'

As Glamorgan coach, Alan Jones has observed Matthew's progress through the county ranks. From scoring a century on his debut against Yorkshire in 1985 to lifting the championship trophy on the Taunton balcony, his career has included everything from unconventional dismissals – remember the helmet falling on the stumps when facing Michael Holding at Swansea? – to unpopular decisions: by joining the 1989-90 rebel tour to South Africa for which he received a two-year Test ban. But throughout it all, his ability to dominate an attack has never deserted him.

'Matthew has definitely matured as a player,' says Alan. 'Over the years, many of us have tried to impress on him the importance of keeping the ball on the ground. He says he gets a buzz once he sees it in the air. To hell with the buzz, as far as I'm concerned! If he keeps the ball on the ground, Matthew will get many many more runs. Last season, he was a fourteen-hundred run man, this year we'll be expecting more – perhaps eighteen hundred.'

Certainly, the departure of Hugh Morris to Lord's as the England and Wales Cricket Board's Technical Director will put more pressure on the captain to maintain his impressive average. His predecessor acknowledges his contribution to Glamorgan's glorious summer.

'Obviously, Matthew did a very good job for Glamorgan because at the end of the day, we won the championship. He had the help and support of senior players and his relationship with the coach was a key one. Duncan is an experienced person who's used to dealing with top-class players and he helped us all – particularly Matthew.

'Nobody can argue with his record of winning the championship and that's a great credit to him.'

Four years ago, Matthew Maynard and Steve Watkin had just returned from a largely disappointing trip with England to the West Indies. The Glamorgan representative in the Caribbean in 1998, Robert Croft, experienced a difficult summer as he alternated between county and country.

'Matthew was superb to me throughout the 1997 season,' recalls Robert. 'We didn't have a lot to say but on the few occasions when we had a beer together, I apologised for being a bit touchy because of my disappointing Ashes series. He told me it was alright and said I was important to the team. He knew what I was going through. I was never allowed to step out of line or take advantage but, at certain times, people were a little bit more understanding.

'As captain and bowler, we have many discussions on the field, which is right. I generally get what I want but if there's something that he'd really like to try then I'll go with that for a bit. It's a lot about learning together.

'I remember the way we got rid of Marcus Trescothick in Somerset's second innings at Taunton. I had a slip and a silly point and Marcus looked OK outside the off stump – nothing much was happening. So I started bowling a little bit straighter and he didn't look so happy then. I suggested that I bowl over the wicket but Matt said he wanted me to stay round. Why not bring the silly point round to short leg? I said Trescothick would work the ball away quite easily but two balls later, after Matthew had altered the field, he was caught at short leg by Steve James. That's just one instance of the way he read the game better than me.'

Steve James was also involved in another fielding change which demonstrated the captain's willingness to consider any option – no matter what its origin – in his search for wickets. After making 159 for Northants in their first innings at Abergavenny, Kevin Curran was targeted as a danger man. His habit of slashing wide outside off stump to Waqar had brought him a number of runs over the slips, so Steve James suggested he should move to fly-slip, a sort of no-man's-land.

'I thought Matthew might pooh-pooh the idea but he told me to go for it. "Wherever you think it's going to go," he said, "stand there!" So I did and sure enough, two balls later, Kevin put the ball straight down my throat. He was out for 2 and we went on to win by 6 wickets.'

After the championship celebrations, Matthew relaxed for a month with his family – wife Sue, 9-year-old Tom and Ceri who's 4 – before spending another winter as player/coach with Otago in New Zealand where he also captained an England X1 in a three-match Cricket Max series.

'I have no doubt that we won the title because we had a balanced side and a great team spirit – on and off the pitch. The backroom staff at the club have been tremendous. Of course, there were times when it got rough and tough with the more aggressive attitude we showed on the field. At times, it spilled over into the dressing room and in the warm-up soccer and rugby matches we had before the start of play. But I think it was a brilliant approach, very, very healthy – not just being nice all the time.

'During the championship, there were outstanding individual performances throughout the season but we didn't rely on one person. I think the key was the consistency shown by every member of the team.

'I was fortunate to have the bowlers to be able to try lots of things in the field. You've got to experiment, you mustn't become staid. When you're trying things all the time, batsmen have to be on their toes because they're not sure what's coming up next. You make sure that batsmen don't settle by moving fielders around a little bit so they start to question what's going on.

'I enjoy having that level of involvement in the game and that's why I've worked so hard on my fielding over the years. I love the game, it's been brilliant to me and I just want to be as big a part of it as I can. I've realised my dream of captaining a county club but I just go out and be the same person that I've always been.

'I don't believe I captained the side any differently in 1997 than I did the year before. We had a better structure in place this year with Duncan and, with Waqar and Dean Cosker, the balance of the side had changed. Duncan's input on a one-to-one basis was tremendous. His work rate with the players was excellent and he was a very good coach.

'I think I have matured as a batsman over the last couple of years – I averaged over 60 in 1996 – but I'll still be playing those cameo innings! If I go on to make 140, then great. If I get out at 70, well, that's the way it is. That's the way I play my cricket and I'll carry on that way.'

Matthew Maynard is a big Manchester City fan so he knows all about backing losers. As the other team in Manchester have swept all before them, Matthew has been on the receiving end of a fair amount of ridicule in recent years. But no more will he be associated with a losing cricket side. The team which finished bottom of the championship five times between 1976 and 1989 have silenced their critics by winning cricket's version of the FA Carling Premiership. They may have been unfashionable but in 1997 Glamorgan proved uncatchable.

In the history of the county championship, only four sides have managed to retain their titles outright. The 1969 Glamorgan team finished third a year later. Matthew knows that making history by emulating Manchester United won't be easy.

'We have to set out to become a consistently good side in the next five or six years. That means finishing in the top six of the championship. If we do that, we're going to win the title every now and then. Our realistic ambition has got to be to stay up there. Saying that we're going to retain the championship is a huge challenge. A top six finish will be quite an achievement. We have to go out there with the same attitude as we had in 1997 – we can't relax, if anything we have to work even harder. The challenge for us is to remain at the top and to play in a Lord's one-day final.'

In Glamorgan's 1997 Year Book, Matthew Maynard thanked everyone for their contribution to his successful benefit season. In an open letter, he observed that he had also been appointed captain and enjoyed an England recall during 1996. His message, short and sweet, concluded with the following wish:

'I hope I can repay all the supporters with a 1997 season to remember.'

Surely not even he can have imagined how significant those words would sound come September? Six months later, benefit buckets of notes and coins had been exchanged for a priceless myriad of memories. Thanks for those, Matthew.

PART 2

Behind the Scenes

WITH RESPECT, MR CHAIRMAN

DAVID Morgan might well go down in history as the most successful chairman of Glamorgan County Cricket Club.

Having marked his elevation to the post by winning the Sunday League in 1993, the players ensured that his swansong would be even more memorable by lifting the championship title four years later. By going out at the top, David will now combine his job as commerical director of one of Europe's biggest specialist steel manufacturers with a burgeoning career as a cricket administrator in London.

The chairman's association with Glamorgan began nearly twenty years ago when Robin Hobbs was parachuted in from Essex to captain the county. David Morgan decided enough was enough and, thanks to scorer Byron Denning, won a place on the committee.

'I was a very dissatisfied member and supporter,' recalls David, 'and we had just imported a skipper from the south-east of England. How on earth can you make decisions like that?' I demanded of Byron.

'Morgan,' he said, 'I'll propose you for the committee and then you'll see how difficult it is to change anything!'

'He did, I was elected and we've been friends ever since!'

After making his mark in marketing, David became deputy to Tony Lewis when the former captain took over as chairman in 1988. Over the next five years, the seeds of Glamorgan's 1997 championship success were sown. They began to bear fruit when Viv Richards first planted his foot down the wicket in 1990 and started knocking the side into shape.

'I've always said that the Sunday League success and the excellent championship performance in 1993 was due to Tony Lewis rather than me,' says David. 'Tony and the then club secretary, Phil Carling, deserve immense credit because they brought Viv Richards to Glamorgan. Viv made the team much better competitors. Tony did a great deal to improve the image of the club and I've taken on the lead he gave.'

Skipper Matthew Maynard also acknowledges the huge debt owed by Glamorgan to the captain of the last championship-winning side. He traces the turnaround to the signing of another international batsman – albeit one less decorated than the former West Indies captain. Alan Butcher may have been another import from south-east England but the new pastures he was seeking were not for grazing.

'Tony initiated the revival by recruiting Alan from Surrey,' says Matthew. 'A lot of positive thinking came through before Viv arrived, and Tony and Alan were responsible for that. It's certainly true that, thanks to Viv, we became a tougher side to beat.

'He had a huge influence on me personally in terms of batting and attitude. Unless you play and you learn, you can't really understand it. It's a bond that you get out there together in the middle. I just looked at the way in which Viv went about things. It wasn't just one thing that he gave me but lots of little things that I picked up.'

Viv Richards spent three years with Glamorgan as their overseas player in the early Nineties. Ravi Shastri, the talented Indian left-arm spinner, had become more effective with bat than ball and the county decided to think big. Richards was the result.

'I think Viv was the turning point,' says Tony Lewis. 'Signing him gave the crowd a lift – they couldn't believe that he would come to Glamorgan. Some of the players, whether it was their pride or their own talent, weren't totally prepared to admit that his arrival was important, because there was a downside to Viv. He had a lot of personal problems at the time and he wasn't perhaps an easy guy in the dressing room. He hadn't been with Somerset, so we knew what we were buying.

'But he was chosen to raise the profile of Glamorgan and to see him bat and field at his best was unbelievable. He wasn't a bad bowler either. He was a consummate world-class professional – which did rub off – but I wouldn't take anything away from the other boys out there.

'When the team arrived at, say, Grace Road in Leicester, I really wanted all the kids to run towards our cars for autographs. I wanted Viv to walk out to bat chewing gum slowly and then spit it out and whack it with his bat as he came back to the pavilion – whether he hit 0, 10 or 110. We just needed a bit of swagger and confidence. In the field, he was terrific – he kept the boys alive. He told me that he'd never been to any county just to fill in the time – he'd actually come to win something – and I was pleased for him that we did.

'The players all developed alongside him and they won some surprising games, but some of them will say that when runs were needed Viv never got them – and that, too, could be right. But he had an arrogance that was bred from self-confidence which had a positive effect on the players around him.'

Having served his time as chairman, Tony Lewis stood down to continue his career as writer and broadcaster, and chairman of the Wales Tourist Board. Bearing a strong resemblance to a bank manager or accountant, his successor David Morgan methodically went about the business of updating the club with quiet, unfussy determination. Less high-profile, perhaps, but just as effective. The championship trophy within four years and an undreamt of expansion of the county circuit's Cinderella club constitute a lasting legacy.

'The role of the chairman,' says David Morgan, 'is to provide the environment for cricketers to succeed. Our biggest achievement off the field has been the purchase of Sophia Gardens. We've had to borrow money and win grants from organisations like Sportlot and the Sports Ground Initiative, as well as keep our bank on side. The Midland needed to be convinced that Glamorgan was being run in a modern, business-like fashion.'

At the beginning of 1997, the administration of the club was streamlined. By reducing the number of committees, Glamorgan speeded up and improved their decision-making process. 'It was a very important thing to do and no one can look at Glamorgan now and say the club is run on an amateurish basis.

'We decided that we would amalgamate the cricket and coaching committees into one – the cricket committee. There was a new business committee, which took over the former responsibilities of marketing and finance, and a management committee. So we had three committees instead of half a dozen.

'We've also decided that certain matters should be determined by the management committee. For example, when we used to recruit or dispense with the services of a player, it was the responsibility of the cricket committee. Their recommendation had to be approved by the management committee and in turn by the executive committee.

'Now, if the cricket committee want to offer a player a certain length of contract, they simply bring that as a recommendation to the management committee who either approve it or refer it back to cricket to think through again. It takes out a link in the chain and enables us to behave in a more business-like way.'

25

This reform will hopefully prevent a repetition of the highly embarrassing incident towards the end of the 1996 season when a number of players were released. That year's beneficiary Steve Barwick, Neil Kendrick, Alistair Dalton and James Williams learned of the decision to let them go while playing for the second team against Worcestershire at Barnt Green near Birmingham, and two of them immediately downed tools.

'It was just the wrong way of doing it,' admits David Morgan. 'Now, these sorts of decisions can be made on the night by bringing the small management committee together immediately after the cricket committee meeting.

'This change – along with a number of others – provides the bedrock for Glamorgan's future. Our cricketers can see that they're operating within a good organisation.'

Another important change saw the twin promotion of Mike Fatkin and Tony Dilloway to secretary and director of marketing respectively. 'When Gwyn Stone retired after five years as secretary in October 1996, we implemented a revised admin-istrative structure which involved the appointment of two senior executives, Mike and Tony, from within the organisation which Gwyn had headed.'

During the course of transforming Glamorgan into the Prince Charming of English cricket, the county enlisted the support of Paul Russell, a partner in Andersen Consulting, one of their major sponsors, and Richard Weston, the corporate director in Wales of National Westminster Bank. 'They've been of immense help to our committees by bringing their business acumen to the club in terms of buying the ground, deciding how to fund the purchase and making applications for grants,' says David Morgan.

'We have also modernised the presidency. Wilf Wooller, even in his later years, did so much to make us believe in ourselves. He was the long-term thread running through the club and when he died in 1997, we decided that the president should serve for two years and not be re-electable. Gwyn Craven was elected to succeed Wilf.'

Having overseen such an overhaul, it seems strange that David Morgan has resigned as chairman. He quit while he was ahead but wouldn't he liked to have stayed for what is likely to be the most exciting era in Glamorgan's history? Yes but no: David felt he had done his bit. In a variation of the club-versus-country theme, his call-up to the national administrative team as chairman of the First

Class Forum – under the auspices of the new England and Wales Cricket Board – meant that his commitment to his county could not be guaranteed. Clearly, Glamorgan's loss will be England's gain.

'I've stood down because I've always thought that five years is about right,' says David. 'You have a certain style of management for a certain period, then I think change is appropriate. In my case, it was easier for me to move aside because I've got these challenging and interesting things to do at Lord's in my role with the First Class Forum and as deputy chairman of the England and Wales Cricket Board.'

1997 proved a busy year for David Morgan and a watershed for county cricket. After the ECB's chairman Lord MacLaurin had suggested a two-divisional championship in his document, *Raising the Standard,* the First Class Forum, representing the MCC and the eighteen first-class counties, put up the shutters on such a radical option. Critics like Ian Botham had wanted to sweep away the cosiness of county cricket but, by 12 votes to 7, the FCF decided the *status quo* should prevail – at least for another three seasons.

But there will be two divisions in a new 50-over national league to replace the Axa Life competition, an enlarged Nat West Trophy and a 'Super Cup' for the top eight teams in the 1998 championship instead of the Benson and Hedges Cup.

'Both my jobs at Lord's are fairly demanding and time-consuming so there'll be plenty to occupy me but I won't stop watching Glamorgan,' says David. 'The club is an integral part of my life – it's one of my three passions – along with wine and reading newspapers.

'I made the decision about a year ago that if I was re-elected to the FCF chairmanship for two years, then I would give up the Glamorgan job. My work as commercial director of European Electrical Steels at the Orb Works in Newport takes me all over the world. We have other companies in Sweden, Canada and America, so it involves quite a lot of travel – mainly from Heathrow.

'I'm obviously sad to have left but I'm sure someone else will come along and do as well if not better. There are pangs – leaving it behind was not easy. If I hadn't have had my Lord's commitment, it might have been impossible to stand down. But if I'm going to do justice to my ECB job and continue to fulfil my business obligations, then something had to go.'

27

As he reflects on his five years at the helm, David Morgan is proud of the progress made under his chairmanship. 'I feel I'm leaving the club in a good state. There's a significant negative bank balance but we have a splendid cricket ground in the making. Five years ago, it didn't look as if we had a hope in hell of actually buying Sophia Gardens. We were looking in Cardiff Bay, Swansea, Pontypridd and Pentwyn in Cardiff but Sophia Gardens was the place we really wanted all the time. We've been very lucky. It's been costly but well worthwhile. The championship win came at absolutely the right time.'

David Morgan also believes the public perception of Glamorgan has changed for the better. By winning the title, the Welsh county struck a blow for the underdog – the country cousins came to town and walked off with the biggest prize of all. Glamorgan met the challenge from the south-east head-on and emerged victorious.

Their long-awaited success may have put Glamorgan back on the map but will it mean more of the county's players being picked for England? Few of the Glamorgan faithful are likely to share David Morgan's view that playing cricket west of the Severn Bridge is anything other than an occupational handicap to England selection. The treatment of Morris, Maynard and Watkin in the early 1990s has hardly been offset by Croft's inclusion in the last two years.

'I'm never happy when Glamorgan members, and Welsh journalists in particular, claim that our cricketers stand a poorer chance of playing for England than those with Hampshire or Sussex or counties in the south-east of England. I know Steve James has been unlucky but when you look at the people who have represented their country at full and A level, we are no longer an unfashionable club.'

Another former Glamorgan chairman with strong links with Lord's supports David Morgan's assessment. 'I don't think that an anti-Welsh or anti-Glamorgan bias existed when it came to choosing the England team,' argues Tony Lewis. 'The only really unlucky one was Matthew because he was picked for that Fifth Test against the West Indies in 1988 and not against Sri Lanka. They played Kim Barnett instead.

'People who think that Welsh cricketers haven't had a fair crack of the whip are wrong. Selectors always look at good sides although I accept that you can rightly question the number of Lancashire and Surrey players in recent England teams – especially as those two counties can't beat anybody in four-day cricket.

28

'But I think our guys have had a chance and a view has been taken of them at that level. Matthew lacked so much self-confidence at international level but I think he could still come back and captain England and bat at number six with great success.'

David Morgan also maintains that the Welsh presence in the corridors of power at Lord's reflects Glamorgan's growing stature within the game. 'Look at the people sitting on ECB committees. Gerard Elias is chairman of discipline, Hugh Davies serves on pitches and Hugh Morris, until recently, was involved in the appointment of umpires. Now he's got a top full-time job as Technical Director at Lord's where he'll be responsible for the whole future shape of cricket development in England and Wales.

'All of those things are important. I don't think we are perceived in the game as the hicks-from-the-sticks anymore and I think our organisation is such that we need never revert to that situation again.'

Everyone – administrators, players and supporters – is agreed that Glamorgan County Cricket Club has come a long way in the 1990s. On and off the pitch, the team looks fighting fit. Tony Lewis, now a trustee who 'just signs the leases', believes the club can look forward to the new Millennium with confidence.

'I think Glamorgan got a few things right some years ago when we reduced the staff and tried to consolidate by paying decent wages but you should always review your set-up to make it more professional all the time. David Morgan was unflappable and his successor Gerard Elias thoughtful and, obviously, as a QC, strong legally. Both have been happy to take on board the opinion of those who know cricket better than they do.'

Hugh Davies has been chairman of the cricket committee for all of David Morgan's term of office. 'David has been a good guiding influence who's played the part of chairman really well. He's well respected outside Glamorgan too.'

In what turned out to be his final season, the retiring chairman managed to see every championship game but one – the 221-run, rain-affected win over Lancashire at Liverpool in the middle of June.

'I never take holidays in the cricket season so I can go to as many matches as possible. I was at Lord's for the Second Test against Australia at the time of the Lancashire game,' he recalls. 'It was raining in London, so I walked around to Gareth Williams' office – he's the man from Pontardawe who runs the ground at Lord's – where a few people had gathered.

'"Glamorgan have won then?" Gareth said to me as I wandered in. This was about five o'clock in the afternoon.

'I looked at him in amazement! He then explained that Waqar had done the business with 7 for 25. I shall never forget the casual way in which Gareth told me – I couldn't believe my ears of course, because there'd been so much rain in Liverpool!'

Among his other vivid memories will be the fightback against Yorkshire in the Nat West Trophy quarter-final at Cardiff in early August. Despite suffering from chicken pox, Matthew Maynard had top-scored with 62 before Waqar, Steve Watkin and Dean Cosker scored the runs to take Glamorgan to Chelmsford and the infamous semi-final defeat. David also witnessed the abortive run-chase at Worcester.

'I saw much of the Worcestershire defeat,' recalls David. 'Matthew had scored a terrific hundred, stylishly and quickly, in the first innings but then was out first ball on the final day. But still, we fought hard and lost by 54 runs. It did look as if our championship chance had perhaps gone but the team had shown terrific spirit even in defeat and bounced back to take the title.

'When the trophy was handed over to Matthew on the balcony at Taunton, my feeling was one of relief. I was simply thankful because I had written in my message to members in the Glamorgan Year Book that we had underachieved so often in the past.

'The season was so rewarding in so many ways that I have a succession of wonderful memories with very few lows. One of the highlights was the trip to Buckingham Palace in November to meet Prince Philip, the permanent twelfth man for the Lord's Taverners charity team. There was the disappointment of Chelmsford, of course, and that's one regret I have – that during my time as chairman, Glamorgan didn't reach the final of a one-day competition.

'On the other hand, when we do, the new chairman will have one hell of a job deciding who's going to go into the Glamorgan hospitality box on the day – that's the poisoned chalice that I'm passing to my successor!

'I've been to every Lord's final for the past twelve years and it would have been lovely to be the chairman of one of the two counties taking part. Winning the championship though is the absolute prize.'

The initial feeling of relief was later followed by quiet satisfaction and then sheer emotion. Having sampled some

Somerset hospitality in the Taunton pavilion, David and his wife Ann returned to their home in Newport. Their son Jonathan and his girlfriend Siân arrived with more chilled champagne. The following day, as the players recovered from the night before, the Morgans attended morning service in the neighbouring village of Caerleon.

'When we won the Sunday League in 1993, the then vicar of St Cadoc's Church, Canon Philip Morgan, was very keen on cricket. About halfway through that season, we were in with a chance of the championship as well and I jokingly asked him to pray for us! It became a running gag until the end of the season and it obviously paid off!

'Halfway through last summer, the new vicar, Canon Arthur Edwards, was told about his predecessor's prayers and he promised to continue the tradition. The most emotional moment of the season for me came towards the end of the service just before the final prayer.

'The choir had processed to the vestry and the vicar and the curate were at the back of the church. Canon Edwards said he thought the congregation would like to congratulate David Morgan on Glamorgan's success. That was real emotion because it was completely unexpected. I was sitting in the pew with Ann and, although there wasn't a round of applause, there were plenty of handshakes on the way out – it was quite something.'

Having helped to galvanise Glamorgan into grasping the nettle, David Morgan has reluctantly resigned as chairman. His leadership was characterised by diligence and discretion. Steel by business, steel by nature. By pulling together the various talents of committed committeemen and dedicated staff and players, David Morgan moulded the county into a thoroughly modern cricket club on the threshold of a brand new era.

According to their promotional brochure, David's company, European Electrical Steels, are in 'pursuit of perfection – efficiency, accuracy and flawlessness'. Glamorgan have still some way to go but at least under David Morgan, they have at last fulfilled their potential. For that achievement alone, he deserves much credit. A trophy at either end of his term of office is no mean feat. David Morgan will prove a hard act to follow.

In the Committee Room

SAME surname, different spelling. Same background, different generation. Same aim, different style.

Hugh Davies and Roger Davis, both former county cricketers, serving on the same committee with one objective – to rid Glamorgan of their record as under-achievers.

Since the championship win of 1969, the county had reached just one one-day final – in 1977 – and won just one trophy – the Sunday League in 1993. The Canterbury Tale's happy ending saw glasses and hopes being raised as a promising crop of home-grown cricketers at last secured some silverware for the Sophia Gardens trophy cabinet. It looked as if the corner had been turned.

But third place in the championship, a Nat West Trophy semi-final and the Sunday League title proved a false dawn. Glamorgan returned to the bad old days of promise, potential but poor performances. Without the inspirational Viv Richards, they finished bottom of the championship in 1994 and 16th the following year.

Under the chairmanship of Hugh Davies, members of the cricket committee braced themselves. Something had to be done. It was time for the Welsh county to deliver – and difficult decisions had to be made.

'We missed Viv's charisma,' says Hugh, who took 115 wickets at 31 apiece for the county between 1955 and 1960 and who had chaired the committee since late 1992. 'His replacement, Ottis Gibson, took time to settle and ended up having quite a good year with 60 wickets but it was generally felt that 1994 was a one-off – we couldn't be that bad again! In 1995, we struggled again with Hamish Anthony returning to the county as a late replacement for Ottis who was on the West Indies tour of England. But it was another bad season.'

In the late summer of 1995, with Hugh Morris having resigned and been replaced as captain by Matthew Maynard, the cricket committee drew up a three-year development plan.

'We looked at the situation and we felt we had to improve as a four-day side,' recalls Hugh Davies. 'We were busy negotiating to buy Sophia Gardens from Cardiff Athletic Club but financial and marketing activity had to coincide with success on the field.'

An outside coach was the number one priority with Dave Gilbert, fresh from a tour with Australia A, being targeted after an audacious but abortive attempt by Roger Davis to bring Ian Botham to Wales.

Roger is the only member of the 1969 championship-winning side and capped player to have been elected onto the present cricket committee. Fellow all-rounder Peter Walker is a co-opted member. Roger's 12-year Glamorgan career ended abruptly and acrimoniously in 1976 when he received a mid-season letter from the committee threatening not to renew his contract. The previous season had been his best: 1,300 runs, including 90 against the Australians.

But in 1992, when then chairman Tony Lewis wanted to increase the number of experienced ex-players on the committee, Roger returned to the fold. Three years later, he was calling for a radical re-vamp of Glamorgan's coaching structure. A loose cannon perhaps, no one has ever doubted Roger's commitment to the county but his impetuosity meant more than a few feathers were ruffled when he contacted England's greatest living all-rounder without approval.

'Before we tried for Dave Gilbert,' recalls Roger, 'I threw Ian Botham's name into the melting pot. I approached his agent Nick Lee because I was so keen to get somebody new. The word came back that Ian was interested so I handed the matter over to the committee. In the end, no agreement was reached with Ian or his agent. His commitments with Sky TV would have limited his availability.

'Later, I drew up a short list of about ten candidates including Desmond Haynes, the former West Indian batsman who may well have turned out to be a mistake in view of what's happened to Sussex.'

David Morgan was less than impressed by the initiative shown by Roger Davis. After contacting Nick Lee, the chairman decided not to bother with Botham. 'In my view,' recalls David, 'it would have been an extremely expensive arrangement which had no chance of working. Once Roger realised that I wasn't prepared to bring Botham to Glamorgan – I just didn't feel he would be right for us – we tried for Dave Gilbert. It became a race between us and Surrey but his wife wanted to be somewhere close to London so I realised that he was going to go to Surrey, come what may.'

'In retrospect,' says Roger Davis, 'I think Ian may have been the wrong person but I just wanted somebody to come and shake up the whole place. I think he may have shaken up too many people but we had to have somebody in to put his finger on why the team weren't performing as a unit and to do something about it.'

With no obvious high-profile ex-international available, Glamorgan turned to one of their own to fill the gap. John Derrick, the second XI coach, agreed to step into the breach. 'Rather than just going and getting somebody for the sake of it,' says Hugh Davies, 'we decided to stick with what we'd got and brought in John as first team coach to help Matthew with the pre-match drills. We made John a sort of support coach to the first team and he did a good job.

'Matthew had his first full season as captain in 1996 and we did win six championship games in our best year – apart from 1993 – since 1975. It represented an improvement.'

Roger Davis was less convinced. He felt the need for an outsider to coach the team was more pressing than ever. 'Matthew was the right appointment but there was still something lacking. We had a good team that was under-achieving and if that had gone on for another three or four years, the players may have finished or retired or got fed up and gone.

'The coaching staff had done a good job in bringing most of the team through but the old system wasn't working – something had to change. We had a newish captain and we felt Matthew needed someone on his shoulder to help him. I thought it was unfair to promote John because that wasn't what we had appointed him for.'

Towards the end of the 1996 season, the cricket committee decided to take the bull by the horns. Three problem areas were identified: the search would begin in earnest for an overseas coach, a world-class strike bowler and cuts in staff.

'We wanted somebody completely from outside,' explains Hugh Davies, 'because we felt that most of our players had a Welsh background, they had all been brought up together and the dressing room was very insular. We talked to every player on a one-to-one basis to ask them their opinion.

'We got the feeling that they wanted someone around to help them on their technique, someone who'd never seen them play and who would have a different approach. We needed new and fresh ideas in Glamorgan because the game was embracing sports psychology and new drills and practices.'

'The players wanted someone with new ideas,' agrees Roger Davis, 'who they could talk to about their performances back in the dressing room. They wanted a motivator, not a big name who would lead from the front but someone they could talk to and confide in to sort out their problems on a one-to-one basis.'

A two-day innings defeat by South Africa A at Cardiff in July helped Glamorgan to see the light. As the tourists' coach Duncan Fletcher took his young charges to Somerset and then Worcester, Hugh and Roger, suitably embarrassed, retreated to the committee room.

'I felt South Africa A were a highly professional, organised outfit,' recalls Roger, 'and I made some enquiries about Duncan. I think Matthew had mentioned his name when we had been discussing Dave Gilbert.'

Peter Walker had also been busy. As well as sounding out the former Australian coach Bobby Simpson, he had spoken to an old friend, Dr Ali Bacher, chief executive of the United South African Cricket Board. Ali confirmed that, in his view, Duncan Fletcher was the man for the job: a strict disciplinarian and an astute tactical brain – just what Glamorgan needed.

'We heard that he was on the short list of two with Bob Woolmer for the South African coach's job,' recalls Roger, 'but he withdrew because he felt he needed more experience.'

When avuncular chairman and impulsive member put their heads together, the penny started to drop. Would New Road provide Glamorgan with a new coach? It was time to find out.

'We went to Worcester to talk to Duncan about the job and what we wanted him to do,' says Hugh. 'He said he was prepared to think about it but because he had to sort it out with his South African employers, Western Province, he wouldn't be able to let us know until November. We were taking a bit of a gamble in waiting but I was so impressed I felt we should stay with it.'

Within thirty minutes of arriving in Worcester, Roger Davis realised the importance of their visit. 'Duncan wanted to be involved in the way that we wanted him to be involved. It had to be like 1969 where the captain ran the show with a coach on his shoulder. We didn't have a coach as such then, but there were some very experienced older players like Peter Walker and Don

Shepherd who were a great help to Tony Lewis. They were the Duncan Fletchers of 1969.

'We were very impressed with Duncan. It's amazing – you meet somebody for just over half an hour – I was convinced. He didn't say much but what he did say had been well thought out. He was very organised.'

Having made their approach, the cricket committee had to sit back, wait and hope. Like the proverbial Canadian Mountie, Hugh Davies was determined to get his man.

'I spoke to Duncan a couple of times before their tour ended. He knew his cricket backwards and came across as very conscientious. As director of cricket for Western Province, he was very aware of the off-the-field influences, like sports science and psychology. It was a question of whether Western Province would be prepared to let him come out of contract for a season.'

'Roger Davis did much to bring about the engagement of Duncan Fletcher,' recalls David Morgan, 'but Hugh was the man who delivered Duncan to Glamorgan.'

'Hugh chased Duncan all around the country,' says Matthew Maynard. 'He was brilliant.'

While negotiations with the new coach were taking place by telephone and finally fax, an official dinner in the heart of London proved the catalyst for the solution to the second problem facing the cricket committee: the need for a world-class fast bowler.

'We decided not to retain Ottis Gibson, who'd been injured for much of 1996,' recalls Hugh Davies, 'and instead look for an overseas player who'd actually win games off his own bat or ball, as the case may be.'

'Ottis wasn't the right man,' recalls Roger Davis, 'and somebody had to have the guts to say that. He was a popular figure and a good player who, if he hadn't have come from overseas, would probably have held his place in a championship side. As far as I'm concerned, an overseas player has got to be world class.'

The committee decided to target a strike bowler to support Steve Watkin. Potential – in the shape of Darren Thomas – was starting to emerge but a proven performer was a priority.

Former captain and chairman Tony Lewis set the ball rolling at an MCC dinner for the Pakistan touring team. Waqar was known to have been unhappy at the Oval so the question was put: would he be interested in leaving London and making his way down the M4 to Cardiff? A bit of a long shot, perhaps, but nothing ventured, nothing gained. There was certainly a lot to be gained, so once contact had been established, the committee moved quickly. Glamorgan would break the bank if Waqar would bend his back.

'Matthew, our secretary Mike Fatkin and I went up to London to meet Tony in an hotel,' recalls Hugh. 'We spoke to Waqar and his agent and he seemed very keen from the start. We had to go back a second time to negotiate and we paid more than we had done for any other player but we felt that Waqar would put bums on seats.

'We felt we had to go for it as part of the overall plan. We knew that other counties were interested in signing Waqar but when you see a house you really want, you don't worry too much about the mortgage! Everybody at the club was delighted and we just hoped the money would come in.'

'In footballing terms,' says Mike Fatkin, 'Tony Lewis was going down the right wing and put a cross over – it was up to the club to bury an open goal. Tony made the initial contact, Matthew talked to Waqar's agent, the committee took a decision to go for him and then I become involved in the nitty-gritty of negotiation.

'After we'd signed Waqar, I came back from London and went for a drink with a few of the boys. I remember the reaction of players like Adrian Dale and Steve James, the buzz they had then. They suddenly started thinking: "Crikey, we've got a world-class player here now at the peak of his game – we can win something!"

'I think it was that realisation that we weren't just adding to a talented pool – we were going out to strengthen it in the best possible way. The overseas player is a county's trump card and I think it was perfectly played. It showed we had ambition.'

The downside of Waqar's signing was the downsizing of the Glamorgan playing staff. When the cricket committee looked at the books, it was clear that some prudent pruning was needed.

'We had to be very careful about the finance because of the ground negotiations,' says Hugh Davies. 'We decided that 25 players was too many. There were marginal players who we felt would never really establish a permanent place in the first team.

'So at the end of the 1996 season, we reduced the staff from 25 to 16 full-time players. We released Steve Barwick, Neil Kendrick, James Williams and Alistair Dalton to make us more professional. They were tough decisions but, at the end of the day, we had to do it. We couldn't have it all – an international strike bowler, a top coach and fringe players.

37

'But we didn't release players just to save money. Now there's a general feeling throughout the country that after the ECB's *Raising the Standard* report, clubs will have to reduce their staffs. They won't be able to carry or justify the financial burden.

'As it happened, Andrew Davies got injured on the first day of last season and didn't play for several months so, effectively, we had a squad of 15 with two others in full-time education. During last season, we were looking to roll on players to new contracts before having a final meeting in September. Promising players like Wayne Law and Mike Powell were offered contracts as the season progressed.'

The committee's judgement appears to have been vindicated because none of the players released in 1996 was taken on by other counties. David Hemp decided to join Warwickshire, while at the end of last season, off-spinner Gareth Edwards and veteran wicket-keeper Colin Metson left Glamorgan. Metson's replacement, 21-year-old Ismail Dawood, from Worcestershire, and 19-year-old Simon Jones, following in his father Jeff's footsteps as a fast bowler, have been added to the championship-winning squad.

Another casualty of the cricket committee's recruitment policy was the traditional pre-season tour. Chairman David Morgan was determined that one of its overseas commitments would have to be sacrificed.

'We didn't have the money for an overseas coach and an overseas tour. An overseas player was a must anyway, so it was really a toss-up between going abroad for pre-season or bringing someone like Duncan Fletcher or Dave Gilbert to the club.

'I made it clear to the cricket committee that unless there was new money to fund nothing but a tour, then there wouldn't be one – and there wasn't. If we had spent money on a tour, we wouldn't have had any to pay Duncan's salary – it was as simple as that.'

Instead, Glamorgan's pre-season preparations involved a low-cost stay at Christ College in Brecon. Low rainfall in April meant an unexpectedly perfect prelude to a season which was to be badly hit by the weather.

The arrival of a new coach heralded another break with tradition. Duncan Fletcher's philosophy meant a less hands-on role for the cricket committee.

'Before last season, as well as the cricket committee, we used to have a small monitoring group, including the captain and the two coaches,' recalls Hugh Davies. 'The captain would have more or less the side he wanted but the group would look at selection in a general sense.

'Last season, Matthew chose the team in conjunction with Duncan and a senior management team drawn from within the side. Periodically, before a cricket committee meeting, we'd have what we called a professional meeting – Duncan, John Derrick, senior coach Alan Jones, Matthew and me – perhaps two or three a season.

'Matthew and Duncan were the cricket managers with power to choose the team but, at the end of the day, they were accountable and if we felt something wasn't right, we would say so. By and large, we went along with their decisions. There was some debate among members about whether Colin Metson should be playing but the side was doing well.'

Roger Davis also welcomed the new division of responsibility between the committee and the captain and his coach. 'I think the job of the cricket committee is to appoint a good captain and good coaches because they are the pros who are accountable for the performance and recruitment of players. The committee are there to question and make those they appoint accountable.'

Having acquired the final two pieces for the new Glamorgan jigsaw, the cricket committee sat back and watched it being put together. Could the captain and coach match up the various parts to produce a team which would first perform and then, perhaps, even win something? From the outset, Hugh Davies realised that everything was in place. 'During three weeks of pre-season, we only had two one-day matches against Wales for Duncan to get to know the whole squad – but he and they were totally committed and enthusiastic.

'Watching the pre-season practice and Duncan's new training routines, I just felt there was a good team spirit, a real buzz. I noticed their fitness and the way they worked with Duncan and Matthew and I realised we weren't going to have a bad season. My view was strengthened by their superb performance against our jinx side, Warwickshire, in the opening game. If it hadn't been for the rain, we'd have won and it just went on from there.'

'We were looking for improvement in a side which over the last three years had come bottom, 16th and 10th,' says Roger Davis. 'That wasn't good enough and we would have been delighted to have finished in the top six. I thought it would take Duncan and Matthew at least two years to sort this side out but they did it in half the time.'

For his part, Matthew Maynard is pleased with the way the new system worked in practice. 'I still get quite infuriated at times at the odd committee meeting but everything we really wanted to get through, we did. They were very supportive of us throughout.'

In retrospect, it could be said that the cricket committee took a double gamble. By opting to go outside Wales for two key figures, their master plan could have backfired. Duncan Fletcher, despite his success in Zimbabwe and South Africa, had little experience of English – or Welsh – conditions. They were taking a risk with an unknown quantity.

Waqar's phenomenal strike rate at county level had been achieved on the Oval's hard, bouncy tracks – he once took 113 wickets in a season for Surrey – but could he reproduce that form on the less lively pitches in Cardiff where most of the home championship matches would be played? And, after the bright lights of London, how would Waqar take to the quieter life of the Welsh capital in particular and Wales in general?

But by September 20th at Taunton, the committee's policy had paid rich dividends. Everything had gone according to plan and the championship trophy was on its way over the Severn Bridge for the first time since 1969.

'Personally, it was very satisfying to win the title,' says Hugh Davies. 'When Glamorgan have done badly in the past, there were plenty of bricks being thrown. A cricket chairman is accountable to the club and its members for the cricketing side of the club. Indeed, I remember being challenged for my position as chairman of the cricket committee a couple of years ago. You have to be involved in development and planning but you can't do anything about what goes on on the field – that's up to the players.

'We couldn't have won the title at a better time. It all seems to have come together – Glamorgan buying Sophia Gardens, the Cricket Board of Wales being formed with Glamorgan as a prominent member, and now us winning the title.'

Roger Davis may not admit it but Glamorgan's championship success was one in the eye for the committeemen who sacked him 22 years ago. It has certainly softened the blow. Now a successful estate agent, his shabby treatment rankled for some time.

'From my experience with the club as a player,' he says, 'I understand that when you release someone, it's a huge, huge setback for that individual. 1975 was my best season for 12 years and, four months into the next season, no one wanted me! What

40

you learn from that is if a cricketer has bad seasons, it doesn't make him a bad player.

'Tony Cottey had a lousy time of it in 1997 after three tremendous seasons when he held the side together. But there would be no way that I would say he can't play. He'll come back with another good four years. I was bitter when I finished but that feeling has mellowed in time.

'I think the committee have got to be congratulated for bravely having the guts to sack Ottis Gibson and recruiting Waqar and Duncan Fletcher but that's where it ended for us – and we understood that. Matthew and Duncan were accountable for the team's performance and they pulled it off. They did a remarkable job.

'All I've ever wanted is for Glamorgan to do well. The club has to be run as a business. When I came on the committee, I always used to say that if the side isn't successful on the field, nothing will work. And there are people at Glamorgan who said yes it will – "We will still make money even if the side isn't successful." I said that was absolute rubbish! You have got to be ruthless, you've got to have the right players and then, once you're successful on the field, it makes it so much easier for everybody else.'

Hugh Davies and Roger Davis do not always see eye to eye on cricket matters. Giraldus Cambrensis, the twelfth-century church dignitary and chronicler, summed it up perfectly when he wrote: 'Put two Welshmen together and you always get three points of view.' Little has changed in the last 800 years: the love of argument is still a national trait.

But in the Glamorgan committee room, with one Welshman shooting from the lip and the other biting his tongue, the problem was solved – the county stopped under-achieving. The amalgamation of determination, tact and diplomacy with passionate outspokenness did the trick. By putting aside their differences and working together as a team, Hugh and Roger and the rest of the cricket committee did Glamorgan a huge favour and now the county are reaping the rewards. Shall we put that to the vote, gentlemen?

The Boys in the Backroom

They're the men with the Midas touch. One of the great double acts. Their names go together like Morecambe and Wise, Torvill and Dean or Edmonds and Embury – even Batman and Robin. They're Mike and Tony. Administration and marketing. Or should that be Tony and Mike, marketing and administration?

No sooner had they been appointed to head up these two sections of Glamorgan County Cricket Club in October 1996, the team went on and won the championship for the first time in 28 years. Like those other two new boys, Fletch and Waqar, everything they touch turns to, if not gold, then silver.

Pure coincidence or pure genius? Speak to the pair and you'll find out the answer. Mike Fatkin and Tony Dilloway could hardly have dared to dream that their first season at the helm would be so successful. The county championship title, their own ground and development plans to take the club forward into the new Millennium.

As well as being secretary and director of marketing, Mike and Tony are two of Glamorgan's most committed supporters: they're crackers about cricket and, after more than a decade in the game, they know where the real credit is due; out on the field.

But behind a championship-winning cricket team lies a very well-run club. In the more spacious part of Glamorgan's portakabin headquarters, the committeemen meet to decide the policy. Down the corridor and around the corner, in homely but cramped conditions, the boys and girls in the backroom put it into practice.

'Good marketing has kept the club afloat during the lean years,' says recently retired chairman David Morgan, 'and now cricket has given marketing the leverage to move to a new plane.

'Tony and Mike are two excellent people of equal status. In fact, we couldn't have a better group of staff running the club. They really are first class. They don't over-engineer. They keep things simple and they're pleasant and, just as in my business, the steel industry, the way customers are treated is all important.'

Mike Fatkin and Tony Dilloway joined Glamorgan at about the same time. Tony was taken on as marketing assistant in 1985 and, apart from spending a year as secretary, has been heading a department which has helped the club's annual turnover rise from £300,000 to £2 million in the last thirteen years.

Mike had just finished a degree in media studies at Trent Polytechnic in Nottingham in 1986 when he decided to try his luck. 'I wrote to all the first-class counties looking for a job,' he recalls. 'The then Glamorgan secretary, Philip Carling, was kind enough to give me a chance – although he didn't pay me any money in the first season! – and after six months, I was taken on as office boy.

'I've always loved cricket and, back then, it was a real thrill just to be involved with a county club – whatever I was doing. Now it's much more of a job but it's still a great job. I'm a lot more conscious of my responsibilities – that's the real difference. I suppose I've just grown up over the last 12 years. When I came here as a 21-year-old, I was mixing with players of my age but, with Hugh Morris and Colin Metson having left, I'm now older than the lot of them!'

'Mike and I see ourselves as a double act,' says Tony. 'We are effectively joint managing directors or partners. I'm responsible for business development and marketing, and he's in charge of administration and cricket. It's an unusual structure but we've been here a very long time and we work closely together. So far, it's going well.'

As Tony was carving out a career in marketing, Mike Fatkin first became assistant secretary and then cricket secretary – a post he held for seven years. 'I started taking responsibility for all the contractual bits and pieces, hotels, travel and the coaching programmes. That's now been extended to cover all cricket and general administration, including more involvement in ECB affairs, managing staff and dealing with the media.

'I had done all the cricket and a lot of the admin for some time but when I realised that, as secretary, I was now the first point of contact, I suddenly had to brush up my act and get it right. Tony's right – we see ourselves as joint heads – we have twin jobs which run in parallel.'

It appears that two heads are indeed better than one – especially when they share a common vision. Cricket is a game of high drama, a piece of loosely choreographed but unscripted theatre.

An intoxicating mixture of entertainment and excitement, bathos and pathos, tragedy and triumph with a limitless number of possible plot twists and a touch of comedy. A match is cricket's equivalent of a play or film.

'We like to use that analogy,' says Mike, 'because there are the star performers, top-of-the-bill players like Matthew Maynard and Waqar Younis, with the rest of the team as the supporting cast who all chip in with important contributions. Duncan Fletcher, as coach, was the director who shaped it and pulled it all together. The rest of us all have roles off the field, off camera or off stage but what you see out on the field is down to the players, therefore the Oscars rightly go to them.

'It won't work if there's anybody off the field pulling in the wrong direction. You have to have the committee, the staff and the players working together. The play or film won't make any money if nobody comes to watch it, so the supporters have a key role to play as well.

'The first question I was asked when I joined Glamorgan,' recalls Tony, 'was "What's the most important thing in the club?" The answer was, and still is, the players, because without them on the field, the rest of it doesn't exist. As long as you never lose sight of that, then you'll be fine. It's great to build academies for the future and to develop the game but our prime objective is to compete in domestic county cricket.

'What makes Glamorgan unique is that the players have invested more of themselves in the club than at other counties. They are committed to Glamorgan, partly because so many of them have come through the Welsh ranks, and that has produced a wonderful team spirit. We have helped them do that by recognising their importance.'

'The personal touch is crucial,' agrees Mike. 'If a player scores a hundred or takes five wickets away from home, then we send him a fax. We make him feel that it's not just the team out there – the team involves the whole club.'

The way to make the playing staff really feel wanted is through their pockets. As in any profession, money talks – via their contracts, they are offered a performing role on the county stage and a range of fringe benefits. Glamorgan follow established Professional Cricketers Association guidelines while exceptional players are able to exploit market forces.

'There's a recommended rate for uncapped players,' explains Mike. 'We've got a wage band for the second XI capped players plus first team appearance money, and then there are rates for capped players year by year. Test cricketers have got to be looked after a little bit better again.

'We've heard recently about some players moving counties for what I consider to be huge money. If one came here, I know we'd have every other member of staff coming in to ask for a pay rise. It would be very difficult for us to defend signing a player for say £80,000 – even if we had it! Money has to be a factor because cricket is their living but it's a happy dressing room and we've got to make sure that the players don't become totally preoccupied with what they're earning – they should also be ambitious on the field.'

The signing of Waqar Younis stunned cricket. It was felt, not surprisingly, that 'The Waqar Factor', as the club newsletter hailed his capture, must have cost Glamorgan megamoney. Why else would one of the world's fastest bowlers have come to a club which had won only one trophy in nearly thirty years?

'Waqar didn't cost us as much money as people think,' reveals Mike. 'He's obviously well paid – you don't get a player like that for nothing – but a lot of it is bonus-related. I think that's the right way of going about it. If he performs well and the team does well, then he earns more money and that's been proved to be right. He earned every penny last year.

'We didn't set him silly targets like 90 wickets for the season. It was more a question of how many games he would win for us. He was on a bonus for individual wickets as well as for winning competitions. Tony Dilloway agreed a deal with the insurance group Heath Wales to underwrite a lot of that. From their point of view, it was great to have the association and at the end of the year it came through for them and him.'

The director of marketing also made sure that the Pakistani superstar was mobile. Following the trend set by one of Glamorgan's main sponsors, management consultants Andersen Consulting, all capped players are provided with cars by the club.

'Andersen were able to sponsor some of the players' cars,' recalls Tony, 'and that lifted the standard. Once we got into that market, we were able to encourage local garages to help out. We have quality Mercedes from Continental Cars in Cardiff as well as other support, such as a kit van from Euro Commercials.

'It's important that the overseas player, and especially someone of Waqar's calibre, has something that he feels special in. He wasn't able to have the Jaguar he wanted – that cost £78,000 and one wasn't available. But with the help of Greens Motors, he settled for a £50,000 XJ Sport instead. One of the first trips Waqar went on was to Canterbury – blissfully unaware that you have to release the handbrake to get maximum performance from the car!'

'Robert Croft and Darren Thomas have got their own cars from local garages but we've sorted out everyone else. We also provide cars for second XI players, although they're not allocated to individuals. But it's not just all about status symbols. We want the players to feel good. Self-esteem is all part of the development of a team because if we don't help them to believe in themselves, they're not going to believe in themselves when they go onto the park.

'A great deal of cricket is played in the mind and if we can help them not worry about the fringe things, then they're going to concentrate more on their game.'

Over the last 18 months Tony Dilloway's concentration has been largely focused on one project. The acquisition of Sophia Gardens from Cardiff Athletic Club was always considered to be the key to unlocking the county's potential. The sale was completed for £2.5 million in October 1997 and the first phase of a £12-15 million redevelopment over approximately 15 years is underway.

Phase one, costing just over £4 million, includes an indoor cricket school, new offices, changing rooms and outside nets, and is being made possible by a £3.2 million grant from Sportslot and £250,000 from the Sports Ground Initiative. Additional private sponsorship is also needed to supply the finishing touches.

During the 1998 season, new seating for spectators will be provided near the pavilion, and the Riverside stand will be replaced in September. The change of ground ownership has already improved the lot of the players.

'They've achieved amazing things considering the appalling facilities,' admits Tony, 'and we've always been the first to hold our hands up in acknowledgement. It hasn't been our fault that they haven't had proper net practice facilities or lockers or all the bits and bobs which, perhaps, other counties have, so we've tried to compensate in other ways.

'As soon as the ground became ours, we built new showers and toilets for the players. It's such a simple thing but so important. We also created their own exclusive dressing room for the first time and we gave them a TV with Sky. We couldn't do much before because it was Cardiff Cricket Club's dressing room.

'Last season, we expanded the players' area in the pavilion by knocking a door through from the caretaker's flat next to the dressing room, onto their balcony. This gave the players an extra room, somewhere where the coach could meet them on an individual basis. There was extra storage place and room for Dean Conway, our physiotherapist, plus some new carpeting. All of that enhanced their quality of life at Sophia Gardens and I know it's those little things they appreciated.

'It took us nine months to obtain planning permission for the whole ground. Rather than doing it in a phased way – we were worried that after granting phase one, they wouldn't let us go on to two and three – we gambled on putting forward the whole scheme but it came off when the project was approved by Cardiff County Council in May 1997. It was an anxious time but worth it.

'Obtaining planning permission, being offered the Sportlot grant and paying the final £950,000 for the ground were our objectives for 1997 and we achieved them all. If we hadn't done so, the ground would have reverted back to Cardiff Athletic Club and we would have spent £1.5 million for nothing.

'We bought Sophia Gardens ourselves without using a begging bowl because we wanted to establish our credibility. Completing phase one will further enhance that, so that when we do have to go out and appeal to sponsors and the public later on, they'll know we can deliver. At the end of the day it's all about delivery.'

With the first part of the development plan up and running, Tony Dilloway's attention can gradually switch to funding the two later phases covering the main pavilion and a new grandstand. Both will cost an estimated £4 million and will take two years each to complete. Money is still very tight but, in the short term, the championship win has provided Glamorgan with some serious financial clout.

'There is a feelgood factor to winning the championship,' says Tony. 'We are a hot property and people have been happy and proud to talk about Glamorgan over the winter. We've seen some benefits – we have serious sponsorship interest in the name of the ground.

'What we hope to do with the ground sponsorship money is gradually repay our loan from the Midland Bank. And then we can, perhaps, borrow the money again in order to trigger phase two of the development.'

As secretary, Mike Fatkin's responsibilities are far more wide-ranging. As well as dealing with the ever-present press and media enquiries, he found himself involved in a number of bizarre incidents during the 1997 season. Before Waqar even joined the club, there was a foot injury scare which came to nothing and then, as Australia were about to arrive, Glamorgan's catering was criticised in *The Daily Telegraph* by the former Middlesex and Durham bowler Simon Hughes.

'Simon wrote a tongue-in-cheek piece previewing what the Australians could expect catering-wise on the county circuit and he really laid into Cardiff. Now, we've actually had a new caterer in Andrew Walker for the last couple of years and he produces excellent, well-balanced meals. Our players leapt to his defence. They wrote a letter to the paper and invited Simon down to sample some of the fare. Sadly, he didn't get the chance to see that the proof of the pudding is in the eating! In our support, Warwickshire were very impressed by the catering during our first championship game.

'It was one of those little things at the beginning of the season around which the club closed ranks. It was nothing personal against Simon – he was writing about the situation five or six years ago, when he played here, but things had moved on. Other journalists, players and umpires all enjoyed the food provided. It's good – Andrew gives them chips one day in the summer and that's the last day of the season!'

As the weather started to play up, Mike ran into another headache by becoming the first county secretary to have to implement the new Duckworth-Lewis system of deciding rain-interrupted games. 'If I hear once more that the "basic principle" is easy, I'll scream!'

At the beginning of June, Mike was lucky to escape injury when a tree crashed onto the groundsman's shed he was using as a temporary office for the Sunday League match against Durham at Pontypridd. 'I was sitting on a roller working at a small desk,' he recalls, 'when past the door – which was kept open because the windows were boarded up – I saw a steward rushing by.

'The next thing I remember was hearing a creak, a bang and a thud – in that order! The wind had brought the tree down and I stepped outside to inspect the damage. It could have been quite nasty because there were children playing nearby a couple of minutes earlier. Had the tree come down on the middle rather than the corner of the shed, I could have been injured. Incidents like that weren't mentioned in the job description – I checked!'

Mike Fatkin is first and foremost a cricket fan and whenever possible, he likes to watch Glamorgan in action. 'I've always thought that administrators should take time off to go to away games. I arrived at Liverpool in June to see the players literally coming off the field and then watched two days of rain. I came back to South Wales early – along with the Swansea Balconiers – and so missed Waqar rolling over Lancashire for 51!

'While I was up there, Matthew Maynard took me out to try to prove that the players' subsistence level isn't enough. When the bill came at the end of the meal, he totted it all up and realised that he'd underestimated it by about £1.50 a head! I'll never forget the look on his face as his hand came down over his eyes when he realised his mistake!'

His next away trip took Mike to Chesterfield for the draw with Derbyshire. 'I saw Adrian Dale lead the fightback in a difficult game with his highest score of the season – 142 not out. The side showed a huge amount of character in saving that match. I enjoy taking days off to watch – it's the only real chance you get to see the players.'

When the show moved on to Colwyn Bay for the Nottinghamshire game, there was a spell of personal heart-searching in store for the secretary. With Dean Cosker on duty with England Under 19s, Glamorgan drafted in Wales Minor Counties captain, Phil North, as their second spinner. Unfortunately, Phil missed his wake-up call and the chance to resurrect his Glamorgan career. He had played 22 games for the county in the late Eighties and his presence on a turning pitch, bowling with Robert Croft, might have won Glamorgan the game. Indeed, his indiscipline could conceivably have cost them the championship.

Phil is godfather to both skipper Matthew Maynard's son Tom and Mike's daughter Hannah but it made no difference. There's very little sentiment in professional sport and Phil was despatched back to South Wales with a flea in his ear.

More difficult decisions needed to be made in the wake of Glamorgan's Nat West Trophy semi-final defeat at Chelmsford. As Essex moved towards victory in the deepening gloom, knife-edge cricket proved too much for Robert Croft and Mark Illott and their minor skirmish, rather than an exciting game, grabbed all the headlines.

'At the time of the incident, I was more concerned about the players staying on, because I thought if they did we would win,' recalls Mike. 'But when I saw it as the third item on *News at Ten* that night I realised we had a problem. Putting it before the volcanic eruption in Montserrat was a bit over the top though!

'We had to act – cricket was expecting us to. Gerard Elias, the chairman of our discipline panel, was at the game, so we called a meeting within 48 hours. We had a procedure and we stuck to it and we fined Robert £1,000. We thought that amount was appropriate.

'Because it was such a high-profile game, I think it was inevitable that the ECB might take it further. They were perfectly entitled to do so in the interests of the game. They just did what they felt was appropriate by giving the two a suspended ban.

'I think the Nat West semi-final probably surprised a few people. Apart from the Croft-Illott incident, there were one or two bad-tempered moments involving Darren Thomas, Stuart Law and Ronie Irani in that game. The players showed a lot of spirit in almost winning. Remember, there was a lot at stake – we hadn't been to Lord's for 20 years.'

A completely different problem arose at the start of Glamorgan's game against Northamptonshire in late August. 'Pitch alignment stops play' neatly summed up the situation.

'It was one of those bizarre things that only cricket can throw up,' recalls Mike. 'Steve Watkin was bowling his first over when the umpires started gesturing towards the groundstaff. The crease lines weren't quite straight. If you'd bowled and appealed for lbw, in theory you couldn't have got it because the markings weren't quite right. The match was held up for 40 minutes while the whole pitch was re-marked.'

After Matthew Maynard had dislocated a finger while fielding, Glamorgan went on to win by 6 wickets before drawing at Leicester. Back in his own backyard for the penultimate championship match, the pressure started to get to Mike. Glamorgan needed to beat Essex at Cardiff to maintain their challenge but ran into some trouble on the last day. When the going gets tough, the secretary heads for the hills.

'We lost three wickets before lunch and after I'd eaten, I just thought: I can't watch this! So I went to relieve the steward behind the pavilion for an hour and followed the game through the cheers and applause for various landmarks. I only came out when we needed 10 to win! I'm just no good in that sort of situation when there's so much at stake. It was like the semi-final of the FA Cup.

50

We had to make sure we went into our last at Taunton with our noses in front of Kent who were playing Surrey at Canterbury.'

Tony Dilloway isn't the best watcher of cricket either. Normally, he has his hands full on match days – either looking after sponsors or helping Mike.

'Andersen and Hyder, formerly Welsh Water, were our main sponsors at the start of the season,' says Tony. 'I don't regard Andersen as a sponsor but a partner. We have worked with them and used their expertise to make us a better organisation. They came in on the back of the Sunday League win when Allied Steel and Wire finished their period of sponsorship. ASW had achieved their aims – they had set up the youth coaching system and really modernised our ability to move forward. It was time for them to move on and we'll always be grateful to ASW for the money they put into the club at a crucial stage of our development.

'We undertook a management review with Andersen which shaped our business objectives for the next five years. We identified three corporate strategies which make a successful county cricket club: success on the field, good facilities, and a strong and loyal support. We've tried to deliver them all.

'One of the benefits of buying our own ground is that we have new streams of income. We've introduced our own catering which is probably our fastest growth area. Until 1996, we didn't have the bar income, and hospitality has always been a small part of our business because we don't have any permanent boxes. Last season we consolidated what we'd put in place but we've tried not to expand too quickly.

'The season always depends on the amount of work we've done during the winter. We like long-term relationships – we're not looking to make a fast buck out of an organisation which comes in just for a year. As someone who's been here during the bad years, I can tell you there's nothing worse than trawling around in the winter when we've finished bottom of the championship. Now it's nice to be wanted for a change!'

Various sponsors – like local councils – are in place for specific matches long before the season starts but there's nothing like a good cup run to generate business. Glamorgan made about £10,000 from their Nat West Trophy quarter-final tie against Yorkshire in Cardiff – thanks to an exciting win over Hampshire in Southampton in the previous round.

'As the season wore on, there was more interest in Glamorgan being shown by companies,' says Tony. 'The championship may be a canter but the thing which makes them gallop is the Nat West Trophy. The Hampshire match was very exciting, it was on television and there was controversy when Adrian Shaw was run out and then recalled by the umpire. People started to think we were going to do well, to believe that we might even win something.

'Between the win at Southampton and the quarter-final against Yorkshire, we sold out the hospitality tents and we could have sold them twice over. We had an attractive product and people were buying in to that immediate success because they knew it was going to be a fabulous day.'

1997 was to turn out to be an absolutely fabulous season for Glamorgan – both on and off the field. Stressful but ultimately very satisfying, it was the year during which the county came of age. By shaking off the shackles of the past, Glamorgan can now look forward to the future with growing confidence. Even now, Mike Fatkin and Tony Dilloway still find it difficult to believe what Glamorgan have achieved.

'I often pinch myself to check it's all true,' Mike admits. 'I keep looking in the cabinet and seeing the championship trophy and thinking: That's ours – we won that!'

'In five years,' says Tony, 'we've won two trophies – the championship and the Sunday League in 1993 – and reached three Nat West semi-finals. We've also earned ourselves financial security to a point where we had enough confidence to pay £2.5 million for a ground that nobody thought we could or should afford to buy.'

That confidence is reflected in the £150,000 record club profit made in 1997. 'It's a remarkable turnaround,' admits Mike, 'and not all of it can be put down to the players' success. I think our treasurer Ron Jones and Phil Pullin, our finance man, deserve a lot of praise. We've had to watch the purse strings very carefully and deliver to budget. It capped a good year all round but we're not naive enough to think our worries have disappeared.'

Not surprisingly, Andersen Consulting are delighted with the way in which Glamorgan's fortunes have been transformed since 1993. And, following the championship success, the management consultants want to extend their relationship with the club.

'It's particularly gratifying for us to see the strategic plan coming to fruition,' says partner Paul Russell. 'We are discussing a restructured involvement with Glamorgan for the next five years because we think there's more to come. The Welsh public have responded magnificently but we have yet to gain the kind of corporate support from businesses in Wales that we need and deserve. In our experience, that's always the last thing to arrive.'

Since moving from their office above Laura Ashley at 6 High Street in Cardiff 13 years ago, Glamorgan have taken huge strides. Their humble portakabin headquarters, parked on the Sophia Gardens boundary, has had a longer-then-expected shelf-life.

'We're working in a building which was put up in 1985 and was meant to last ten years,' says Mike. 'If you drive into Edgbaston, you get lost it's so vast. You drive into Sophia Gardens and all you can see is the portakabin. Seeing what we've achieved in the last year with the ground and the championship just goes to show that it can work – despite the circumstances rather than because of them.

'We've only got an administrative staff of seven but we'll need more as we develop the ground. We would hope that by the World Cup in 1999 that the first phase will be finished – with a brand new shop, reception and office building. If we hadn't bought the ground, we would have had to carry on as we are, perhaps in perpetuity.'

The poor relations of county cricket hit the jackpot in 1997 – against all the odds and to the delight of most of their competitors. The warmth with which their championship success was generously greeted reflected Glamorgan's position as one of the most popular sides on the county circuit. But will the development of the ground spell the end of the cosy, club atmosphere they have fostered at Sophia Gardens?

'There'll be no chance of us losing our friendly, homely feeling if I have anything to do with it,' insists Mike Fatkin. 'I don't think that intimacy will evaporate just because we all happen to be in a plush new building rather than something that's freezing cold in winter and boiling hot in summer! We have got to expand but we've got to be sensible in the way that we do it. I wouldn't like to think we'll ever need, say, 35 staff. You have to keep a balance.'

'We all know each other so well. Everybody knows everything about everybody else's jobs because they have to. We're not like other counties who have got dedicated teams of people in different areas. Everybody mucks in here and I don't see any other way of doing it – it's a pleasant place to work.'

'Our strength as an organisation is that we are creative and we have courage,' says Tony. 'We are prepared to take risks as any business must while trying to make sure that we don't overexpose ourselves. We also have a feeling of family. The staff really believe in the club – that's why so many of them have been here for so long.'

During his career with Glamorgan, skipper Matthew Maynard has sometimes worked in the marketing department during the winter. He – and his players – appreciate the support they receive from the club's administrative staff.

'I've always had a good relationship with everyone there, but since I've been captain, I've got to know them even better. They probably felt pressure at times to intervene but, to be fair, they stayed away and enabled us to get on with our cricket.

'The whole operation is well run by Mike and Tony. We now own the ground, Tony's got something he can use to sell Glamorgan and the whole club's moving forward in the right direction. We've given them success on the field but it shouldn't stop here. Just as Warwickshire were the side of the early Nineties, let's try and make Glamorgan the side of the late Nineties.'

Former club captain and chairman Tony Lewis admires the way in which Mike Fatkin has developed into a first-class administrator. 'If there was a difficulty for Mike it was that he was quite close to the players and that's not good when it comes to discipline or sacking people. On the other hand, his closeness to them has really helped us because he's been able to understand their aspirations. You can't run a club without taking the players with you.'

And according to Mike and Tony, Glamorgan's special relationship – the bond between those on and off the pitch – will always be at the heart of the operation.

'We don't bat and bowl – they do,' says Mike. 'I've always tried to deflect the credit because we just push paper around. It's the players and the people who put that squad together who deserve the praise. We do what we can by coming up with things like personnel plans, and balancing budgets can be difficult as we try to invest in the ground and yet still pay the players a proper wage. Everybody at the club deserves a degree of credit.

'One of the main reasons for our success is that the personalities of all the people concerned clicked and gelled – including Waqar, Duncan, all the committee members who brought those two to the club, and the staff. It was a real team effort.'

An important ingredient of the Glamorgan collective is its unique Welshness. The majority of the team were born and bred in Wales and the club represents not only a county but a country.

'We had congratulatory telegrams from all over the place,' says Mike. 'It was a Welsh triumph for exiles everywhere. Our former overseas Indian Test star Ravi Shastri rang from Canada to say well done. West Indian Ottis Gibson, who followed him, phoned in too.

'My wife and I are from Yorkshire and it's up to other people to say whether I'm an adopted Welshman or not but we feel happy and comfortable enough here for our children to attend a school where they learn Welsh. I'm glad I've played a part. I suppose I would be saying the same thing if I'd working for Leicestershire when they won the championship in 1996 but to see what it means to the Welsh people gives me a special kind of warm glow.

'I can't think of any other county, apart from Yorkshire, who would have taken so much pride in what is essentially a home-reared success. It was hard work but it's certainly a lot easier when you're first as opposed to last in the table. It's incredible when you think we've had enough wooden spoons in the last 20 years to open a kitchen superstore!'

With the championship trophy back in Wales for the first time since 1969, it would be appropriate for Glamorgan's latest triumph to be celebrated, perhaps, with a commemorative canteen of cutlery? Hopefully, the days of collecting crumbs from the rich man's table are gone forever.

TAKE THREE GIRLS

(Nicer than Spice)

IT'S Monday morning on the 22nd of September – two days after Glamorgan's victory at Taunton. The phone rings in reception at Sophia Gardens and is immediately answered.

'*Bore da*! Good morning! Britannic Assurance County Champions!' says the receptionist with undisguised glee.

'Sorry,' says the caller, 'wrong number!' and promptly hangs up.

Ten seconds later, the phone bursts into life again.

'*Bore da*! Good morning! Britannic Assurance County Champions!' repeats the receptionist.

'Oh! I've dialled the wrong number again.'

'Did you want Glamorgan cricket?'

'Yes.'

'There you are then! You're through to the Britannic Assurance County Champions.'

'Oh!'

Pause.

'Right.' The penny has finally dropped. A conversation to celebrate the championship success ensues – one of many to take place during the next week. The three girls who make up the public face of Glamorgan County Cricket Club have known nothing like it – but are prepared to milk the county's success for all it's worth.

'It was incredible,' recalls Caryl Lloyd Jones, the club's membership secretary who joined Glamorgan four years ago. 'That Monday was our day – especially in the morning. It was like first day at school after the holidays – we didn't do a stroke of work. We were all like excited schoolchildren!

'The fax machine didn't stop, there were loads of telegrams and congratulations cards arriving from all over the UK and then the world, and once they'd got over the shock of our announcement, people were ringing up just to say "Well done!"

'Matthew brought the trophy in for us to have a good look at it and then there was the champagne and the wine and the chocolates – all given to us by members!'

The bouquets made up for the brickbats handed out to the girls in the office during the course of the season. Life at the sharp end is often . . . well, sharp, the language often bad. It's no place for delicate souls, a thick skin is a prerequisite when serving on the front line.

Any caller to Glamorgan – at reception or on the phone – is normally dealt with by either Caryl, Victoria Snook or Joan Pockett. The three girls are sweetness and light personified, politeness is their watchword. They refer to themselves as 'general dogsbodies'. In truth, they are the vital link between players and public.

Keeping both sides happy is a delicate task for the club's administrative staff but, thanks to the county's third championship win, they finally achieved it last summer. Having made sure the players would want for nothing in terms of cars and creature comforts, the staff's attempt to keep the customers satisfied occasionally turned out to be a slightly more difficult operation.

Victoria Snook started working for Glamorgan as a shorthand secretary in 1989 and is now assistant to director of marketing Tony Dilloway. 'The worst day is a Sunday when it's raining. We have loads of calls about when the game's going to start, with people asking about the weather and the state of the pitch – it tries your patience a little sometimes.'

Membership revenue is Glamorgan's largest single source of income – it brings in about £250,000 a year. Thanks to some shrewd trendsetting, membership has risen from 3,600 in 1992 to the current 12,200 – peaking at 13,200 in 1994.

'We were receiving an average of £17 per member per year across 18 categories and decided to introduce a value-for-money membership,' recalls Tony. 'We felt a flat, across-the-board fee of £15 was a lot more in keeping with what the public wanted. It was as good value being a member as it was to pay at the gate. We made it possible for this huge reservoir of support for Glamorgan out in the shires to contribute towards the growth of the club. It really set up the platform for the success of the last four or five years.'

The fee was increased to £30 in the middle of January 1998. But more members means more aggravation.

'We're always the first ones to be approached by angry

spectators when they want to sound off,' says Caryl Lloyd Jones. 'That's fair enough, they're upset and they feel they have to say something but, at the same time, I think they forget that we work here. The players are friends of ours, they're not a bunch of blokes that we don't know. And we're upset too – for instance, it hurts us too when we see them being bowled out for 31!'

That collapse against Middlesex in the middle of June provoked an angry reaction from spectators – both at the front desk in reception and on the phone. One of the county's regular callers soon had the lines humming.

'This man had a very strong Welsh accent,' says Vicky. 'I want to speak to Matthew Maynard!' he said. 'What the hell does he think he's doing? He shouldn't be captain, it should be Hugh Morris and Colin Metson should be in instead of Adrian Shaw! What the hell is he playing at!'

'He rings up after every game when the players have done badly and genuinely thinks Matthew is going to call him back. We suspect he might also be the author of some cranky letters we keep getting.'

'He signs himself "John Williams" or "David Jones" with an address,' says Caryl, 'and I spend hours trying to trace him because we want to write back. They're disgusting letters – really foul. He's very much anti-Matthew and Adrian Shaw. He basically thinks Colin Metson should be captain, so we wondered if it was Colin at one point! But only jokingly – we didn't think Colin knew words like that!

'I sometimes lose my temper with angry callers. If I think they're being totally unreasonable, and perhaps start calling me names, I'll thank them and put the phone down. "The team's a disgrace!" is a familiar complaint. They pick on individuals by saying they're not first-class players – how dare they be in the Glamorgan side. What are we going to do about it?

'Having said that, I wouldn't want to give the impression that all we deal with are complaints. Most of our members are as good as gold but I suppose it's the complaints that you tend to remember!'

Joan Pockett is the newest recruit to Glamorgan's backroom staff. She joined in October 1996 and is officially employed as an accounts assistant. 'I wanted a new challenge and a change of environment,' says Joan, 'and I realised that it would be like having two jobs – one in summer, the other in winter. The winter job was as I expected but I couldn't imagine what the summer one would entail.

'The two girls tried to warn me and the first championship game against Warwickshire was pretty quiet. On the Sunday though, I realised Vicky and Caryl were right. It was very busy, with supporters taking out their membership for the season. Basically, I realised I would have to put my normal job on hold on match days.

'The people who ring up during play seem to think that we're sitting out there watching the game with a wonderful view. They appear to be quite surprised if we don't know the latest score because we haven't had time to look up, but occasionally we can help them.'

The last-gasp win against Yorkshire in the Nat West quarter-final in Cardiff at the end of July gave Joan the opportunity to show her versatility. As Waqar and Dean Cosker edged Glamorgan to an improbable victory, an excited member rang up wanting to know what was happening. Joan took the call in Caryl's office at the front of the portakabin, overlooking the ground. To the list of revered cricket commentators – Arlott, Johnson, Benaud, Blofeld and Martin-Jenkins – a new name can now be added – Pockett.

'It was the last ball,' recalls Joan, 'so there was no alternative – I had to give him a running commentary! Waqar and Dean walked to the middle of the wicket, they had a little chat, they went back, the fielders took up their positions and the bowler ran in and bowled! When the game was won with a wide, I just screamed down the phone and slammed it down! From what I can remember, the caller was screaming too at the other end!'

Not every conversation has such a happy ending. Whether in person or on the phone, awkward customers have to be dealt with. They come with the territory.

'I think you have to be polite but firm,' says Joan. 'You say what you have got to say – "I appreciate your position" – and just keep repeating it. We always get somebody complaining about something after every match – they are never happy!

'There was one member who came in towards the end of the season to complain about the number of hospitality tents and cars at the bottom end of the ground – he couldn't sit there and have a barbecue with his family! But these types of comments tend to be in the minority. We're at the front line dealing with the public and I suppose it's part and parcel of the job. People don't complain if they're happy!'

A more legitimate criticism resulted from Essex's curious

decision to restrict the capacity at Chelmsford to 3,600 for the Nat West Trophy semi-final. It led to stormy scenes in the Sophia Gardens reception when the tickets went on sale. Only 1,200 were available for Welsh supporters and as the temperature started to rise, the three girls were in the firing line.

'Some supporters had been camping out since six o'clock in the morning in the pouring rain,' recalls Joan, 'and when the last ticket was sold, everyone still waiting in the queue suddenly realised that they didn't have one. I felt very sorry and, as fate would have it, I handed out the last ticket. There was a moment's silence and then they blamed us for everything!

'They were going absolutely potty, shouting things like "This is a terrible way of selling tickets!" Some of them became quite hysterical. We tried to explain but the voices just became louder and louder and then suddenly I heard someone say: "I really think we ought to stay more calm about this." It was me. There was another moment's silence and then it started all over again.'

'We'd had to get extra people in to help us man the phones and reception,' recalls Vicky. 'It was quite frightening when we ran out of tickets for that semi-final.'

'Some of the spectators almost laid siege to the office,' recalls Tony Dilloway, 'but you can only sell the tickets once. We know we upset a lot of people and it was disappointing because we had great sympathy for them but there was nothing we could do about it. We would have had the same problem had we been at home. The tickets were allocated on a priority basis for members, there were none on sale to the general public, and the last ones were shared between people who called up and booked by credit card or who came here on the day.

'The idea of staging semi-finals at neutral venues is somewhere on a back-burner because of the ECB's *Raising the Standard* report but I'm sure it will come up again. Intimacy is important to a team like Glamorgan – 3,000 at Sophia Gardens is more use to us than than 3,000, say, at an empty Oval.'

Variety is certainly the spice of life for the small Sophia Gardens staff. They all have their own specific duties but everyone mucks in – whatever the task – because they have to. As well as dealing with the club's growing membership, Caryl is also PA to secretary Mike Fatkin.

'I get involved in all the cricket side – organising the players' clothing, accommodation – anything and everything. Even though it was a bit of a *coup*, we didn't seem to get more members as a result of signing Waqar. I think we have a base of about 10,000 all-weather supporters and it didn't fluctuate straightway but probably picked up during the season. We've even had letters from people who lapsed as members 20 years ago and now want to re-join.

'One of the first things people said to me when I told them I'd be working here was, "Great! You'll be able to watch a lot of cricket!" but it hasn't worked out like that. There's never a dull moment off the field either.

'I remember the Sunday League game against Durham at Pontypridd at the beginning of June. Ponty's a very popular venue and people are always complaining about the parking problem. We didn't have the shop souvenir trailer up there – it had died a death – so in its place we put up a marquee which the wind was causing havoc with.

'We were getting covered in twigs because we were having to sit outside and I remember Waqar getting a lot of stick from the crowd when he asked them if it was always this windy in England! Then we heard about that tree falling on our temporary office.'

There was more drama to come. The combination of Sunday sunshine and alcohol produced a succession of streakers. 'We sometimes have the odd one and it's usually hospitality people who get tanked up. But at Ponty, it was one after the other! All five of them! We did nothing – we just asked the stewards to sort it out, which they did.

'Streakers disrupt the cricket and spoil what is meant to be a family day out, and quite a few people let us know that. They ask what we're going to do about the streaking, the bad language and the drunkenness. We have a zero tolerance policy and the stewards are told to approach the offenders and ask them to stop.'

With director of marketing Tony Dilloway inevitably concentrating on the purchase and development of Sophia Gardens throughout the summer of 1997, his assistant Victoria Snook found herself heavily involved in Glamorgan's hospitality programme.

'It was our best ever – we were rushed off our feet. The three-day game against the Australians in July in Cardiff was a sell-out. We occasionally had a spare day during the season but, most of the time, the suites were taken.

'Our faithful clients such as Konica and Welsh Brewers come back season after season. Then there are accountants, solicitors and building societies who like to be associated with the club. Most of them are interested in cricket but there are the odd few who are invited along as guests just for the day out and the drink. Some of them make it obvious and it can be difficult when one or two guests become a little rowdy.'

It's pretty obvious that Caryl, Vicky and Joan must have the patience of saints to handle some of Glamorgan's more difficult supporters. And there's no pleasing some people. As the championship race neared its climax, Essex arrived at Sophia Gardens for the penultimate match. The result was in the balance before Matthew Maynard and Tony Cottey finally saw Glamorgan home by 7 wickets. On the third day, one member wandered into reception bemoaning his bad luck to Caryl and Joan.

'He'd put a £1,000 on us to win all four competitions,' recalls Caryl, 'and the only one left was the championship. He started complaining that he'd lost £4,000. We tried to gee him up but he felt that the £1,000 on Glamorgan to win the championship at 20-1 had gone down the drain.

'I was livid,' says Joan. ' "For goodness sake!" I said to him. "What are you doing in here? Get out there and cheer them on!"

' "Oh no," he said, "We're not going to win this one!" And off he toddled.'

The pessimistic punter wasn't seen again at Sophia Gardens after that but the girls presume he collected his winnings.

Like several hundred Glamorgan supporters, Victoria Snook didn't make it to Taunton where the title was won. She had intended going down on the Sunday but ended up watching the drama on television.

'I felt really out of it because I wasn't there,' recalls Vicky. 'It was an unbelievable feeling – I was just jumping up and down and crying. I couldn't help it – the emotion just overcame me. It made all the lean years worthwhile.'

Television also provided Victoria with her one abiding memory of the 1997 season – an example of the new toughness which took Glamorgan to the title. During their Nat West Trophy win over Hampshire at Southampton in July, the game turned a bit nasty when Adrian Shaw was run out before eventually being recalled by the umpires.

'I remember Steve James squaring up to the Hampshire captain John Stephenson after the stumps hadn't been broken properly. Steve is one of the most placid people in the world and I thought:

Good for you! It was totally out of character for such a nice bloke but I was so proud of him for taking a stand.'

Joan travelled down to Taunton with her husband Howard on the Saturday while Caryl went with Mike Fatkin. Both deliberately attended the game as supporters rather than staff.

'It's nice to go to away games just as a spectator,' says Caryl. 'I normally sit with the home supporters and keep my distance from the Glamorgan crowd – if you go near some of them, there's a chance you'll get your ear bent! I like to be reasonably anonymous and just watch the cricket. That said, I do keep an eye on things like programme prices and the stewards.

'As soon as the first ball is bowled, then I just sit there – I'm just worried sick about all the players! When I got to Taunton with Mike, there was a nice buzz about the place. Everybody was saying that if the weather held, we could well have a day off on Sunday.'

'I felt we were going to win,' Joan recalls, 'it was just a question of when. At one point in the afternoon, I went out of the ground for a walk along the river bank just for a bit of calm. When we bowled out Somerset, tears overwhelmed me even though I knew we still had to score those 11 runs. When Steve hit them, I felt more like a supporter than a part of the club – probably because I wasn't working. It would have been a different feeling had it been a home game.'

'I felt part of it because we know the players so well,' says Caryl. 'I was on the other side of the ground when the runs were hit and stood back from the celebrations for a while. You know who the stars are and when to keep your distance. I eventually went over to the balcony and later had complete strangers coming up to me and hugging me and nicking champagne.'

Glamorgan's championship success was nothing if not a team effort. From the players to the committee members to the staff and the supporters, everyone did their bit. The team rightly received the plaudits but the behind-the-scenes staff should not be forgotten. They joined in the celebrations by going on the open-top bus ride around Cardiff and the trips to Buckingham Palace and Highgrove to see Prince Charles. Mike Fatkin thinks it was no more than they deserved:

'While this is a job of work like any other, I think it's a reflection of the "team element" we have here that the championship success means so much to all the staff – not only Caryl, Joan and Vicky but to Phil Pullin, our financial controller, the two Andrews – Walker (catering) and Jenkins (shop) – Gail Hartridge, our catering assistant and the three groundstaff lads, Len, Andy and Mark. They all put in the hard work so why shouldn't they enjoy a little of the limelight?

'I don't think it's right to be throwing praise around like confetti but we're well aware that our staff do a great job with the minimum of fuss and what the players achieved in 1997 makes the whole effort all the more worthwhile for everyone.'

1997 was also the year when Girl Power strengthened its grip on the nation. The Spice Girls were everywhere – in the charts, on the silver screen, even on crisp packets and handkerchiefs. It was impossible to escape them, however hard you tried. But there was an alternative, more low-key all-girl band who also did the business last year.

As the Glamorgan Spice Boys – Old, Skinny, Skeleton, Fat, Pixie, Little, Drunken, Strut and Speedy – performed out on the pitch, a less spectacular but equally important contribution was being made back at Sophia Gardens. By beavering away in the portakabin, far away from the glare of publicity, Membership Spice, Marketing Spice and Accounts Spice kept the show on the road and, when necessary, irate supporters at bay.

'*Bore da*! Good morning! Britannic Assurance County Champions!'

Part 3

From the Balcony

WHAT THE HELL
AM I DOING HERE?

DUNCAN Fletcher likes to act on impulse. After a distinguished career as captain of his native Zimbabwe – which included a famous victory over Australia in the 1983 World Cup – the all-rounder decided to end his playing days with Western Province in Cape Town before becoming one of the most respected coaches in South Africa.

When he was offered the chance to work in English cricket, he did it again. Different distance, perhaps, but same sudden decision and again his intuition was rewarded. Under Fletcher's guidance, Glamorgan won the county championship for only the third time in their history. But as he waited to disembark at Heathrow Airport with his wife Marina in April 1997, the gut reaction which had brought him to Britain was temporarily transformed into a terrible sinking feeling. Self-confidence replaced by self-doubt.

'I had made a huge decision to come over here,' recalls Duncan. 'It was quite scary because I was putting myself on the line. I didn't know how I was going to relate to a side playing in English cricket. It wasn't that easy, they might have treated me differently and I was very, very nervous about how this was going to pan out.

'We were also worried about leaving our kids, Michael and Nicola, to look after the house in Cape Town where there is a bit of violence. But I've always tended to behave in that way. I moved from Zimbabwe to Cape Town and that proved to be the right decision. I came here to Glamorgan because of the same gut feeling. That's probably why I relate to Matt Maynard so well, he has a similar approach.

'But when we arrived at Heathrow, I remember confiding in Marina. "What the hell am I doing here?" I asked her. "What am I letting myself in for? Why don't we just get on the plane and go back to South Africa?"

'I'll never forget walking into the Glamorgan offices in Sophia

Gardens rather nervously on my first day and meeting Peter Walker, from the Cricket Board of Wales, in reception. "Don't worry," he said, "you've come to a place where you'll meet no nicer people and you'll be involved with a team that you'll enjoy working with."

'He wasn't wrong. I realised I had made the right decision three or four days before our opening game against Warwickshire when we came back from our weekend in the Brecon Beacons. I just enjoyed the people. I realised what I'd been told was the truth – they were a good bunch of guys.'

Over the course of the next six months, Duncan Fletcher set about helping to explode the great sporting myth that nice guys always come second. That 'good bunch of guys' were turned into hard-nosed winners by the softly-spoken Zimbabwean who, by the end of the season, had become an adopted Welshman – complete with a Welsh rugby shirt presented to him by his appreciative players.

Duncan Fletcher never played cricket professionally. A left-handed middle-order batsman and right-arm fast-medium bowler, he represented Old Hararians and Mashonaland while pursuing a career in computers. Five years ago, he joined Western Province after coaching the University of Capetown side.

'At Western Province, I was in charge of everything, not just the coaching, and I was busy setting up structures and reorganising cricket in the Western Cape. It was lucky that when Glamorgan approached me, I had just finished the job.

'My first experience with Glamorgan was when I was coach to the South African A tourists in 1996. We played in Cardiff but I'd been so wrapped up in our performance that I didn't look much at the opposition. I wasn't concerned about Glamorgan and I didn't even remember who the individuals were. In fact, when we'd played the MCC, I didn't realise they were captained by Hugh Morris and that Robert Croft was in the side! I was totally focused on the South Africa A team.'

After a win inside two days over Glamorgan, the tourists played Somerset and then Worcestershire, where Duncan received a phone call from Hugh Davies, Glamorgan's cricket committee chairman. 'When I heard of their interest, I was keen to know more because I had really enjoyed visiting Cardiff and Swansea, where we had played the Wales Minor Counties side earlier on the tour, and I had always wanted to coach in English cricket.

Glamorgan approached me at just the right time. If some other county had come in instead of Glamorgan, I would have gone there.

'The other reason I accepted their offer was because I'd been involved with Western Province, a top South African side, for three years and there had always been pressure – with everything to lose and nothing really to gain. I thought I'd like to see how I fared with a side sitting in the bottom half of the table. I wanted to test myself to see if I could be successful. It would be an ideal opportunity for me to improve my perspective of how I should coach. I wanted to see how it would affect me as a person and how I could develop my coaching ability.'

When negotiations had been concluded and contracts exchanged, Glamorgan secretary Mike Fatkin travelled up to Heathrow to collect the Fletchers in April 1997. The new coach immediately made an impression on the new man in charge of running the county.

'What struck me was that Duncan just wanted to talk about cricket all the time. He was full of ideas, he'd done his research over the winter and knew all about the players and obviously saw building a good relationship with the captain as vital. I thought if he was half as good as he sounded, then he'd be excellent. He was affable and charming and although I don't always hold with first impressions, my initial impression of Duncan was that he'd do a good job. I came back and told everyone so.'

Having broken the pre-season ice at Brecon, Duncan set about the task of producing a team to win Glamorgan the title. His low-key but firm approach struck just the right chord with the players and they responded to the new regime. The first championship challenge came from Warwickshire.

'When I got here,' recalls Duncan, 'I detected a certain fear of big Warwickshire coming to Cardiff and it was strange working with a smaller county who felt this way. I started to understand why we at Western Province were feared by smaller sides back home. I couldn't believe the feeling because no one is better than you – you can beat anyone if you put your mind to it.

'As it turned out, we gave Warwickshire a good hiding, the so-called best team in England were given a real cricketing lesson. Straightaway, I could see that we had something we could work with. The other thing I noticed immediately was the team spirit. It was brilliant and I realised that I had eleven or twelve individuals who were going to be a pleasure to work with. I had been with a lot of teams where you can have eight such players – with one or two problem children – but I had never met a squad like this.'

After outplaying Yorkshire and then thrashing Kent, the picture became even clearer. Duncan knew precisely why he was right to have followed his instincts. 'I realised that we could go somewhere in the four-day game. The balance wasn't quite right for the one-dayers – I felt we lacked experience in vital departments – but from then on I always thought we had a very good championship side.'

A lifetime spent working in computers had given Duncan an insight into the world of business. As a cricketer, he found the experience came in very useful. 'I was in data processing all the time I was playing the game. In business, I always used cricket as an analogy to make it clear to people how I saw things. And then when I became involved in cricket, I used business strategies because cricket is also a business as well as a sport.

'I decided to set up a management team involving Matthew Maynard as skipper, myself, Hugh, Steve and Tony. It was based on business lines and is something I've done with every team I've coached.'

While the management team looked after the day-to-day running of the side, pre- and post-match training was the coach's domain. The players were encouraged to play football and rugby and they relished the opportunity to try out new training drills instead of more traditional methods like catching practice.

'I've always believed that cricketers train incorrectly,' says Duncan, 'so I introduced systems or routines that are required for cricketing purposes. Instead of just running around a field, players should be training all the time by picking up balls and throwing them and getting tired that way. All the time, I try to think of new routines so the players don't stagnate and get bored.

'There's one called the Roundabout, which is a training and warming-up exercise at the same time. Players practise some-where in the region of six important features that could happen in a real-life environment.

'For example, you roll the ball out into the covers, a guy swoops in and throws at the stumps and there's got to be a guy backing up or the routine breaks down. Once the guy in the covers has picked the ball up, he carries on running towards the stumps and – like a run out – the backer-up throws the ball to him at three-quarter pace. People never practise that. He catches the ball and throws it to the other end – like when the two batsmen have run to the same end – and then it's rolled out to another position where another guy comes in and throws it underhand at the stumps. And then everyone moves round a place so everyone has a go at every part of the routine.

'Games of touch-rugby and football were already being played but I encouraged them because I'm not in favour of cricketers just dedicating themselves to the one sport. They have to play other games to improve their cricket. The guys asked me to play football at the start of the season and I found that my balance was funny. After my third game, it suddenly dawned on me that soccer was great for improving your balance.

'Cricketers always practise running forward or sideways – as in touch-rugby – but in soccer, you actually run backwards as your opponent comes towards you with the ball. In cricket, you're doing that when you're running back and taking catches – to do so you have to get your centre of gravity right – so why not play soccer and lots of it? These kinds of specialist things are so vital but sometimes we don't realise it.

'In my view, kids should be told to play hockey or soccer in the winter and forget about cricket. They must have a break and come back fresh. The soccer and rugby games were a way of relieving the players' frustrations and easing pre-match tension rather than sitting in the dressing room. These warm-up games became very competitive with the young ones taking on the oldies. I was always the referee – I made sure I never got involved!'

From the outset, everyone was delighted with the new coach's approach. For his part, Matthew Maynard felt the appointment freed him to concentrate on the captaincy.

'Although I didn't know too much about Duncan beforehand, he fitted in with our job description for a coach. We were looking for someone to run everything pre- and post-game and to work with the players on a one-to-one basis. The coach would have little say about what happens on the field but he would work within the team strategy and be a good communicator. Duncan proved to be all those things.

'I knew it was going to be a tough enough job captaining the side so why complicate it further by having to organise warm-ups in the morning and getting the guys to do this, that and the other afterwards? Fletch was the perfect man for the job.

'I think he was a similar kind of animal to me when he was

71

captain, so that obviously helped. As well as coaching, he·sorted out things like the players expenses and clothing. It was superb because I was left to deal with selection and things on the pitch.

'Duncan was a pro-active coach, he didn't talk in negatives – it was all about giving the players confidence. We talked a lot and although we had some disagreements during the season, say on selection, when we went to a cricket committee meeting, Fletch would back me all the way. And that's where he was brilliant. I would have a discussion with him and although occasionally I'd come round to his way of thinking, I felt selection was my area.'

Members of the cricket committee were to share the captain's enthusiasm for Duncan Fletcher's impact on the side. Chairman Hugh Davies recalls a conversation he had during Glamorgan's game against Yorkshire at Headingley.

'Darren Thomas had been a little expensive – 32 off 5 overs – but he looked quite good and we knew he could bat a bit. Duncan said to me: "This boy has got to come through because he's an important cog in this team."

'It was only the second game of the season but Duncan realised Darren's potential and worked with him to fulfil it. He improved his action and Darren became exactly what the coach had predicted.'

'Duncan made training interesting and fun for the players,' says Roger Davis. 'People were horrified to see them playing football and touch-rugby before and sometimes even after a game but he kept them competitive. They bonded with each other – he built team spirit.

'Duncan's job was 95% psychological and 5% technical. At first-class level, there are very few players whose technique can be radically changed – it was all about motivation. He was a business-man who was very good at man-management. I thought there might be one or two players who were set in their ways and wouldn't go with the flow but Duncan impressed them so much in the first three or four weeks that, from then on, they did exactly what he wanted them to do.'

'Duncan was so conscientious,' says Hugh Davies. 'You never saw him walking down the corridor with a piece of paper in his hand during a game – he watched every ball. He was always in the dressing room, talking to the players – he was absolutely committed.'

Opener Steve James welcomed Duncan Fletcher's arrival at Sophia Gardens as a breath of fresh air. 'He was an outsider who knew very little about the players and their past. We all realised that we'd have to prove ourselves all over again.

'The other coaches we've had – Alan Jones and John Derrick – have been from the inside and we've grown up with them. They've been very helpful but having someone from outside who didn't know what we were all about maybe got another two per cent out of each player. Everyone was trying to impress Duncan. His fielding exercises were completely new, good fun and helped us improve.'

As he prepared to face Allan Donald in Glamorgan's opening championship match against Warwickshire, Steve James had first-hand experience of the new coach's methodical *modus operandi*. Steve and Hugh Morris had wheeled out the bowling machine to simulate the South African's speed.

'When facing someone like Allan you have to rely on pure reflex action,' says Steve, 'so we set the machine at 90 miles an hour – the speed he bowls at. Duncan said it was a great idea but he changed the position of the machine. We had it straight on – where the bowler normally delivers the ball from – but Duncan pointed out that Donald bowled from very wide of the crease so we should put it there. That struck a chord with me – it was so professional, a tiny point but so important.'

Duncan Fletcher soon realised that he only needed to fine-tune the technique of the more experienced members of the Glamorgan squad. His influence in this area would be felt more when working with the youngsters.

'The senior players had mainly fallen into some bad habits. Steve James, for example, was sometimes playing a little inside out and this wasn't using the full face of the bat. Darren Thomas's action looked all wrong but I just left it at first. Then I advised him to go back to his old action and open up a bit more. And I changed Gary Butcher's run-up. The older guys, on the other hand, understood their game and could correct their faults themselves.'

'I had spent the winter working on my action,' recalls Darren Thomas, 'trying to get closer to the stumps and get more side-on. It had gone well and I got my away-swinger going again but Fletch could see that my head was way off centre and I was in danger of doing myself an injury by bowling this way. We spent hours in the nets working at it together and eventually it came right.'

Robert Croft also warmed to the new approach to coaching as he moved from county to international and back to county cricket.

73

'Initially, Fletch seemed to target the younger players. The older players had an in-built discipline which maybe the generation coming behind didn't necessarily have. He tried to instill into them the importance of getting the cricket skills right first – everything else would follow.

'For the first couple of months, he generally left the senior players to their own devices. He stood off and watched. He homed in on Darren, Dean Cosker and Gary. But for us, if we needed help, he was never too far away.

'It would be fair to say that we had the odd argument but that's to be expected over an intense six-month period. I have the utmost respect for him. It would be nice to say everything was a bed of roses but it wasn't. We had a couple of disagreements but they were all sorted out in the dressing room. We made a point of keeping everything out in the open. We didn't have people not saying things in meetings and then going off afterwards and complaining in a corner.'

'Duncan was good at building people's confidence,' recalls Steve James. 'He inspired people in a quiet sort of way. When we were driving back from Taunton having won the championship, he mentioned a couple of things that I really needed to work hard on – like the initial movement of my front foot. He felt that towards the end of the season, my foot was going too far across the crease. That's probably why I was lbw to Andy Caddick in the first innings against Somerset and again in the second although, luckily, I wasn't given out.

'There was also something about my back foot twisting around – just tiny little things but he was so sharp.'

Duncan Fletcher not only made his presence felt out in the middle. He introduced a series of regulations to tighten up discipline – including a dress code.

'Our players had pretty much gone with blazers and coloured ties most days,' recalls secretary Mike Fatkin. 'Duncan was prepared to give them some leeway but he expected them all to conform and if they didn't, he'd come down heavily on them. It worked superbly.

'Number Ones, as he called them, were chinos, blazer, white shirt and benefit tie. Twos were chinos and denim shirts embroidered with a daffodil. On Sundays, there was a little bit more latitude with a polo shirt or T-shirt and for one-day cup games it was the full uniform – Number Ones.'

'You can't succeed anywhere in life without discipline,' says Duncan, 'especially in sport. When I arrived at Glamorgan, I noticed there was a culture of the twelfth man running onto the field with his boots undone or wearing a sweat shirt. If that happened, the players were fined. If the dress code was violated, there was a £5 fine.

'The players responded well, especially to the lighter side of the system. It wasn't exactly a dictatorial thing although it served a serious purpose – it was a bit of fun. I would treat the fines as something of a joke. The guys weren't sure precisely what they might be fined for, so they went out their way to make sure they did things right.

'We had one rule that you weren't allowed to sit with your girlfriend during the hours of play. We caught Waqar kissing his girlfriend once, so he was had up for public indecency. It was very funny because he thought we hadn't seen him!'

Physiotherapist Dean Conway also fell foul of the fines system when the coach decided that the full uniform would be replaced by T-shirts for the Sunday League game against Durham at Pontypridd.

'Dean had been away on an osteopathy course at Oxford on the Saturday,' recalls Mike Fatkin. 'He turned up at the ground fully attired in Number Ones and was fined twice – once for wearing the wrong clothes and once for not checking!'

There was a change, too, in the players' perception of their role within the club. Glamorgan's director of marketing Tony Dilloway was excited by the new approach to sponsorship introduced by the coach.

'Duncan educated the players about the importance of keeping the customer happy – he recognised that sponsors are the lifeblood of a club like Glamorgan. On match days, he allocated two players – one senior, one junior – to visit all the hospitality tents – to meet the sponsors and their guests and sign whatever needed signing. They were a little sceptical at first but they – and the sponsors – soon started to enjoy it. Duncan was a conduit – the link between Glamorgan on and off the pitch.'

As the season unfolded, Duncan Fletcher's optimism about Glamorgan's chances of winning the championship proved well-founded. The county were there or thereabouts throughout the summer and crowned their coach's debut in English cricket in spectacular style with a performance of real panache against Somerset.

'The whole season was like a dream for me,' reflects Duncan. 'The game against Warwickshire started it and it just continued from there right through to Taunton. There's no doubt that we were the side most affected by rain. Kent always seemed to be playing when we were rained off. We would have thrashed Warwickshire in Cardiff and Nottinghamshire in Colwyn Bay but for the weather, and I think the game against Yorkshire at Headingley was 70-30 in our favour.

'I don't think there was one side that outplayed us in a championship game even though Middlesex beat us in Cardiff. We did play badly against Derbyshire at Chesterfield and I said to the guys then that we'd have to wake up and drastically improve.

'You'd be hard pressed to write a book with an ending like the championship climax – we had to win our last game. Kent had already beaten Surrey to put us under pressure. Someone had to go and play a brilliant innings, which Matt did, and someone had to knock five wickets over, which Darren did. It's always nice when a junior player like Darren does it for you – especially as we were all expecting Waqar to take the wickets.

'More pressure was put on us when one day was lost to rain but then we went and clinched it in front of all those supporters. I was glad Taunton was an easy drive from South Wales. If it had been at, say, Headingley, we probably wouldn't have had that kind of backing but Taunton was overrun by Glamorgan supporters. It was very nice to win in that fashion. Much better to win it that way than, say, with four games to go.

'We'd realised it was going to take a huge effort to beat Essex and Somerset – especially after the way Surrey were behaving. It was no surprise when they "rested" Graham Thorpe against Kent. We had to earn the title and we did.'

Throughout the six months he spent with Glamorgan and wherever he went in Wales, Duncan Fletcher was made to feel very welcome. He appreciated the warmth of the reception and by September he was as Welsh as the next man. In fact, Wales was a sort of home from home. Sophia Gardens, Cardiff Athletic Club and Glamorgan have much in common with Newlands, Western Province Cricket Club and Western Province Cricket Association, Duncan's full-time employers.

'In Cape Town, we have huge problems in trying to develop the Newlands ground,' explains Duncan. 'We want to build an indoor cricket school but it's very complicated because, unlike

Glamorgan and Sophia Gardens, we don't own Newlands.
Negotiations are now underway for the Western Province club to
sell us the ground on a 99-year lease. Fortunately, Glamorgan now
own their home and can go ahead with their development. It's
very tempting to stay part of such an exciting future.'

In the end, Duncan allowed his head to rule his heart. After four
months of intense deliberation, he decided he could not return to
help Glamorgan defend their championship. Three years of non-
stop cricket had taken their toll.

'I just need a break. I've had a hell of a lot of cricket and I don't
know if I could go through another six months and make sure that I
did the right job for Glamorgan. I wouldn't want to get tired of what
I was doing. I wouldn't be doing justice to Glamorgan or myself.

'Three-quarters of the way through the English season, I felt I
would like to do this a bit more often and there's a good chance
that I'll come back to Wales in 1999.'

With the South African season having just ended, Duncan will
spend his winter looking after Western Province's youngsters. 'A
lot of players start changing their techniques at this time of year
and I will be helping them with their preparation for next season.'

Duncan Fletcher's decision to stay in Cape Town this summer
was not entirely unexpected. His commitments with Western
Province meant his return was always going to be in the balance.
There was no gnashing of teeth at Sophia Gardens – just a quiet
acceptance that the county would have to manage without him.

In his absence, the cricket committee reverted to the 1996
arrangement. John Derrick was promoted from second XI coach
to help Matthew Maynard with the first team.

'There were several options open to us,' says committee
chairman Hugh Davies, 'but probably the most important factor
was the need for continuity. We made some enquiries but it was
clear to the committee that John Derrick has all the right
credentials to be able to work with the first XI players this
summer. He's been on the coaching staff for four years, he devotes
a lot of attention to players and is a fine technical coach. We have
some experienced and knowledgeable senior players who'll have
learned much from Duncan and I'm sure John will pick up on
that.'

John Derrick's reappointment has been welcomed by skipper
Matthew Maynard and his team. 'Having worked closely with
Duncan, I can say that the players are one hundred per cent behind

the club in their efforts to secure his services again in 1999, but, in the meantime, we feel that John is the right man to work with us this summer. He's a very good coach and organiser and, having worked alongside him in 1996, I know he'll do an excellent job.'

'I was disappointed but not surprised to hear that Fletch wouldn't be returning this season,' says Matthew Maynard. 'He put a lot into our cricket, he gave it his best and it was bound to catch up with him. He had a very long, hard season with us, then he was back to South Africa for their A side series against the West Indies, and he's blown out. He's understandably very tired and I'm sure the rest will do him good. We just hope he will come back to us again in 1999.

'Coaching's not like playing – it's very intense all the time. There's no respite. I told him there was no point in him coming back if he's not one hundred per cent right mentally. But I would have loved to have had him back – he was a huge asset to me and I really enjoyed working with him.'

As Matthew Maynard's team attempt to make history by becoming the first Glamorgan side to retain the county championship, how great is Duncan Fletcher's legacy? Did he do enough to bring about a permanent transformation of the county's fortunes? Having taken Cinderella to the ball, has he made sure of an invitation to next year's event?

The committee's decision to invest in an outsider paid off handsomely. Shrewd Zimbabwean nous, traditional Welsh *hwyl* and a dash of Pakistani pace proved a potent brew in the hands of a quick-witted captain. Matthew Maynard remains as upbeat as ever.

'Duncan obviously left an impression and the guys have learnt a lot,' says the skipper. 'Now they've got to do it for themselves. They took a great deal from him last year and Fletch can't be there to mother them all the time. I'm sure they'll survive – they're a keen set of lads and always willing to learn. They won't rest on their laurels.

'At the end of the day, a coach can only help you in practice and before a game – once you're on the pitch, it's entirely up to you. The guys responded last year and I'm sure they will do so again with John.'

'Duncan made a huge impression on the club,' says Hugh Morris, now the England and Wales Cricket Board's Technical Director based at Lord's. 'He was a very approachable person who fitted into the club magnificently. And he really was the person who knitted the team together.

'I don't think we necessarily needed somebody from outside Wales or from outside English cricket, but a really good cricket brain was vital. Duncan had that and was also very well-versed in man-management techniques.'

It was obviously a difficult decision for Duncan Fletcher to sever his connection with Glamorgan – however temporary it may turn out to be. Having proved himself in English cricket, he now wants some time to reflect on his future, to indulge in some personal man-management.

'It was an outstanding feeling to win the championship. People were very patriotic in Wales and it was nice to be involved in that passion but the thing I enjoyed most was the team spirit – on and off the field, from the players to the administrators. It was a great pleasure to be involved in a set-up like that.

'It's impossible for me to say what sort of effect my absence will have on Glamorgan. It's a bit like making a cake – I'm just one of the ingredients. I'm sure they are capable of retaining their title. Losing Hugh Morris, however, is a major blow – he was extremely influential – but if they can replace him, there's no reason why the side shouldn't be able to perform as well as they did in 1997.

'The team can get better. There are still three or four years good cricket left in the older players like Matt and Steve James, while Steve Watkin will keep going for another couple of years. I think this side could be successful until the end of the Millennium and there's a lot of talent underneath waiting to come through and continue that success – as long as it's managed and planned correctly.'

For a season at least, that job will not be carried out by Duncan Fletcher. For once, he didn't act on impulse in deciding to stay in South Africa. After careful consideration, he felt that a change of scenery was not, after all, as good as a rest. But there are no regrets or recriminations. In six short months, this unassuming, unflappable coach helped Glamorgan put three decades of championship disappointment behind them and, for that, the county will always be grateful. Have a good break, Fletch – look forward to seeing you in 1999.

KEEPING IT IN THE FAMILY

I F Peter Walker, as head of the Cricket Board for Wales, is the godfather and Tom Cartwright, as national coach, the stepfather, then Alan Jones and John Derrick could reasonably be described as the father and big brother of Welsh cricket.

All but three of the fourteen players used by Glamorgan to win their third county championship title came up through the family firm. It may have taken a couple of outsiders from Pakistan and Zimbabwe to help Glamorgan light the fire but it was the boys from Cimla, Cowbridge and Cardiff who kept it burning through the summer of 1997.

Ever-present veterans and occasional up-and-coming youngsters all had one thing in common: they had been brought up in the Glamorgan way. By marrying natural talent to good habits in their cricketing offspring, Alan Jones and John Derrick were able to sit back and enjoy the fruits of their labour last season. Home-grown talent had brought the championship title back home to Wales.

Like a proud and relieved parent, Alan Jones drew immense satisfaction from the graduation of so many former Glamorgan Colts and Welsh Schools players to the first-class county stage. A member of the 1969 championship-winning side, Alan retired in 1983 after scoring a record 34,956 runs in a 26-year Glamorgan career. He's now the county's Director of Coaching with special responsibility for the Under 19s, Under 17s and Colts sides.

'I went straight into coaching,' he recalls, 'with the help of Tom Cartwright, who played for Glamorgan in 1977, after a successful career with Warwickshire and England. We coached together at the indoor school at Neath and at the National Sports Centre in Cardiff.

'We thought we had some very good players in the squad in 1984 – people like Robert Croft, Steve Watkin, David Hemp and Tony Cottey – and they've all fulfilled that promise. In fact, there's a young kid coming to Neath now who's just like a miniature Robert Croft.

'His name's Arwel Thomas, he's under 13 and also from Hendy, near Llanelli. He's a big spinner of the ball with a lovely action and he's a very useful batsman too. He reminded me a lot of Robert when I first saw him.'

So, with no sign of the production line fault which hit Welsh rugby's outside-half factory, the tradition of developing cricketers from Wales to play for their country side seems assured. John Derrick trod the familiar path from Welsh schools through Glamorgan Colts into the first team.

He joined the county in 1981 after spending three years on the Lord's groundstaff. Ten years later, after scoring nearly 2,000 runs and taking 137 wickets, the all-rounder retired to become cricket development officer for Blaenau Gwent Council when the new indoor school opened in Ebbw Vale. In 1993, he returned to Glamorgan as second XI captain and coach before moving up to the first team in 1996.

'I wouldn't say the committee asked me as a last resort,' recalls John, 'but they were looking to bring the Australian Dave Gilbert here and it all fell through. My role was not intensive coaching but someone to be on hand to help out – just to be there if players needed one-to-one discussions. Matthew Maynard did all the work out on the field. I enjoyed it tremendously but I did miss playing.'

With Duncan Fletcher's arrival, John reverted to second XI coach and didn't miss a game all season. 'I batted eight, nine or ten – whatever the situation required – and I bowled a few overs, especially if somebody got injured.

'With the staff having been cut, I think the first team picked itself at the start of the season but we had three players – Alun Evans, Mike Powell and Wayne Law – who were knocking on the door and the first two of them were allowed in. Wayne will surely follow.

'I was in regular touch with Matthew, especially when Tony Cottey ran into some bad form and Mike made his debut. Mike had returned from wintering in Australia with a very positive attitude – he was a completely different player. He felt he was the bee's knees as a batsman and just took everybody on. Two of his best second XI innings saw him get hundreds against Durham and Warwickshire against three or four bowlers who had played regular first team cricket.'

After hitting a double hundred against Oxford on his debut, Mike Powell was eventually given his championship chance in the match at Worcestershire in mid-August – and made 0 and 8. 'Mike was delighted to break into the first team,' says John, 'but probably felt at the back of his mind that perhaps he should have had a chance a fortnight earlier. After all, Cotts was the first one to admit he was struggling.

'I saw Mike score 41 not out against Northamptonshire at Abergavenny and from then on, I thought he'd have a decent run. But he made 3 and 0 in the next game against Leicestershire. It's a hell of a big step and I don't think second XI cricket is as strong as it used to be, mainly because the staffs have been reduced. I would have picked Mike a fortnight earlier but after dropping Cotts, Matthew went for experience for the run-in and it proved the right decision.'

Alun Evans played in just one championship match – thanks to a simple twist of fate. In the rugby warm-up before the 6-wicket win against Northamptonshire at Abergavenny in late August, Hugh Morris went over on his ankle and Alun went into the team. The right-hand batsman from Glanaman celebrated his 22nd birthday by opening the innings with Steve James and contributed 31 to a stand of 84 as the country's leading batsman moved on to score the first of two centuries in the match. In Glamorgan's second innings, Adrian Shaw was promoted to opener and Alun didn't bat.

'A lot of people have formed their opinion about Alun on one shot – that hook into the tent at Pontypridd off Wasim Akram in the Pakistan tour game in June 1996,' John recalls. 'Everybody starting raving about him – that's fine because he'd taken on one of the best fast bowlers in the world and knocked him for six, and not too many people do that – but he's still got a lot of hard work in front of him.'

When the cricket committee decided to import Duncan Fletcher, it would have been understandable if the existing coaching staff of Alan Jones and John Derrick had felt slightly miffed – especially as John had helped the team to their second-best season for twenty years in 1996. Their pride may have been hurt but the pair behaved in a thoroughly professional way by supporting the new man.

'You've always got your doubts when somebody comes in from overseas to take over the first team,' says Alan Jones. 'You always wonder whether it's a good idea. But I must admit that Duncan Fletcher did a hell of a good job.

'I didn't know much about Duncan but I had heard good reports about him from South Africa and during the three weeks we spent pre-season, as well as a weekend away in Brecon, we got to know him quite well.'

Back with the second team, John Derrick was quickly impressed. 'When he arrived, Duncan didn't dive in straightaway. He sat back and watched for three or four days and gave little ideas to each and every one of the players. My only regret is that I didn't have enough time to spend with him because, wherever the first team were playing, I was away somewhere else with the seconds. I would have liked to have spent a lot more time in his company. During the summer, he was always willing to listen to my view on a particular player.'

Alan Jones soon realised the importance of team-building to Duncan Fletcher. It was needed both out on the pitch and in the nets. 'The good thing about Duncan is that he always came for advice. He didn't take it all on his own bat.

'For example, down at Taunton, we talked about whether we should declare fifty in front – so we could try to bowl them out and have another go at it – or go on and score the big total like we did. We all came to an agreement that we should get the runs on the board and bowl Somerset out.

'The three of us got on really well and we both felt involved, part of the team. There was no animosity at all. At the end of the day, after listening to John and me, Duncan would make up his own mind.

'He had something about him which meant he was well respected by the players. He was a hundred per cent man, he introduced interesting fielding drills and he was prepared to spend time with anybody.

'I must say that he was helped by the type of cricketer he was dealing with. In every dressing room, there's at least one awkward one but all the Glamorgan players are easy to get on with.'

When Duncan Fletcher decided to stay in South Africa this summer, Glamorgan mounted a holding operation. By promoting John Derrick again, the county left the back door open for the Sports Council for Wales' 'coach of the year' to return – perhaps in 1999. In the meantime, John is delighted to have been given another opportunity to work with the first team.

'I think I did the job reasonably well in 1996 – we finished six places higher in the table than the previous year – but I think, more than anything, the committee didn't really want to upset the applecart after the way things had gone last year.

'I've done the job before, I'm a similar coach to Duncan and I think the committee just wanted to keep it rolling. I'm standing in for Duncan this year but I've also got my own ideas as well. I realise he's going to be a hard act to follow. I know people will compare me with him but I'm prepared to take that on my shoulders.

'If Duncan doesn't come back, then I see myself as the person who could take the job on for the next four or five years. It would be nice to finish in the top six of the championship and, having spent three years on the groundstaff at Lord's, there's nothing I want more than to take the side back there for a one-day final.'

With John moving back to the top job, Alan Jones will be in charge of the second XI this summer. He was pleased to see that, in toughening up the side in 1997, Duncan Fletcher and Matthew Maynard continued to emphasise the disciplines drilled into their former charges from an early age.

'We have always tried to teach the players to play fair,' says Alan. 'Unfortunately, there's a lot of cheating going on now – the game is completely different these days – and when you challenge the players about cheating, they won't accept it as such. They call it gamesmanship.

'We've always told our boys that it's better to play the game fairly and be good sports. Anyone you might speak to about Glamorgan would bear that out. Umpires and opposition players never have any hassle with Glamorgan – which is a nice thing to hear.'

Neither director of coaching nor second XI captain were too surprised when Glamorgan lifted the county championship trophy. Both felt the signs were there in 1996 when, without Ottis Gibson for half the season, the side won six matches and finished 10th in the table.

'We had four blokes in the dressing room who had scored 1,500 or 1,600 runs,' recalls John, 'so obviously the base was there. The balance of the team was better with Darren Thomas and Dean Cosker coming through in leaps and bounds, and Waqar and his physical presence helped to gell everything together.

'You've got to have a settled side – remember, we only used fourteen players last season. Continuity is the key – and a fantastic team spirit – something we've always had at Glamorgan. Winning obviously helped and there were no cliques within the team.'

As the crowd poured onto the pitch at Taunton, Alan Jones was immediately transported back to 1969 and similar scenes at Sophia Gardens. 'I remembered going into the dressing room in Cardiff. The first person I saw was Phil Clift who was in tears. He just couldn't believe that Glamorgan had won the title – he was coach at the time. I felt exactly the same at Taunton. It was out of this world. There were so many Welsh boys in that side and so many of them had come through the indoor schools at Neath and Cardiff – I felt very proud.'

As Glamorgan attempt to hang on to their hard-won title, will the homespun philosophy of 'Made in Wales' mean the championship will stay in Wales? Both coaches are confident that, despite Duncan Fletcher's absence, the side will do well again this summer.

'Having been involved with the boys for the last four years,' says John Derrick, 'I think the big difference between Glamorgan and other counties is that there's no first or second XI squad here – just one big happy squad. All the youngsters still feel part of what goes on at the top, so when they become more involved, they're more relaxed. I feel we can retain the title although Hugh Morris will be a huge loss – not only as a player but as a team man.

'Alun Evans has opened the innings before but I suppose a case could be made for Adrian Dale partnering Steve James and one of the youngsters coming in at three or further down the order.'

After Alun Evans and Mike Powell, the newest rising star hoping to make the first team this summer appears to be right out of the Maynard mould. A right-handed bat and occasional off-spinner, Wayne Law hails from Llanelli and comes very highly recommended.

'Wayne is very talented and I was banging the drum to get him a contract here,' says John. 'In fact, I've stuck my neck on the line a little bit. He went to Lord's on the groundstaff but didn't like it after a year. I think the kid's got something special but it wasn't until Duncan saw him playing at Oxford that we actually signed him.

'Wayne's a hot-headed sort of character – a young Matthew Maynard, if you like – but he's got so much ability and so much time. His best knocks were against our best opponents. I think he's got as much chance of succeeding in the first-class game as the other two.

'Owen Parkin is the main back-up fast bowler and Gary Butcher the all-rounder. We are short of a bit of depth but we've also got Simon Jones coming through – Jeff's son. Like father, like son. He's a big, strong lad who's been injured quite a bit but he's as quick as anybody when fully fit.

'My main concern though is the gap between people like Alun,

Adrian Shaw and Gary Butcher and the first XI players who are probably going to be leaving in the next three years. Obviously David Hemp was a big loss to us, because we have many players in that middle age bracket. What we've got to do this season is back Alun, Mike and Wayne and make sure at least one of them comes through and does a good job for us.'

Not surprisingly, Alan Jones is optimistic about the future of Glamorgan cricket – both in the short and long term. The championship win put the past in its place. No more will Glamorgan players be haunted by the ghosts of 1969, as Tony Lewis, Alan Jones, Peter Walker and Don Shepherd were by their 1948 predecessors. Three decades of frustration can be laid to rest – along with the premature obituaries of Welsh cricket.

'It's great for the players that they've won the championship,' says Alan, 'because it's been hard for them over the years since 1969. As a joke, Cotts summed it all up when he said, "Thank goodness! We've finished hearing about the 1969 side now!" But I know what he meant because he'd been listening to it for 28 years!

'I'm pleased, too, because, at the end of the day, we all want Glamorgan to do well and you're not going to be doing well if you're thinking about 1969 all the time. It's nice to see these boys coming through in their own right and in their own way.

'This side could be together for another four or five years and it wouldn't surprise me if they won the championship again – they believe in themselves now. When you've been so long without winning the title, you always wonder if the team is going to be good enough to do it again.

'As we celebrated at Taunton,' recalls Alan, 'Peter Robinson, the Somerset coach, came up to me. "Brilliant, Alan," he said, "I wish we could have done something like this. We don't know if we can win anything down here! We won one-day trophies with Viv Richards, Joel Garner and Ian Botham but we don't know what it's like to win the big one, the championship."

'The only sad thing is that I wish Wilf Wooller had been alive to see it,' reflects Alan. 'I would have loved that. He would have been proud of them all, the Welsh boys doing it for Wales.'

PART 4

At the Crease

NOT GOOD ENOUGH
FOR ENGLAND?

H E scored over 1,700 runs for the second successive season –
more than any other batsman in domestic cricket – and was
the first player to reach both the 1,000 and 1,500 milestones . . .

He won so many awards – the outstanding cricketer of 1997
according to his fellow professionals – that his mantlepiece was in
danger of collapsing . . .

He nearly scored a hundred against the touring Australians . . .

And he just happened to hit the runs which won the Britannic
Assurance Championship for his county for the first time in nearly
30 years.

With such an impressive track record, you could be forgiven for
thinking that Steve James must be a pretty good player. The type
of batsman, perhaps, that England might be looking for to partner
skipper Mike Atherton?

But that's where you'd be wrong. The England selectors *did*
look at Steve during the summer of 1997 but were loath to give
him a game. Having run the rule over the batsman of the year, they
broke the rule of picking the man in form by refusing to let him
show what he could do at Test level.

Passed over for the Ashes series and the winter tour to the West
Indies, Steve was finally rewarded for his remarkable achievements
with a place – and the vice-captaincy – on the England A trip to
Kenya and Sri Lanka. Just a sop? Perish the thought! And just to
show that his name was still in the frame, the selectors put Steve
on stand-by in the event of any England batsmen having to
withdraw from the front-line after falling foul of Curtly Ambrose
and Co.

In fact, Steve's belated international call-up quickly paid
dividends. 'Sid' or 'Jamo' or 'Jamer' acquired a new nickname at
pre-tour nets. The youngsters, for whom A trips were specifically
designed, decided to christen the oldest member of the squad

'Grandad'. Luckily, the 30-year-old from Lydney in Gloucester-shire could see the funny side of both his sobriquet and his selection.

'I didn't think I'd be considered for the A tour because of my age!' he admits, 'and I found the hullabaloo in the press about my being selected for England a complete joke. When they first mentioned it, I was just laughing – I thought they were off their heads!

'I had no thoughts whatsoever of playing for England at the start of last season. I just wanted to build on my good 1996 and try to do as well as I could for Glamorgan.'

And didn't he do well! Although Steve narrowly missed hitting the magic 180 three times during the season, he seemed to be performing on the oche rather than the square. After opening with 83 against Warwickshire, he scored a 150 in the second rain-affected draw at Headingley before making exactly 100 runs in two innings to help Glamorgan to their first victory of the season against Kent. Steve then hit 73 in a drawn game with Hampshire before making 153 in the innnings defeat of Durham.

'It was technically my best knock of the season,' he recalls, 'the one when I felt most in control. It was nice to score a hundred before lunch because it doesn't happen to me very often! I remember Tony Cottey saying to me as we sat down for our meal: "Oh my God, I don't believe it! I never thought I'd see this day." I was out for 153 at about three o'clock and I was really gutted because I should have gone on to get a really big score – I could have batted all day. I threw it away. I was hitting the ball so well.

'I was eventually caught and bowled by James Boiling, a good friend of mine who'd actually dropped me when I was on about 50. For once in my life, I really did feel in control that day. It was funny because I'd said to James before the game that I never seemed to score any runs against Durham and then, suddenly, I did.'

A rare double failure in the Middlesex defeat was soon forgotten as Lancashire were put to the sword at Liverpool. Waqar stole the headlines with his 7 for 25 but Steve's 152 not out laid the foundations for an unlikely victory. The show was back on the road.

'When I started to get a few runs, there were one or two comments in the press but as I started to score more, and some of the England guys didn't, it sort of escalated. It seemed to upset a lot of other people a lot more than me, because my sights have always been set a bit lower than that.'

Having impressed on the winter A tour to Australia, Mark Butcher seemed the most likely replacement for the injured Nick Knight. 'There was no stage of the season when I honestly thought I'd get picked. The selectors obviously felt Mark was the next guy in line after Nick and they were going to give him a good chance against the Australians. Remember, too, that he was a left-hander.'

As the debate over the perplexing treatment by England of yet another Welsh cricketer continued, Steve James just kept on doing what he does best. A 48 and 82 not out against Sussex set up victory by 234 runs, while Morris and Maynard took over the run-scoring responsibilities during the 10-wicket win over Gloucestershire.

'My knock against Sussex, in terms of importance to the team, was significant,' Steve recalls. 'It was made on quite a dodgy wicket where both sides had struggled. Waqar had bowled them out for 54 and we obviously needed to get a decent score to bat them out of the game. It was a difficult track and we seemed to be losing wickets quite regularly at the other end.

'Matthew and I put on 119 for the third wicket before he was run out. I thought I'd played quite well and it must have been a good knock because Watty came up to me afterwards and told me he thought it was one of my better innings! Anything he says to me I listen to, because he knows his stuff about cricket. He did his bit with two wickets, Darren Thomas picked up five and Crofty chipped in with three.'

Steve dropped the England selectors another huge hint when the Australians visited Cardiff in the middle of July. His 91 meant he was the first batsman to reach 1,000 runs for the season but it did little to impress the great and the good of Graveney, Gooch and Gatting. After all, the tourists had fielded a weakened team with Shane Warne, as twelfth man, spending the match signing autographs and coaching a local, budding leg-spinner. Warne had just returned from Australia that morning after visiting his newly-born daughter. Facing the Aussies was obviously a test but not that great a challenge. Nice try, Steve, shame about the strength of the opposition.

After a mere quarter-century against Derbyshire, Steve posted a season's best 162 in the drawn match with Nottinghamshire as he entered the most prolific period of his first-class career. Purple?

This patch was nearer vermilion as Steve went on to paint the circuit red. Innings of 69 and 130 against Worcestershire were followed by 103 not out and 113 as Glamorgan beat Northamptonshire by six wickets at Abergavenny.

'After the Worcester game, when the side had just been picked for the last Test against Australia, David Graveney, the chairman of selectors, came down specifically to talk to me. He saw me score my second hundred of the match, so really I couldn't have timed it better.

'I tried to stress to David that my batting had changed. I explained that, at the start of my career, my technique wasn't quite what it should have been. I had a reputation for playing a lot of balls down to third man and, to be honest, a lot of them were going down there unintentionally! I was opening the face of the bat quite a lot when I was driving as well as defending but, over the last two and a half years, I've worked hard to try to play straighter and hit more balls in front of the wicket and more through the "V". As my technique has got better, I've become more confident.

'I told David that I felt people wrongly thought I was still playing everything down to third man, as I did earlier in my career. He told me not to worry – he knew I'd changed. He said he was impressed with the way I was batting and was pleased that, despite the clamour for me to be picked by the press, I hadn't actually come out and had a pop at the selectors. I didn't want to because I didn't feel bitter. To be honest, despite my good form, I didn't think I had much chance of playing.'

Skipper Matthew Maynard, another Glamorgan batsman to have suffered at the whim of the selectors, recalls the chairman's visit to New Road. 'I remember him telling Steve that he was close to being picked and that he should keep going because he was in the frame.

'In our very next game against Northamptonshire, Steve made another two hundreds to win us the match by six wickets. That was a very important contribution because Hugh Morris had twisted his ankle in a pre-match game of rugby, and I'd dislocated my finger against Worcestershire and then took another knock which meant I couldn't bat.'

'We were chasing 196 to win in the second innings,' recalls Steve. 'Apart from Hugh and Matthew, Adrian Dale had a bad back, so we were a bit thin on batting. I felt that I had to score runs if we were going to win. It was the first time I'd scored two hundreds in a game, which was obviously a big milestone, and there was quite a bit of pressure in the second innings. I tried not to think about it too much at the time but afterwards I sat down and realised it had been a very important innings.'

'Steve played superbly,' says Matthew Maynard, 'and I think he deserved to win his full England cap after that.'

As did most of the country. But the selectors stood their ground and were perversely vindicated by the calm after the storm. Deluge – 567 in five knocks – was followed by drought as Steve managed just 105 runs in his last eight championship innings – including the final historic four at Taunton. The bad run began when David Graveney and co-selector Graham Gooch arrived at Grace Road to see Steve caught at the wicket for 14.

'I could sense something was going a little bit wrong with my technique,' recalls Steve, 'and maybe that's why the runs dried up. Leicestershire and Surrey – two of the more vocal sides in the championship – were wading into me, trying to make the most of it and putting pressure on me with some choice comments like "He wants to score a hundred today to impress the England selectors!"

'I don't think the sledging really got to me but it was the sort of hassle I could have done without, to be honest. And then I dislocated my finger at the Oval about two overs before the close on the third day. Cotts had just dropped Graham Thorpe in the slips when he was in the 80s and then he cut one off Watty to me at backward point. It was a catch I should have taken but it seemed to keep going away from me as it hit me on the end of the small finger on my right hand.

'I batted the next day when Glamorgan were set a target to win, which we initially went for and then declined. After I had made 28, Matthew asked me what I thought and I said the wicket was doing too much for us to get them. If we went for them, we'd probably be bowled out as we were at Worcester a couple of games before. When I was holding the bat, the finger wasn't too bad but an injury like that is always in the back of your mind. Adrian Dale couldn't bat because of his bad back and Adrian Shaw was promoted to number three against Surrey.

'For the rest of the season, Matthew was hiding me away at either third man or mid-off. I couldn't field where I would normally – I was just trying to stay out of the way. In the mornings, I couldn't do any fielding practice but I'm not trying to make any excuses. When I actually dislocated my finger, it went almost unnoticed by the press because most of them were writing their reports on the day's play and not many of them saw the incident.'

Steve realised his chance of making the West Indies trip had all but disappeared when the selectors made it clear that Jack Russell would be going as wicket-keeper. 'Alec Stewart was obviously going to be considered as an opening batsman and they'd only be taking three – Atherton, Stewart and Butcher.'

Not for the first time, the selectors received the support of former England and Glamorgan captain Tony Lewis. 'Steve was really too old for the A squad – because that's meant to be for the future – and if he was going to be picked, he should have gone with the full side to the West Indies.

'There have been doubts about Steve's technique – this habit of angling the ball down – and I think he might have got into terrible trouble against the very quick bowling. If he really has changed, then I'd like to see him score another hatful of runs next season. Mark Butcher got the nod because of his age and his ability to play against fast bowling. I think Steve would have been a risk but Mark can't afford to fail now. All the selectors are asking of Steve now is, "Is this really true?" after two seasons of runs. I think that's a fair question to ask of someone whose technique has previously been in doubt.'

Opening partner Hugh Morris, another Glamorgan batsman to have been under-used by England, was full of sympathy for Steve's predicament. 'I think he coped very well with the disappointment of not being picked for England. He scored more runs in the last two seasons than anyone else and by virtue of that, he deserved an opportunity.'

'I'm desperate to play for England,' says Steve. 'That's got to be every cricketer's ambition – and it could still happen. Then again, it might not. All I can do is look back on last season with an immense feeling of satisfaction. At the moment, I'm just happy to be involved in the England set-up.'

Pre-tour training in Lanzarote provided David Graveney with another opportunity to explain Steve's international prospects and priorities. 'He said that if I made a lot of runs on the A tour – like Mark Butcher had done the previous winter – and became the number-one contender, then I would get a chance if the England batsmen don't perform this summer.'

In the event, Steve failed to emulate Mark Butcher in Kenya and Sri Lanka. At one stage, the whole future of the tour was in doubt because of political unrest in Sri Lanka and eventually the players returned home ten days early. Steve made three successive half-centuries and played in the first two unofficial Tests against Sri Lanka, before missing the third as England A wrapped up the series 2-0. The vice-captain was rested so that Northamptonshire's David Sales and Owais Shah of Middlesex could be given a game.

'It was disappointing not to score more runs,' says Steve, 'because I had gone there with high hopes of putting a good case forward to Mike Gatting and Graham Gooch, the team's coach and manager. I think I did OK – my average was 35 – but I would liked to have done a lot better. I didn't really get any big scores – I maybe should have made one of my three fifties into a hundred and done more in the Test matches but I got a 20 and 30 and that was about it.

'Mike and Graham told me they were impressed by my attitude, how I worked hard at my game, but, like me, they were disappointed that I didn't score more runs. Obviously, one or two other guys pressed their claims on the tour – Darren Maddy came from nowhere – but I think a lot depends on what happens at the start of the season. I don't want to worry about that – I just want to do as well as I can for Glamorgan.

'My county form has always been my priority – if I start scoring runs and an opportunity presents itself, then so be it. If I don't get a great start, it won't be the end of the world.'

In a delightful twist to the debate over his possible selection for England, mischievous speculation about Steve's relationship with captain Mike Atherton started to circulate during the summer of 1997. The pair had played together for Cambridge University in 1989. Had they fallen out? Had Steve, perhaps, run out the captain? Was that why he wasn't being chosen for England?

'It was my first year at Cambridge and his last,' recalls the former land-economy student. 'We were the only two professionals in the Cambridge side so we practised and trained a bit harder than the rest. They were happy-go-lucky students who were good cricketers. I opened and Athers batted three.

'At that time, he felt it was the best way to get into the Lancashire side because they had Fowler and Mendis as their established opening partnership and there was a gap at number three. Mike felt that if he got runs for Cambridge at three, then he'd go straight into the Lancashire side, which is what happened.

'I spent a lot of time with Athers in 1989 – we became good friends. He helped me quite a lot with my mental attitude towards the game. He doesn't feel that any bowler is capable of getting the better of him and bowling him out.'

Barely a week after the championship win, the England captain was among a hundred guests at Steve's wedding to Jane Parker, a physiotherapist with Cardiff Rugby Club. Cricket bats and crutches made up the guard of honour at the church in Llanishen but the West Indies tour wasn't on the agenda when the two openers met at the reception.

'I felt awkward and didn't really want to speak to him about my England prospects,' says Steve. 'In fact, he doesn't have a vote now. I only spoke to him once during the season and that was just before the West Indies squad was announced. I rang him up to check if he was coming to the wedding. During the conversation, he said he thought I had a good chance of making the tour. I didn't want to be seen to be tapping up a friend for a favour.

'At the wedding, I didn't get the chance to have a really good chat with him – there were so many things going on. I thought Athers was really good because, during the speeches, there were a couple of humourous mentions about me not getting picked for the West Indies but he took them all in good heart. Everyone I spoke to realised what a nice down-to-earth chap he is.

'I wouldn't say the wedding was playing on my mind as the season drew to a close. Obviously I knew it wasn't far away and I was very nervous about it – more so than trying to score those winning runs against Somerset – and I certainly didn't enjoy making my speech. A lot of the Glamorgan boys turned up – those who were still in the country – and I think the wedding rounded off the championship celebrations quite nicely!'

Steve and Jane should be celebrating again in late September – their first child is expected almost a year to the day that Glamorgan beat Somerset.

One member of the championship-winning team who had to miss Steve's wedding was Hugh Morris. He had left for a family holiday in Greece almost immediately after Taunton – and he won't be around this summer either. The lure of Lord's – and the post of Director of Coaching with the England and Wales Cricket Board – proved too much, so Steve is on the look-out for a new partner for a very special relationship.

'As an opening batsman,' he explains, 'you can't clap the

opposition off at the end of their innings – you have to rush off because you've got to get ready and go to the toilet.

'For some reason, Hugh always liked to sit outside quietly while I would stay in the dressing room doing my stretches and getting quite hyped-up. When the bell went, it was always me followed by Hugh, who didn't like going out first. After the applause from the crowd, we'd meet for a chat and basically say the same things every time: "Good luck!" "Be positive!" "Good running!" "Enjoy it!"

'I always took the first ball – Hugh preferred it that way. I'm always quite happy to do so – you might as well get it over and done with. During our partnership, we discussed the bowling and occasionally helped each other out with our techniques but it's basically routine to go and have a chat at the end of every over. It's eleven against two and you meet to get a feeling of togetherness.'

But the two openers didn't share a love of statistics or targets. 'Unlike Hugh, records, goals and aims aren't something I place a great deal of emphasis on. They kept him going towards the end of his career – he liked to sit down and set goals.

'All I can worry about is the next ball – that's as far as I can look. At the start of last season, all I knew was that Warwickshire's Allan Donald would be bowling the first ball at me and I didn't want to think any further than that – I've got to survive that first ball to the best of my ability, then the next, and the next and so on.

'I wouldn't even want to think about breaking Hugh and Alan Jones's record of fifty-two centuries for Glamorgan. For the last two seasons, I've got seven hundreds but this season I might only get one – or none! You just don't know. There are so many things that can go wrong for a batsman that I wouldn't like to put too much pressure on myself by setting goals.'

Like all the Glamorgan players, Steve James retains one or two special memories of the 1997 season. Apart from his seven centuries and his eventual England A recognition, he temporarily lost his bat during the post-victory celebrations at Taunton – until a public appeal touched a guilty conscience and the trusty blade was anonymously returned. Then there was the incident in which he behaved completely out of character – and nearly did a spectator an injury.

'During the game against Gloucestershire, Hugh and I were chasing 48 to win. The spinners were on and it was turning and, for some reason, I came down the wicket to Richard Davis and hit him over the top. Amazingly, the ball went for 6 and hit some poor chap on the head! It was the winning shot and I just walked off, so I didn't realise what had happened. I should have gone to see him afterwards but I didn't get round to it. He probably didn't expect me to hit a six – I certainly didn't!

'My one real regret of the season was that my runs dried up in the last four games – that does rankle. In fact, it probably disappoints me more than not playing for England! I'm annoyed about not scoring runs when we really needed them.

'If somebody had said to me at the start of the season that I'd be hitting the runs to win us the championship, I would have just laughed. From a personal point of view, winning the Professional Cricketers Association's Players' Player of the Year Award was a massive thing for me. To earn the respect of your fellow cricketers with such an overwhelming vote was indeed overwhelming.'

The decision by his peers to honour the game's leading run-maker was entirely expected by one of the two men who masterminded Glamorgan's championship win. 'Steve is a top professional and a top person,' says former coach Duncan Fletcher. 'I was surprised and disappointed for him that he didn't win an England cap but glad for Glamorgan and Wales.'

Amen to that.

WHAT A WAY TO GO!

HUGH Morris began and ended his last season with Glamorgan by making history. A career-best of 233 against Warwickshire in the opening championship game of 1997 was halted only by a ball from the world's fastest bowler. Five months later, one of the most prolific batsmen ever to wear the daffodil bowed out with another monumental innings to help steer Glamorgan to their third championship title. In doing so, Hugh equalled his mentor Alan Jones's achievement by scoring 52 centuries for the county. For the moment at least, his name will join that of his long time coach in the record books.

During most of his sixteen years as a professional cricketer, Hugh Morris was, like Emrys Davies in 1948 and Alan Jones in 1969, the rock on which a Glamorgan innings was built. Solid and occasionally spectacular, he frequently had to drop anchor as the good ship Glamorgan found her bearings. On the bridge or below deck, Hugh was always a methodical accumulator of runs. 1997 was the tenth year in which he passed the 1,000 mark and one which the Milestone Man sensed would be special.

'I always like to set myself targets for the summer and I knew I was on 48 hundreds when the season began. One of the things I was hoping to achieve was to overtake Alan's record of 52 for Glamorgan.'

Number 49 wasn't long in coming. It ended with a bang and a whimper. Half a stone lighter, thanks to a punishing pre-season fitness programme, Hugh knew he would have to be at his most mobile to prevent Allan Donald leaving his calling card somewhere on his body. Time was of the essence.

'It's always a great challenge to play against someone like Allan who, day in and day out, is probably the quickest bowler in the world. You're always a little bit apprehensive – and not just because of his pace. He's also a very fine bowler and it promised to be a very difficult start to the year. Playing Warwickshire is never easy and it was Alan's first game back with them for two years, so he was obviously up for it as well.'

Even more so after Warwickshire had been dismissed for 151 in fewer than 40 overs! But Hugh and Steve James could hardly have given Glamorgan a better start – 190 for the first wicket.

'I set myself mini-targets within the innings, initially trying to collect runs in tens and then aiming for 50, 75 and so on. Early on, I felt quite tight defensively and after I hit my first couple of boundaries, my confidence started to flow a little bit and I moved steadily towards my century.'

Towards the end of the opening day, Donald finally struck. James was bowled for 83. Near the close of the next day, he again struck – Hugh Morris on the head. After ten hours at the crease, the Glamorgan opener was just 17 runs away from his first-ever 250.

'The ball that ended my innings was short,' recalls Hugh. 'I ducked to try to get under it but it didn't bounce as much as I expected. It was fairly obvious that as soon as it had pitched, I was going to be in trouble. I turned my head and the ball hit me just behind the right ear. Suddenly, everything just went black.

'I remember people rushing towards me and our physio-therapist, Dean Conway, was on the field very, very quickly. I was obviously very shaken by it. When you're hit on the head by a ball travelling at 90 mph, you're going to be shaken! I'd had a few glancing blows before but this time I took the full force of the ball.'

After being stretchered off, Hugh was taken to hospital to receive good and bad news – the X-rays were clear but his innings was over. 'I was very disappointed that I couldn't carry on because I was in striking distance of a very big total. I realized that I was on track for the highest score of my career and I was entirely focused on trying to make the most of it. But, after being hit, there was just no way I could continue. Looking back though, it's important to try to get off to a good start to any season, so I was delighted to hit my career-best in the first game.'

It turned out to be a sporadic sort of season for the stocky left-hander. Knocks of 55 and 96 against Yorkshire maintained his three-figure average but they were followed by a couple of quiet games in the draws with Kent and Hampshire. Hugh reached his career half-century of centuries with 135 in the innings defeat of Durham in Cardiff but in his next four knocks, he mananged just 35 runs as Lancashire and Sussex were soundly beaten.

'As an experienced batsman, I realised that there were going to be times during the season when things wouldn't be going well for me and halfway through I did go through a lull. It was very frustrating but, when you look back over the season, the good thing is that it really was a team effort. Different players chipped in with performances that actually won games.'

When Gloucestershire visited St Helens in early July, Hugh was back to his best. For once, Steve James failed to reach double figures but his partner top-scored with 173 as Glamorgan won by 10 wickets. Fifty-one down, one to go to equal the record. Another mini-slump followed against Derbyshire, Nottinghamshire and Worcestershire, while a twisted ankle in a pre-match touch-rugby game meant Hugh missing the 6-wicket win over Northamptonshire. Despite his lean spell, Hugh was still heavily involved in Glamorgan's championship campaign – as part of the team's management committee.

'The idea of the senior management structure that Duncan set up with Tony Cottey, Steve Watkin and me was ideal,' says Hugh. 'I was very happy because I felt I still had a lot to offer as a former captain and we were encouraged to voice our opinions at meetings.'

Duncan Fletcher was delighted with the way Hugh contributed to the committee throughout the season. 'He was a sound individual who never tried to impose himself but was willing to offer advice if asked. Having been captain before Matthew, he was in a difficult position, but he wasn't left to worry that Matt would ignore him because of that. The management team created a bonding of good players whose ideas would be listened to.'

Despite their former rivalry, Hugh gave Matthew his full backing throughout the season. When Lancashire were set what some considered a rather generous 273 to win in the rain-affected match at Liverpool in June, Adrian Dale remembers the former captain's attitude.

'Hugh said that if we didn't agree with Matthew, we could have a word with him afterwards. But we had to do the business for the captain now, and back him when he made a decision like that. It was no good moaning about it behind people's backs – we had to believe the captain had done the right thing and that attitude helped us to win that game.'

More low scores at Grace Road and the Oval in August and early September were soon forgotten as Hugh played a crucial part in the defeats of Essex and Somerset.

'I returned to form with 82 in the first innings against Essex in

Cardiff and then made 165 at Taunton. I was fully aware that I needed just one more century to draw level with Alan.

'It was evident that we were going to have to bat really well because of the uncertain weather. The forecast wasn't good over the weekend, so we knew we would have to score our runs very quickly. We lost a couple of wickets early on and it was extremely dark, but we knew that we had to stay on. If we'd have come off, we wouldn't have got back on because the light wasn't going to get any better – in fact, it got progressively worse!

'Matthew played an outstanding innings, so I didn't really feel that much pressure at my end. It was a vital partnership because we were the two senior players and it was important for us to show the way to the team. We needed to put ourselves on a solid footing, a platform for us to win the game. I just concentrated on what I do best and it worked.'

Peter Walker was taking a break from his job as Director of Development with the Cricket Board of Wales to commentate on the match for BBC Wales. As darkness descended, the former captain's performance helped set up victory.

'Hugh's innings at Taunton personified the man,' says Peter. 'He is the canvas upon which the Maynards of this world throw a few brilliant spots of colour. His contribution may have dimmed in comparison with Matthew's but without it, I don't think Matthew would have had the confidence to launch himself as ferociously as he did at the Somerset attack.'

'It was the type of pitch,' says Hugh, 'that if you bowled well and in the right spots, you could easily get people out. But if you got it slightly wrong – the outfield was so quick and one boundary was quite short – it was also possible to score runs very quickly.

'Matthew and I are different types of players and we've got different qualities and a different approach to batting. It was important that we complemented one another. Matthew had to play his way and I had to play mine.'

For the second successive season, Hugh Morris was to start with a double century and end with a hundred. But this was no ordinary hundred. It was the one which took him into the record books. In front of his parents, Roger and Anne, and Ted Crowe, the master at nearby Blundell's who helped nurture and shape the prodigious schoolboy talent, Hugh reached the magic milestone with a boundary.

'I remember getting through the 90s reasonably quickly,' says

Hugh. 'I then got a widish delivery which I managed to cut through backward point and it was just a relief to see the ball going through the gap and beating the field.

'It was a very satisfying moment to savour when I equalled Alan's record. At that stage, I knew I was on the short-list for the vacant Technical Director's job with the England and Wales Cricket Board at Lord's, so there was a bit of pressure on me. It had taken me a while to reach 52 centuries but I was enormously proud to do it.'

Alan Jones led the applause from the Taunton balcony. Like Hugh, he had been a loyal and successful Glamorgan servant. 'I was delighted when Hugh equalled the record. He's a lovely boy and a very fine player. It's a disgrace that he didn't win more than three caps for England.

'The way the game is going today, I think Matthew Maynard will be in with a shout of breaking the record, and I'm sure Steve James has got a lot of cricket left in him. The record will be safe for a few years but eventually it could go to one of those players but it'll take a lot of effort.'

Hugh's innings finally ended when Andy Caddick bowled him for 165. He departed the County Ground square to a standing ovation with Glamorgan on 404 for 5. A total of 527 all out meant Somerset needed to score 275 to avoid an innings defeat and they just made it. The winning target was a mere 11 runs.

With no chance of breaking his recently-acquired joint record, Hugh strode to the wicket with the country's leading scorer for what turned out to be the very last time. Who would hit the historic runs to bring the county their third championship title – James or Morris? Both deserved the honour but only one would have it – unless extras intervened. After the fickle finger of fate had spared Steve James being given out lbw, he ended it all with that boundary to fine leg.

'As the ball sped towards the rope,' recalls Hugh, 'I grabbed a handful of stumps and then had second thoughts! How many did we need? Had we actually won? In a flash, I realised we had won and dashed back to the pavilion, dodging supporters and hanging on to the stumps. Back in the dressing room, the feeling was one of relief. I was so happy to have made a major contribution to such a great achievement.'

Soon after his invaluable innings ended, the rumour which had been circulating around the County Ground was confirmed. Hugh was on the short-list for the director of coaching job with the ECB. His 165 suddenly acquired an added poignancy.

'At the start of the season, I felt that if a really good job was in the offing then I would be interested, but it was only in the back of my mind. At that stage, I didn't know that Micky Stewart was retiring.'

A month after the Taunton triumph, Hugh was appointed the ECB's new Technical Director. The job might have been made for him. With a brief to improve the standard of coaching and oversee the board's development of excellence programme, Hugh could hardly have been better qualified. A former England A and county captain, he was unfortunate to face the West Indies at their peak. He stands fourth in Glamorgan's list of all-time leading scorers with 18,520 runs and is also an ECB advanced coach. In every cricketing sense, Hugh Morris has been there, done that and has the T-shirt to go with it.

Personable, affable and dapper, Hugh has always been driven by a gutsy determination to succeed. He will undoubtedly uphold the best traditions of the game with far less condescension, even prejudice, than the conventional blazer-and-tie brigade. Part of the Establishment, yet disestablished enough through a lifetime spent in Glamorgan, Hugh will give all counties – rather than just those in the metropolitan south of England – a fair crack of the whip as he seeks out the most talented young cricketers.

He may be working at the revered headquarters of the game, but Hugh Morris is a moderniser. Although the First Class Forum rejected the idea of a two-divisional championship, he was advocating such a split – run along the lines of American football. Hugh views his new job as a long-term commitment.

'I could have stayed on for another season and probably broken the Glamorgan hundreds record but hopefully I might have this job for 20 years! When you put that on the scales, it doesn't really equate.

'The Lord's job is very much a new chapter in my career. To be honest, it wasn't a difficult choice because as soon as I was offered the job, I accepted it. I had no hesitation.'

Edward Bevan, the BBC Radio Wales commentator, advised Hugh to turn it down. He felt that other opportunities would present themselves in Hugh's career and wanted him to stay with Glamorgan.

'He couldn't have written the farewell script better but Hugh was playing so well,' says Edward. 'He scored a double hundred against

Allan Donald and, after his terrific start to the season, he was very close to an England recall. The chairman of selectors, David Graveney, rang me to say he was coming down specifically to watch him but, because Hugh was 34, Mark Butcher got the nod. Had he played for England and done well, then he would have been on that plane to the West Indies and then what would have happened?

'I know a lot of people were hoping against hope that Hugh wouldn't be offered the ECB job! He's so highly thought of that I'm sure that other big jobs like managing A sides would have come his way. I told him he had plenty of cricket left in him but in the end, he had to do what he felt was best for him.'

'I know I'll miss certain things,' admits Hugh, 'like the feeling of success, the pride you get from performing well against top bowlers and the dressing-room atmosphere. Most of all, I'll miss the people I've known for a very long time and lived with for six months of the year.'

The feeling will undoubtedly be mutual. Glamorgan will miss Hugh Morris – the man and his runs. Just how much won't become clear for a while – perhaps not for two or three seasons.

'Hugh has been a magnificent servant to Glamorgan,' says skipper Matthew Maynard. 'We won our first trophy since 1969 under his leadership when we were Sunday League champions in 1993. He's been a credit to the club and a great ambassador for Welsh cricket.

'We will miss Hugh hugely this season. He formed a great opening partership with Steve James and got us off to some wonderful starts all year. But things move on and one of the youngsters will get the opportunity to take his place. We need someone to strike up a similar partnership with Steve. Obviously I can't ask for it to be as successful as theirs was from day one but it would be nice to get, say, 75 per cent of their opening partnership record on board this season.'

Steve James began batting with Hugh six years ago when Alan Butcher was forced to retire through injury. Despite their avalanche of runs in recent years, the relationship has not always been as harmonious as their running between the wickets.

'When Hugh was captain, he left me out of the side a couple of times when I wasn't getting enough runs. I wasn't very happy about it at the time but it was a turning point in my career – I realised I had to buckle down.'

Alan Jones is pleased that Glamorgan have not signed a high-profile established batsmen to replace Hugh in the side. By staying in-house, he believes the county's loyalty to their young pretenders will be repaid.

'In 1992, when Alan Butcher left, people wondered who was going to open with Hugh,' recalls the director of coaching, 'because they had been such a great pair. But Steve James has never looked back. He was given the opportunity and took it with both hands. I think the same thing can happen to either Alun Evans, Wayne Law or Mike Powell. I'm a great believer in giving youth a chance – these players have to be given a run in the first team. If these sort of players have too much second XI cricket, they get stale and they don't come on. They need to play at the highest level.'

Steve James has no preference for his new partner. He can well appreciate the frustration of sitting on the sidelines, waiting for a chance to impress. 'I remember I was kicking my heels in the second team when Hugh and Alan were opening and, after scoring a few runs at Cambridge, I was desperate to play first team cricket. Unluckily for Alan, he got injured and I was in – although it's taken me a few years to fulfil my potential!

'It was only in the last two-and-a-half years that I've really started to contribute to my partnership with Hugh. He's been dragging me along while doing most of the scoring – I've been getting runs in fits and starts.

'Sometimes a bit too much can be made of a partnership. When you go out to bat, you're on your own anyway. It doesn't matter who's at the other end, you've got to face the ball and sort it out. I think the fact that I was right-hand and Hugh left-hand did help – it probably mucked up the bowler's line. But, then again, Hugh and Alan were both left-handers and successful too!

'You've only got to look at the figures to realise the contribution Hugh has made to Glamorgan cricket. His temperament was the big thing – Hugh was always so calm about everything. He wasn't a great worrier. A bad shot or a good ball didn't seem to affect him. He would just get on with facing the next ball.

'The biggest compliment I can pay Hugh is that I was always very surprised when he was out. He always looked so in command.'

It won't be the same without Hugh Morris in the Glamorgan team. A fine opening bat, a sharp slip fielder and a wonderful team man, he was also a jolly good fellow, one of the lads. A smile was never far from his lips and he always had time for a chat and a laugh.

'Hugh was a top role model to everyone during last season,'

says Duncan Fletcher. 'For a guy who had done everything, he still got out there and worked at his game and practised hard. He seemed to really enjoy himself during all the routines. There's no doubt that you win more games off the field than on it. You often win your games in the dressing room with the team spirit and the fun you create – the enthusiasm you can build up. And Hugh just got stuck in.'

After his 40-year connection with the club as player and cricket committee member, Peter Walker is well-placed to assess Hugh's overall contribution to the county cause.

'Hugh has been the Emrys Davies and the Alan Jones of his generation. Around such players a successful side is always built. Along with Graham Gooch, he's been consistently the best opening batsman in English cricket for the last ten years. Hugh's contribution to the championship-winning side was huge and it couldn't have happened to a nicer guy. He's a super bloke who's going to have a tremendous influence on the game into the next century. What a fairy-tale end to a career!'

More than anything else, despite his links with Lord's, Hugh Morris has never been afraid to fly the flag for Wales. Born and brought up in Cardiff, he remained loyal to Glamorgan when other counties came a-courting and was rewarded with a testimonial in 1994. The proceeds gave him the financial security every professional sportsman craves and now the blow of retirement has been softened by his ECB appointment.

As the man responsible for setting standards across the country, Hugh has the opportunity to put something back into the game he loves. Opening the mail at his office at Lord's may not be as exciting – or tiring – as opening an innings for Glamorgan but Hugh Morris is unlikely to become buried beneath a mountain of paperwork. He'll be out-and-about, very hands-on, scouring the country – England *and* Wales – looking for the next Hugh Morris and hoping that 1997 was the start of something big for his beloved club and country.

'I think Glamorgan are fortunate to have an identity as a county and a national side. It opens the club up to a whole nation rather than just a county, judging from the reaction I've had from a lot of people – whether I'm walking down the street or shopping at Marks and Spencers! People who I've never met before tap me on the shoulder to say "Well done!" – it's been fantastic!'

IMMORTALITY IN THE PRINCIPALITY

As the 1996 season drew to a close, Adrian Dale was a worried man.

Despite having played more than a hundred games for Glamorgan – making nearly 6,000 runs and taking more than a hundred wickets – Arthur, as he is affectionately known, feared for his future. He may have shared the county's highest-ever partnership of 425 not out with Viv Richards against Middlesex three years earlier, but now he was struggling.

Apart from a season's best 120 against Northamptonshire in May, Adrian's highest championship score had been 65. Having not been approached about a new contract, he knew his career hung in the balance.

'Some people had been told about their contracts half or three-quarters of the way through the season,' recalls Adrian. 'As I looked around at the players who also hadn't heard, I realised that we all came into the category of being on the fringe.

'It was getting quite scary and it wasn't until the Durham game in late August – when I made a match-winning 69 – that I was told I would be getting a two-year contract. The uncertainty did play on my mind – there's such a fine line between success and failure.

'Fair enough, I accept that I put myself in that position by not getting enough runs but it wasn't through lack of effort. It just became more and more frustrating and the longer you go without scoring, the harder it becomes. I wasn't surprised that the committee waited so late in the season – to be honest, I hadn't done enough to deserve anything else.'

At the end of the 1997 season, the cricket committee's decision to back him had been fully justified. Although overshadowed by James, Morris and Maynard, Adrian Dale rediscovered his form to play a crucial role in Glamorgan's championship-winning campaign.

His 840 runs, at an average of just over 38, included a majestic 142 not out and a crucial collection of innings during the run-in.

'I didn't quite reach the 1,000 runs mark but in a lot of matches, we only batted once. At the end of the day, I was happy with my season but my school report might read "could do better". I think I made a solid contribution.'

Coach Duncan Fletcher is full of praise for one of the most committed members of the Glamorgan squad. 'Adrian under-estimates his ability. He's got to realise that he's a better player than he thinks he is.

'I have never met a more enthusiastic cricketer. He loves the game and he just wants to be on the field, which is brilliant. We tried to build up his confidence and to make him believe more in his own ability.'

Like all the Glamorgan players, Adrian welcomed the arrival of an outside coach with new ideas. He felt the county had become too insular and someone from a different cricketing system was needed to shake up the squad.

'Fletch stood back for at least a couple of weeks as he sized everybody up,' Adrian recalls. 'I think the players respected him for that – nobody wanted him to dive in straightaway. We always enjoy new fielding drills and we could see a point to Duncan's – there was a definite aim. We tried to copy as many of the match situations as we could. We were getting fit the fun way, with the ball in our hands.

'I think Duncan made us twenty-five per cent more professional in our approach to the game. He found out what motivated people as individuals and either talked to or practised with them to improve their game.

'He told me to look at what I'd achieved and be more confident on the field. It wasn't a case of waving a magic wand and suddenly scoring more runs but it certainly helped. I realised I had to back myself all the time to play my shots – I should never be afraid to fail. Both technically and in the way he handled me as a person, Duncan was a great help.'

David Hemp's departure to Warwickshire left Adrian relishing the start of the 1997 season. Buoyed up by the security of a new contract, he realised there was an opportunity to stake a claim to a permanent first team place.

'There was less competition and I knew I was going to get a run at the start of the season,' he recalls. 'Matthew Maynard was very positive in the way he spoke to me and I felt I was starting the season under less pressure. I saw an opening, the door was ajar and I just had to push it wide open.'

The door was almost detached from its hinges as Adrian set about re-establishing himself. After dismissing Warwickshire for 151, Glamorgan built up a first innings lead of exactly 400 with first wicket down making 106.

'We had a pre-season which wasn't what we'd been used to – we normally go on an overseas mini-tour – and although we'd been lucky with the weather, we wondered whether we were really ready for the season. Warwickshire had been our bogey side over the years but we absolutely blitzed them off the park. Without Waqar, we bowled them out cheaply and our batsmen just ground them down. I made a dream start to the season.

'It was one one of my best knocks ever for Glamorgan – I felt totally at ease right from the start of the innings. It was the perfect start to what turned out to be a pretty patchy sort of season. I went off the boil in the middle but I was particularly happy to hit some form during the last few games – apart from the one at Taunton.'

Adrian capitalised on his first century by scoring 44 in the draw with Yorkshire but missed out in both innings as Glamorgan beat Kent. He made 1 against Hampshire but his 73 in a total of 597 helped see off Durham in Cardiff by an innings. Another pair of low scores in the defeat by Middlesex was followed by another solid knock – 78 – as Lancashire collapsed at Liverpool.

Adrian wasn't amongst the runs during the comprehensive back-to-back victories over Sussex and Gloucestershire at St Helen's but returned to save the match at Chesterfield. After their opening pair had put on 247, Derbyshire made a massive 513. With Glamorgan wickets tumbling at regular intervals, Adrian's 142 not out saw them to safety.

'Derbyshire had outplayed us from the start but we knew that if we avoided the follow-on, there was a slim chance of winning the game. I was particularly pleased that, with some support from Gary Butcher and Adrian Shaw, I managed to stay in long enough for us to squeeze past the target of 363, but then the rain came down and the match ended in a draw.

'It was a different sort of knock to my first hundred of the season. I was under more pressure because, unlike the Warwickshire game, we had our backs up against the wall, we were just trying to survive. It was a good pitch and we should have reached the follow-on target quite easily but we didn't play too well.

'It was very satisfying because I hadn't scored a hundred since that opening game and it was nice to prove to the people who had put their faith in me that I could get big scores.'

Another mini-slump followed in the games against Nottinghamshire and Worcestershire before Adrian confirmed his class with a succession of invaluable innings. After making 71 against Northants, he scored 69 (Leicestershire), 72 (Surrey) and 49 (Essex) – almost a third of his season's runs in four knocks.

'I had that feeling in the run-in that when it came to the crunch I was doing the business. We were playing under more and more pressure with every passing game and I knew that I hadn't contributed as much at that stage as Steve, Hugh or Matthew. I knew my poor form would be forgotten if I performed from now on. I was the strongest mentally that I've ever been and I really felt my time had come.

'There were no hundreds in the run of good knocks but some of them were made in low-scoring games – I should have made a ton against Surrey but threw it away. The innings against Leicestershire was the most satisfying because they were the reigning county champions and our 226 on a tricky track was a good score. My half-century was probably the most beneficial of them all but we didn't get to finish that game either, because parts of the square weren't protected overnight.

'At the time, we didn't know that rain was going to ruin the game and it was another knock under pressure. Steve, Hugh and Matthew missed out but because they managed to get high scores when I'd failed, it was nice to repay the favour!'

Adrian Dale was one of five ever-presents in Glamorgan's championship campaign. Regularly batting at number three, he was more than happy to spend hour upon hour watching James and Morris confirm their position as the country's best double act.

'The idea is for the opening batsman to get as many runs as they can,' says Adrian. 'If you don't like sitting around waiting for a wicket to fall, then you should open. Actually, if you've had a long day in the field, you want as long a break as possible to recover.

'Sometimes the wait gets too long – when the openers are putting on a ridiculous number of runs, partnerships of 200 to 300 or more – but, to be honest, Hugh and Steve's starts were brilliant for me and the team.

'I had no preference for batting with either of them – they both had their good and bad points. With Steve, I can play tip-and-run –

111

like garden cricket – because he's very, very quick. We have a very good understanding and we can score quickly without having to hit the ball all over the ground.

'When I batted with Hugh, I had more opportunities because, with Hugh being left-handed, the bowlers weren't always able to find the right line. I scored more off my legs when batting with Hugh.'

Over the last two seasons, Adrian Dale has become less of an all-rounder and more of a batsman who bowls. He once took 6 for 18 against Warwickshire at Cardiff in 1993 but picked up only 12 championship wickets in 1996 and none at all last year, when he bowled fewer than fifty overs.

'I'm not really an all-rounder,' admits Adrian, 'more an eighty per cent batsman and a twenty per cent bowler. There were times when I wanted to bowl more in 1997 but the five bowlers did such as great job that my opportunities were limited. When I did have a chance, it was usually on the flatter type of wickets.

'I did ask Matthew if I could bowl more but it became a bit of a joke in the dressing room. A one-over spell before lunch and tea and another so that people could change ends was all that I was allowed! My first 20 overs in 1997 were bowled in eight different spells! It was all very light-hearted but I wanted to be much more involved because that's the sort of player I am. Gary Butcher came into the side for nine games and started swinging the ball quite a lot – he was bowling more wicket-taking balls than me. At the end of the day, I had no complaints.

'But I want to bowl more this season, because if you're not batting well then bowling is a second string. It's so important to keep it going, if possible.'

Whatever his role in 1998, Adrian will be hoping to have won himself a new contract by the time he reaches 30 in October. When Glamorgan lifted the Sunday League title in 1993, Adrian's international star shone briefly with a winter tour to South Africa with England A, before fizzling out. A recall by his country may be unlikely but last season's success augurs well for his county. The building blocks are in place.

'1997 was the year in which a maturing team finally peaked,' says Adrian. 'It was the proudest year of my life. The nucleus of the team's been together for so long that you felt something bubbling there all the time. It seemed to have come to a head in 1993 but we knew we were more than one-trophy wonders.

First wicket down . . . Adrian Dale, the bricks-and-mortar man for all seasons.

The Cottey comeback . . . a vice-captain's innings against Essex.

A 'Welsh' poet in motion . . .

Watty reaps the 'benefit' of bowling line and length.

No doubting Thomas . . . high-fives for Darren in another five-star display.

Take three Welshmen . . . Crofty and a couple of mates.

Dean Cosker . . . an old head on young shoulders bowls himself into the history books.

Butch appeals . . . 'Why not let me open in place of Hugh?'

'Howzat!' The selectors were sure – and Adrian was in.

'The great team spirit was down partly to the Welsh identity – thirteen or fourteen guys bonding together – and partly due to the mix of good cricketers and decent blokes. There are some great characters in the dressing room – Adrian Shaw and Tony Cottey are very funny but everybody has their moments.'

Adrian appreciates the support the squad have received from the backroom staff at Sophia Gardens. From carpets to cars, the players have been made to feel comfortable – at home and on the road.

'Little things do help – like having carpets in the dressing room as opposed to cold, stone floors and a place to store our kit, rather than having to take it home and then bring it back every day. When you travel the distances we do – two or three players together – it's great to have decent cars. You don't want to feel as tired as you would be if you'd driven to an away game in an old banger!

'I'm sure we can repeat our success next season – it'll be harder without Hugh and Duncan but it's an opportunity for more people to come in. They know the standards that are expected of them. We need to get on a roll but as long as we're in contention with a third of the season left, we know we can do it because we've done it before!'

Adrian's nickname, Arthur, comes from the former television character Arthur Daley played by George Cole in the *Minder* series. It was wheeling and dealing of a different kind which kept Adrian busy between the post-Taunton celebrations and pre-season.

'I don't mind being associated with Arthur Daley although, during the winter, I was selling houses rather than cars for Darlows the estate agents. I must admit, I enjoyed it a lot more than I thought I would. It was the first "proper" job I've ever had because I normally go abroad coaching in New Zealand, but this time my girlfriend Ruth and I decided to spend Christmas at home. Anyway, I needed a rest – I've played cricket non-stop for eight years.

'I'm not sure which is the harder – making a sale or a century. To be honest, when I sold my first house, there was some elation but it doesn't come close to scoring a hundred at Cardiff!'

Although born in South Africa, Adrian Dale is a proud and patriotic Welshman. His father John played for Glamorgan Seconds and Adrian went to school in Pembroke and Chepstow before gaining an economics degree at the University College of Wales, Swansea. His love of his country played an important part in Glamorgan's championship victory.

113

'Towards the end of the season, I invented a catchphrase "Immortality in the Principality" which I used to to gee up the guys during the run-in, especially out in the field. We like to motivate each other while we're fielding and it came about as a way of shouting encouragement to the guys – probably from the Surrey game onwards. It was also used a few times in the dressing room.

'It wasn't meant to be as profound as it sounds but, in a way, it did have a serious undertone. It was, in effect, what we were all working for – we were looking to achieve something in cricket. That's what makes you walk tall and feel very proud of yourself. Immortality in the Principality was what we were aiming for.

'My motivation in cricket is to win for the fans, the people who come to watch us play day in day out – the cricket supporters of Wales. Then, in my list of priorities, it's the team and then me, a faraway third.

'We knew if we could win the championship that we'd be in the history books forever. We knew how much recognition the 1969 side had received and it was great to achieve something similar.'

Immortality in the Principality. It does has a nice ring to it. The 1997 team certainly will be famous for all time if they manage to retain their title.

ON THE BACK FOOT

THE summer of 1997 was almost a nightmare for Tony Cottey. Glamorgan might have eventually fulfilled their dream of winning the county championship for the third time but most of the season was a personal disaster for the diminutive middle-order batsman. In fact, diminutive pretty well summed up his contribution as he staggered from one low score to another.

During 1996, Tony had averaged nearly 50. A year later, that figure had been halved. His highest score had plummeted from 203 to 76 not out – his only half-century of the summer. After three sparkling years which had seen his career average rise to nearly 40, Tony appeared to have lost it. When he was dismissed for 0 against Nottinghamshire at Colwyn Bay in August, the vice-captain was dropped. His season appeared to be over. He had arrived at cricket's equivalent of the marathon runner's wall.

In the end though, the small man with the big heart came through. When push came to shove, Tony emerged fighting – dogged, doughty and determined to play his part in Glamorgan's run-in to the championship. In four late-season knocks – including a match-winner against Essex – Tony provided a happy ending to what had been his own particular tale of woe.

'It was very difficult to remain upbeat,' he recalls, 'because over the last six or seven years, I'd never had to worry about my place. Everything had gone well and to play in a side that was always going to push for a trophy and then see my form go to nothing was very hard. It was difficult for me because I had such a poor year in a team which did so well. Sometimes that's harder than doing badly in a poor side when other people around you are feeling the same. I was in the depths of depression – I couldn't understand what had gone wrong.

'Steve, Hugh and Adrian had started like there was no tomorrow – as if runs were going out of fashion. Early on, Matthew and I were having a laugh and a joke about it because, after three championship games, he'd made 40 runs and I had 41. We were laughing because we thought that when the time came for us to score some runs, things would turn. They did for him but not for me.'

Just why Tony Cottey lost his form so dramatically in 1997 is difficult to say. The former Swansea City footballer with the idiosyncratic batting style feels the problem might have been the result of a combination of wet weather and a change of preparation.

'Not having gone abroad during the winter for the past few years, pre-season was always a big fortnight for me – the chance to find some form in the outdoor nets before competitive cricket starts. Last season, we didn't go on tour.

'Although the weather was wonderful in April, there was a lot of rain about early on in the season, so I was going for about five or six days without either a net or an innings. I didn't get into any rhythm and the season just seemed to slip away. But there was no particular point when I thought, God – I'm struggling here!

'Another game would go by and I still wasn't scoring when I got in. It didn't matter too much because the runs were coming from Steve, Hugh, Adrian and Matthew. That was the thing I found hard to take – I couldn't score any runs but the side was still successful. There were plenty of times when I would go back to my hotel room or home and say to myself: Things have got to change here – I can't suddenly have become a bad player after six decent years.'

There was little sign of improvement as Tony struggled to find his touch. He managed 15 against Durham and then 19 in the first innings against Middlesex at Cardiff. For the only time last summer, he top-scored with 12 as Glamorgan collapsed to 31 all out in their second innings. The humour within the Glamorgan camp helped keep Tony's spirits up as the wickets kept tumbling.

'We did really well for two days against Middlesex and then were skittled out on the Saturday that the British Lions rugby team were playing in South Africa. I was batting and Crofty came in when we were 11 for 4.

'"It's a disgrace!" he said, "so unprofessional. I can't believe it – they just want to watch the second half of the Lions against Natal match!"

'Then, first ball, Crofty was lbw to James Hewitt, we were 11 for 5 and he was on his way back to the pavilion! I think his comment was a little tongue-in-cheek but we gave him some stick later. That result was probably the kick up the backside we needed. The very next game we went up to Liverpool and bowled out Lancashire for 51 and then watched the second half of the First

Test in South Africa when Neil Jenkins kicked the Lions to victory! Looking back, the Middlesex defeat was a one-off. Sometimes you need incidents like that to kick-start your season.'

It worked for Glamorgan – three successive wins followed – but not for Tony. Try as he might – and nobody tried harder – nothing seemed capable of getting his season going. In fact, frustration turned to embarrassment because of his position as vice-captain and a senior player on the team's management committee.

'I think I played in the first team too long,' reflects Tony. 'I should have been dropped a lot earlier to try to re-discover my form in the seconds. If I'd got a hundred and spent three or four hours in the middle and then regained my place, my season might have flourished more than it did.

'Being on the team management committee made it a little more difficult for me and, as the season progressed, I went to see Matthew a couple of times to discuss the problem.

'"Look," I said, "we're good mates and I'm your vice-captain but I don't want to put you under any pressure. I know I'm struggling for form, so don't ever think you've got to hang on in there for me."

'I pointed out to Matthew that Mike Powell and Alun Evans might be able to come in and do a better job but he pointed to my career record and assured me that things would turn.'

But they didn't – even with the help of Duncan Fletcher. The new coach had initially kept his distance but was on hand to help out when Tony's form continued to desert him.

'Duncan must have been in a very difficult position – looking at my statistics for the previous seasons and then seeing me have a nightmare. I've got my own rather unconventional way of batting which has always worked for me in the past, and Duncan tried all sorts of things with my technique. The biggest problem was that my confidence had gone.

'Duncan made me feel very much part of things – he could easily have slid me off the management committee. He was a very positive person and was brilliant to have around. He didn't talk about losing. He was always upbeat with me when we had throw-downs in the morning, and when I hit a few in the middle of the bat, he would tell me that my feet were going well and this would be the day that I turned it around.'

As Tony attempted to come to terms with an increasingly barren run, his wife Gail was having problems with her second

117

pregnancy. She hadn't been well for three of four months before Seren was born in early August.

'There's no doubt that Tony was struggling,' says Duncan Fletcher, 'and I believe his wife being pregnant affected him mentally. One of the rules I introduced was that no mobile phones were allowed to ring in the changing room. If they did, the player was fined £5 but Tony asked if he could have special permission while his wife was expecting and, of course, I had to agree in the circumstances. I think the pregnancy really played on him.'

'I was obviously concerned about Gail,' Tony explains, 'but I don't believe that was the reason for my loss of form. It would be me looking for an excuse – scoring runs was the only thing on my mind when I went out to bat. Duncan's attitude was very helpful – me worrying about the pregnancy was a nice way of explaining why I had lost form but it wasn't true.

'I have nothing but admiration for Alan Jones and John Derrick but I think someone coming in fresh from a different country with new ideas gave a few people the kick up the backside they needed. It was good to have someone around all the time who didn't know too much about us and whom we wanted to please.

'He was great at instilling confidence and my performance in the last three or four games was down to him – even though I knew deep down that I wasn't playing as well as I could, at least I did make a contribution.'

Tony hit rock bottom in, of all places, his home city of Swansea in late June. Glamorgan were playing Sussex in the first of two championship games at St Helen's. Surely this was the perfect opportunity to launch his comeback? It seemed tailor-made for Tony – especially in view of his record at the ground.

'In my last thirteen knocks at St Helen's, my lowest score had been 51. I walked out against the bottom side of the championship and I bagged a pair – only the second in my life on what had been a great ground for me! You can imagine how depressed I felt!'

The demolition of Sussex was followed by the complete annihilation of close rivals Gloucestershire and, at last, Tony made runs – 76 not out in a total of 400 for 5 declared.

'I wasn't in very good nick but I finished the second day on 26 not out and the most relieved I'd been all season. I'd actually got a start and battled it out. I hit a few decent shots the next day but generally it was a case of grinding out the runs because I knew my place was in jeopardy. It was just a question of putting together a decent score.'

The nightmare seemed over but for how long? In fact, there was little respite. After being run out for 14 in the draw with Derbyshire, Tony failed again against Nottinghamshire at Colwyn Bay. His close friend and captain Matthew Maynard had to bow to the inevitable.

'I was dropped after the draw with Nottinghamshire when I was lbw for 0 to Nathan Astle. Matthew knew my confidence had gone and I needed a break. That was fair enough – I'd been lucky to hang on for as long as I did. Even so, it was a very bitter pill to swallow.'

Throughout his disappointing run, Tony had been sitting on the team's management committee. Meetings had been difficult for the out-of-form vice-captain but none would match the one held before the Nat West Trophy semi-final against Essex at Chelmsford in early August.

'Funnily enough, I'd done pretty well in the one-day competitions – batting at five, averaging about 30 and scoring runs quite quickly. I thought I deserved to play against Essex. But I also knew that it was a 60-over game and the Nat West isn't that far removed from championship cricket. You always play your championship side in the Nat West because it's such a long game.

'The discussion about the team covered questions like whether we should play Dean Cosker or bring in Gary Butcher. It was the only meeting in 1997 at which I didn't say a word. I was thinking that if we needed to drop a batsman, I was the one who had to go! I wanted to play but I decided not to get involved.'

In the event, Tony justified his selection by scoring a quick 56 as Glamorgan went down to a dramatic one-wicket defeat after bad light had forced the players off. During the Essex innings, fate intervened. 'I tore a ligament in my little finger and I couldn't field for Darren Thomas's final over the following morning. I couldn't hold a bat, so even though I knew I'd been dropped for the next championship game at Worcester, I wasn't fit anyway.

'I then had a ten-day break during which I couldn't play second XI cricket either. I got away from it all and decided that when I started again I would have to work on a few things.'

When Hugh Morris withdrew from the Northants game after twisting his ankle before play began on the first day, a fit Tony Cottey might have been called up. But his injured finger ruled out a return and with Mike Powell replacing him, Glamorgan strolled to a six-wicket win.

Having dropped his vice-captain, Matthew Maynard then decided to recall Tony for the run-in. Four games – against Leicestershire, Surrey, Essex and Somerset – would decide the destination of the title.

'By his own very high standards,' says Matthew, 'Tony had a poor year, but he still contributed – especially in the Nat West semi-final and then in the vital championship match against Essex at Cardiff. I felt experience had to be the key at that stage of the season. Mike Powell had shown glimpses of what might be in store in the future but, in my view, not enough self-control out in the middle to convince me that he was ready for it then. Mike is a huge talent and he'll come through but I went for Tony and I was delighted that he didn't let me or himself down.'

'Matthew said we were going to play an extra batsman,' recalls Tony. 'We needed runs on the board to make sure we were in the game at Leicester, so I was recalled. It was like a bolt from the blue because I didn't expect to play again that season. It was like starting all over again.

'After all the self-doubts and lack of confidence and really being on the floor, my recall gave me a huge boost. Although I didn't get a big score in any of the matches, I made 25 against Leicestershire and then 34 at the Oval, and 46 and 35 not out against Essex at Cardiff.

'The best thing was having those ten days off. The break was a shot in the arm and I actually felt my form returning. Obviously, my second innings against Essex was part of an important stand but it's sad that I keep being reminded that my best knock of the season was 35 not out!'

There had been signs in the first innings that Tony was on the way back. Apart from Steve James, the first five batsmen had made runs, with Hugh Morris scoring 82, Adrian Dale 49 and Matthew Maynard 71. Tony weighed in with 46 – his second-highest innings of the season so far. A rare top-order collapse as Glamorgan chased a winning target of 149 demanded that the little man walk tall.

'It was very quiet when I went out to bat,' recalls Tony. 'It was very tense around the ground. The wicket, as usual at Cardiff, was slow and low, Matthew had just been dropped on 0 and, at 26 for 3 in a game we desperately needed to win, there were a lot of nerves jangling in the dressing room.'

Many of them belonged to Glamorgan's opening batsmen who, after their unusual double failure, were watching anxiously from the balcony. Having removed their gloves, pads and protectors, they could do nothing but wait and hope.

'Maybe we had tried to score a bit too quickly against Essex,' suggests Steve James. 'With a small target, there's always the temptation to blast away and get off to a bit of a flier. That obviously went wrong because Hugh and I were out with only 13 on the board.

'Hugh had really tucked into Ashley Cowan in the first innings – with five fours in an over – and we weren't expecting him to bowl in the second innings because of problems with his knee and shoulder. I was disappointed to be bowled for 4 but I was confident somebody would get the runs – that was the strength of the side throughout the season.

'When Adrian was bowled by Peter Such, Matthew and Cotts were struggling at the beginning and Hugh turned to me and said, "Bloody hell! Every run will be like gold dust now." That's how it turned out. The crowd were clapping every single. It was a funny wicket, probably the slowest I've ever played on in Cardiff, because of all the rain we'd had. As it was, Tony produced a brilliant innings. He's a class player and I had a feeling he would score some runs that day because he excels in that type of situation – he's a battler.'

'I didn't feel under any more pressure than normal,' says Tony, 'because I saw it as an opportunity to do something significant in the championship year. Probably, I was the best person to go into bat at that time! Essex's tails were up and a lot of banter was flying around – especially after our acrimonious Nat West semi-final against them. They felt they were the team who were going to stop us winning the championship!

'I remember flicking my first ball away for a single through the covers – it was then a case of keeping my end up. We just decided to bat the overs down one by one and the longer Essex went without getting a wicket, the quieter they became. Once we got up to about 70, we felt a bit safer. I just got on the front foot and played from there.'

Slowly but surely, and then with increasing confidence, the skipper and his first lieutenant edged Glamorgan to their winning target. In the first innings, they had put on 127; this time, their stand was worth three fewer. A nudge here, a glide there, by turns watchful and combative, the pair took Glamorgan to a seven-wicket victory and a one-point lead at the top of the championship table.

As he watched this enthralling struggle from his office at the Cathedral Road End boundary, the Cricket Board of Wales's director Peter Walker recalled a recent conversation with Tony Cottey, one of his CBW winter development officers.

'I'd seen him play in Aberystwyth where he'd come with me to open a cricket pavilion on a Sunday. He was telling me how hard he found being out of the team but how, as a former footballer, he fully appreciated that professional sport can be cruel. He was desperate to get back in and start performing.

'He didn't play at all well in scratching 30-odd at Aberystwyth but he was recalled to the side because Mike Powell hadn't quite produced the goods. In the real crisis point – rounds 11 and 12 of a heavyweight title fight, if you like, when you're out on your feet but you've got to stay upright and keep punching – Tony delivered the goods.

'The second innings he played against Essex with no form at all, to support Matthew, was comparable to his captain's. Tony only got 35 but had he gone cheaply, then the whole pack of cards could have collapsed too. I don't care how experienced you are, you get terribly nervous. He came in and ground out his runs. I thought it was a memorable innings in its own right, full of guts and determination – totally in character.'

'When Matthew hit the winning run and we came off,' says Tony, 'I just felt so relieved. It was very emotional on the balcony because we knew we could now go to Taunton and win the championship. Two hours earlier, we could see the wheels coming off again – don't forget we had lost three Nat West semi-finals in the 1990s. This was just like a semi-final and two of the three batsmen out, when I joined Matthew, had been the mainstay of our season.'

Peter Walker believes the two sessions before and after lunch were the key passages of play in Glamorgan's run-in to the title. Defeat would have rendered the result at Taunton irrelevant.

'I remember spending a lot of time looking at the home balcony as well as what was going on out on the pitch during the Essex game. I could recognise and share, through long-distant memory, the ball-by-ball anxiety. It's almost impossible to convey in print what it's like to sit and watch, when every ball is like a game of Russian roulette – a wicket might go down and there's still a hundred runs to get. Emotionally and physically, it's like running a marathon at 1,500 metres speed. As you watch, your heart's in your mouth with every ball. Funnily enough, by the time you actually have to go and bat yourself, it somehow clears.

'I'm not sure why, but as you walk out, it gets easier because now you are much more in control of the destiny of the game. Even though you might be out first ball, you're doing something and it's pro-active. Just to sit, waiting your turn, that's the hard part about cricket. I also felt very tense that day and I wasn't even playing!'

The former Glamorgan all-rounder had another good reason to remember the match-winning fightback. Indeed, it will be difficult for him to forget because of one particular cricketing superstition.

'If a stand begins – especially after a couple of wickets have gone down – people are reluctant to leave their seats in the dressing room because it might change the team's luck. During the Maynard-Cottey partnership, I found myself at one stage listening to one of the great bores of Glamorgan cricket in the committee room.

'I'm not going to name him but the conversation started when we were 26 for 3 and when we'd reached about 40, I was looking for an excuse to move but decided I daren't. Fortunately, he had a business appointment which he couldn't escape and after about an hour and a quarter, he left. I stayed where I was until we'd won about 90 minutes later!'

After his leading role against Essex, Tony had a walk-on part in the final act of Glamorgan's championship-winning season at Taunton. Maynard and Morris had savaged the Somerset attack as he came out to join his former captain.

'It was pitch black when I went out to bat and because we had to make up time, it was just a case of playing like a one-day game. I started to push the ball around and make sure that we were still scoring. I got 13 off about ten balls and I felt in pretty good nick. It was just nice to be part of it all.

'The partnership between Graham Rose and Andy Caddick was very frustrating because of the uncertainty about the weather and we all felt the tension rising. When Dean took the final wicket, my first thought was: Shall I keep the ball? It had flown off Ben Trott's pad into my hands at first slip! I decided I would, so I put it in my pocket – everyone else had grabbed a stump. But after Darren's fantastic performance in taking five Somerset wickets, I had the ball mounted and his figures engraved on a plate and presented it to him at a dinner the following week.

'Although Steve James hit the four to win the match, we'd actually won when Dean had Ben Trott leg-before. It's always nicer to win a game when you're fielding because all eleven of you are out there together, having slogged your way through the opposition for four or five hours. To come off knowing we'd won was wierd. There was a strange atmosphere in the dressing room because Steve and Hugh were trying to psych themselves up to go and score the 11 runs – the other nine of us were going bananas!'

When the winning runs were scored, one of the jokers in the Glamorgan pack could at last relax. The life and soul of the party could enjoy the party after putting on a brave face for much of a season of huge personal disappointment. 'I'm one of the mickey takers in the dressing room – one of the loudest voices, along with people like Robert Croft and Adrian Shaw – but when you're struggling for form, it's very difficult to maintain that.

'About a week after the end of the season, we all received in the post a summary of our performances from Duncan. Mine pointed out a few minor things to work on and congratulated me on my attitude in the changing room. Duncan said I didn't go into my shell and he wouldn't have thought that I was the one struggling for form. That was probably the nicest thing he said to me, because it was very difficult to stay upbeat when I was feeling so low myself.'

Throughout the season, the team's spirits were kept high by a weekend ritual on away trips. A player would be chosen as 'Fool of the Week' for one particular misdemeanour and received the award at the team meal on either the Friday or Saturday night.

'After the day's play, we would have a quick meeting where everybody said what each player had done wrong, the things they'd got up to which had backfired. The winner would receive a jester's hat, an Hawaiian shirt and the current beneficiary's tie – all of which had to be worn for the entire evening.

'Second XI coach John Derrick won it once for a comment he made during a meal we were having in an Italian restaurant. He'd ordered a pizza and the waitress asked him if he'd like it cut into four or six slices? "You'd better make it four," said John, "I'll never manage six!"

'Hugh Morris picked up the award for going out to bat in green pads on the Monday after a Sunday League game and again for turning up at Headingley with the keys of Gary Butcher's car in his pocket – Gary managed to organise a lift from Cardiff to the ground with another player. They were silly things which added to the camaraderie. It's a long season and you spend more time with the boys than you do with your own wife – it's important to be able to let off steam occasionally!'

Along with Steve Watkin, Tony Cottey is now the longest-serving player on Glamorgan's books although they both made their debuts in 1986 – a year after Matthew Maynard.

'Cricket's changed a lot since we started,' says Tony. 'We train harder, we're more professional and we're looked after well. One of the things that I think has changed for the worse is that we play most of our games in Cardiff. Swansea seems to have fallen away but I'm delighted that – thanks to the efforts of the Balconiers – there'll be cricket at St Helen's in 1998 – a four-day and Sunday League match game against Surrey.

'We are a national team and we've got great support all over Wales. I'm from the west, as are a lot of the boys who have come through the ranks, and it's a bit sad that everything's starting to be centred in Cardiff. Glamorgan are a bigger county than that, we're Wales in cricketing terms.

'I understand that you need a headquarters but it's unfortunate that cricket has been taken so far away from a lot of people in Pembrokeshire who are big supporters. I wish we could play a few more fixtures in Swansea.

'The Welsh identity is a big thing for Glamorgan – the more you push that, the more support you'll get and when things are a little bit ropey on the field, this helps you to pull together and produce that extra five per cent that can win you a game.

'Now, I feel very much part of a squad whereas when I started it was a team and I was always worried about losing my place. Everyone felt at the beginning of last season that they were in with a chance of playing first team cricket. There was a gelling of all the boys – we're all mates off the field anyway, there's nobody you wouldn't have a drink with. It didn't matter about your age or generation – from Hugh Morris, who was 34, to Dean Cosker just 19, we were all together.'

Tony Cottey is a real all-rounder. As well as spending three years with Swansea City in the Eighties, he has taken part in two marathons – New York in 1995 and Athens the following year. Like all long-distance runners, he knows all about lasting the course. During 1997, Tony was down but never out. His self-confidence may have gone but his team mates, administrators and commentators never lost faith in him.

'Tony knew in his heart of hearts,' says Adrian Dale, 'that he was getting the full backing of all the other players. We have all gone through it and everybody respected him as a good player because he'd done it consistently over a number of years. Watch out for him in 1998!'

'I think you just have to write off last season as a blip,' says secretary Mike Fatkin. 'He'll come back fighting because he's that sort of player. He's the guts of the side. If you're in a spot of bother, he's probably the best guy to dig you out of it.'

'A lot of plaudits should go to Tony,' says Peter Walker, 'who, after three good years, had a desperate season. He suddenly lost it – that happens to every player. It also took a lot of strength of character for Matthew to leave him out because he's such an inspiration in the field. We should never undervalue fielding. This was a great fielding side – away from the wicket, particularly – and Tony was in the front line of that. He was worth 15 or 20 runs before he even walked out to the crease.'

After the worst season of his 12-year first team career, Tony didn't pick up a bat for three months – apart from during his coaching sessions as a development officer for the Cricket Board of Wales. But he was back in the nets at the beginning of January and felt his confidence returning as he prepared for the pre-season trip to Jersey in April. 'Nets are different to outdoors but my feet moved well. The break over the winter probably helped wipe the memory slate clean.

'When my career comes to an end, 1992 – the year I was capped – 1993 and 1997 will stand out as the highlights, even though they weren't the best years for me personally. Three sides have won the championship for Glamorgan – I was in one of them – and only half a dozen players have ever won two trophies with Glamorgan – and I'm one of them. I was also vice-captain of a championship-winning side – despite the fact that I had a poor season myself. I'm very proud on all counts.

'I'll start back this season with a career average of 38, and 1997 will be forgotten if I get a hundred in the first game.'

With Tony's track record, not too many people would bet against him doing just that.

PART 5

Behind the Crease

WAQAR IS A WELSHMAN

Two hours after Glamorgan had won the 1997 Britannic Assurance County Championship at Taunton, the trophy was on its way back to Cardiff for safe keeping and the celebrations in the Somerset clubhouse were well underway.

Six months of hard work had ended in triumph and the players were justifiably starting to let their hair down. In front of the most appreciative of audiences, they were going through their choral repertoire. It was a moment to savour. Clapping and cheering, hurrahs and hoorays greeted every song as the players, having bonded together throughout the season, now consummated their relationship with their loyal supporters.

For possibly the first time all summer, the side was divided into two camps. The main group consisted of the Welsh contingent – the elder statesmen like Matthew Maynard, Hugh Morris, Steve Watkin and Tony Cottey who, with bottles or glasses in hand, whooped it up with the youngsters – Dean Cosker, Darren Thomas, Alun Evans and Adrian Shaw. It had the makings of a long night!

Just behind them, to their left, standing on a couple of chairs with their arms around each other's shoulders, were two men. Part of the revelry but separate, alone but not aloof. One wore a Welsh rugby jersey, the other his casual but smart Glamorgan uniform – club denim shirt and chinos. Both were outsiders who had crossed the border to help Glamorgan re-tread the path to victory. Duncan Fletcher via Zimbabwe and South Africa, Waqar Younis courtesy of Pakistan and Surrey.

The players had given their new coach the jersey as a mark of acceptance and affection. The world's fastest bowler was in no need of such a gift. From Cardiff to Swansea to Abergavenny and Colwyn Bay, one thing was clear. Anyone who had followed Glamorgan in 1997 knew it already; some supporters sang it every time he made an appearance. The truth is out there: Waqar is a Welshman. He may have been born in Pakistan, educated in Sharjah and played a lot of his cricket in London, but during the summer of 1997, Waqar 'Wicky' Younis became one of the boys.

'I signed for Glamorgan,' recalls the Pakistan Test bowler, 'because they offered me the best contract and I felt I would be playing not for just another county but another country. They came across as a really hard-working national team and my first impression proved to be right.

'I really enjoyed my first season with Glamorgan – the guys were very nice and they really helped me out. The Welsh people were very good hosts, they looked after me well and I was very happy for them when I helped Glamorgan to win the championship.'

Waqar's connection with Wales originated at Lord's in the summer of 1996 during Pakistan's visit to England. As a member of the MCC committee, the former Glamorgan captain and chairman Tony Lewis found himself sitting next to the unsettled former Surrey star at a welcome dinner for the tourists.

'I had commentated on Pakistan around the world and had seen quite a bit of Waqar,' says Tony. 'I felt we badly needed someone to bowl teams out and help Steve Watkin – a fast bowler who could knock over the leading batsmen, roll over the tail and then get some runs down the order.

'I started chatting to Waqar and he said he'd be interested in joining Glamorgan. He'd first played for Surrey in 1990 but told me that he wouldn't be going back there – apparently, they didn't understand his particular needs. The Middlesex chairman, Alan Moss, was sitting opposite us and he approached me as I walked out at the end of the evening.

'"So you've signed him have you?" Alan asked. "I heard every word!"

'"No," I replied, "you can't do it over dinner!"'

But you can if you move, like Waqar on the field, very quickly. Having made the initial approach, Tony set the wheels in motion by contacting skipper Matthew Maynard and Glamorgan secretary Mike Fatkin. 'They met Waqar in the next couple of days but during the Oval Test, Surrey then decided to have another nibble – Robert Croft kept coming up to the commentary box to tell me what was going on! I kept ringing Waqar's agent, Jonathan Barnett, and in the end, after Mike had returned to London for more negotiations, we signed him.

'I suppose I was the catalyst but I don't deserve any special praise – the decision was Matthew's and his advisers. Mind you, if I hadn't seen the potential of having Waqar in our side, I'd have been as thick as that table!'

The signing of Waqar was a stupendous *coup* for Glamorgan. It was on a par with those of two other Pakistani predecessors in the county colours, Majid Khan and Javed Miandad. Here was a Test bowler at the top of his form, coming to play in Wales! The 90 mile-an-hour speed merchant, complete with reverse swinging yorkers, would be plying his trade on the strips of Cardiff and Swansea. It seemed incredible, unbelievable – but it was true. Waqar was coming and the rest of English cricket had better watch out!

'Waqar just lifted the dressing room,' recalls Matthew Maynard. 'After we'd signed him at the back end of 1996, the lads just couldn't wait for the new season to start.'

'Matthew himself was very excited,' recalls secretary Mike Fatkin. 'We had barely pulled out of Paddington before his address book and mobile were in use – Matthew was ringing anyone and everyone to tell them that Waqar was a Welshman! You have to speak very loudly into a mobile phone on a train and about fifty people had moved away from us by the time we reached Reading!'

'Waqar took a lot of weight off Steve Watkin's shoulders,' says Matthew. 'Watty had carried the burden of the Glamorgan attack ever since breaking into the first team ten years earlier and Waqar relieved some of the pressure on him, as well as bringing out the best in Darren Thomas. On his own, I reckon he won three games outright for us.'

Robert Croft had more reason than most to welcome Waqar to Wales. At their only previous meeting in 1996, the Pakistani pace man had bowled Crofty a bouncer as his first ball in Test cricket.

'I remember speaking to Alec Stewart at an England get-together before Waqar came and he told me how disappointed Surrey were not to have re-signed him. "He's a great guy," said Alec, "the only thing you may have to do is learn to accept that he may be late on the odd morning. Not for the start of the game but for the pre-match warm-up." Alec's prophecy proved to be right.

'Sometimes Waqar would indeed turn up a bit late but all the boys ignored it. Had he not been such a great fella, it could have been the start of a bit of friction. We all knew he was a great cricketer but he was also a fantastic fella and everyone just warmed to him straightaway.

'He was superb. Obviously there was a lot expected from him early on, not so much from the players but by the public. It was said he was coming in on a high wage to clean up the town!'

Coach Duncan Fletcher had mixed feelings when he heard about Glamorgan's other new close-season signing. 'I wanted to work with this international bowler but I didn't know how he would relate to me.'

After assessing Waqar's potential contribution to the side and the reaction of the other players to their new colleague, Fletcher decided that Waqar should become a special case.

'I treated him differently to the rest of the team because he was a superstar. I was more lenient about when he had to pitch up at the ground. He didn't have to be on time but he still got fined on certain occasions for minor, jokey misdemeanours but he responded brilliantly and took it all in good spirit.

'I think Waqar fitted in fantastically – he related well to everybody. He was very keen to discuss the way a game might be going and spoke when he felt certain decisions had to be made. He was a first-class individual, a very nice man.'

When he arrived in Wales, Waqar was in plaster. It was thought he had suffered a stress fracture of his left foot while playing for Pakistan in Sri Lanka, and Glamorgan feared the worst. But a scan at the BUPA Hospital in Cardiff, under the watchful eye of club physiotherapist Dean Conway, dispelled the gloom.

'He'd been in plaster in Colombo for three weeks,' says Dean, 'and as soon as he came to us, we took it off. His injury had been diagnosed on the back of a simple X-ray in Colombo but after talking to Waqar we were hopeful. If it had been a true stress fracture, there was no way that we as a club could have taken it on – he would have needed three months to recover.

'The scan confirmed there wasn't a stress fracture. We also had his lower back checked out. The scans were relatively clear but for normal wear-and-tear markings. Both the surgeons we consulted said Waqar was fine, so we were happy to take a punt on him. There was a slight risk involved but he seemed in pretty good nick.'

With the help of club coach and physiotherapist, Waqar's return to fitness was merely a matter of time. He appreciated the help given by Duncan Fletcher after receiving the all-clear from the hospital.

'I really needed somebody to help me out in the first couple of weeks,' Waqar recalls. 'We met at the ground three or four times and Duncan came with his gloves and was telling me where I was going wrong – I was struggling with my rhythm in the early season.

'Fletch is one of the best coaches I have come across. He was basically a very nice gentleman and he kept the atmosphere in the dressing room very cool. He always helped the guys out – especially the youngsters – but when I needed him he was always there. He was a hard-working guy and, like him, I love my cricket – I really put everything into it when I'm on the field – so we formed a good combination.

'Waqar was keen to play straightaway,' says Dean Conway, 'but we held him back to work on his muscle wastage – particularly on his calf – and he made his championship debut against Yorkshire at Headingley. From the first game, you could see he was going flat out and he wasn't a problem for me.'

The opposition batsmen weren't so lucky. After making a quiet start with a wicket in the draw with Yorkshire, Waqar took 3 for 52 as Kent were beaten by 87 runs at Canterbury, and 7 for 154 in the innings defeat of Durham in Cardiff. But it was in the rain-affected match against Lancashire in Liverpool that he really started to repay Glamorgan. Set 273 to win on the final day, Lancashire were skittled out for 51, thanks to Waqar's 7 for 25 from 7 overs – including his first first-class hat-trick.

'That result was the sort that wins teams the championship,' recalls Waqar. 'We were nowhere when, suddenly, the rain stopped and we played for three hours at the most and won the game! I was delighted with my hat-trick. Actually, I didn't know I was on one! I took a wicket with the last ball of one over and the next two with the first two balls of the next over. After the third wicket, all the guys were really happy and I realised what had happened. I probably got the hat-trick because I didn't know I was on one – there was no pressure on me, so I was just bowling normally.'

Waqar went one better in Glamorgan's next game by taking a career-best 8 for 17 from nearly 16 overs, as Sussex collapsed to 54 all out and eventually lost by a huge 234 runs. 'To be fair,' says Waqar, 'the wicket at Swansea was pretty helpful, the cloud cover made the ball swing more and the guys in the slips caught everything that came by.'

Modesty forbad Waqar from revealing that half his victims were either bowled or lbw. He then picked up another five wickets as Gloucestershire were put to the sword. The Waqar Factor was certainly making itself felt.

'Waqar took his wickets at precisely the right time,' says

Duncan Fletcher. 'Even though he sometimes didn't take many in a game, if you look back, he did pick up the vital ones. In Gloucestershire's second innings at Swansea, he got rid of their last two batsmen who had scored 41 and 10 respectively, and put on 39 for the ninth wicket. It was vital because we knew we had to get them out and get back onto the field to win.'

Waqar continued to collect wickets during the draws with Derbyshire and Nottinghamshire and the defeat at Worcester, before picking up his first 10-wicket haul against Northampton-shire at Abergavenny. A devastating spell of three in eight balls in the Northants second innings set up the victory and Waqar fleetingly took over the captaincy when Matthew Maynard dislocated a finger while fielding. 'It was my easiest big haul of the summer because their batsmen weren't in form. My bowling was sharp, with lots of rhythm, and I really enjoyed the day.'

After the draw at Leicester, Glamorgan travelled to Waqar's former stamping ground, the Oval. He took two wickets in both innings on his return but not even Waqar could prise out Graham Thorpe whose 222 kept Glamorgan at bay. Matthew Maynard's decision to abort a run-chase left Surrey fuming – and out of the championship race.

Glamorgan knew that maximum points in their last two games against Essex and Somerset would bring them the title. Again, Waqar did the business when it mattered. Three wickets in the Essex first innings were followed by a couple in their second, including that of danger man Ronnie Irani.

'There was a crucial moment in that match,' recalls Steve James. 'Ronnie had showed in the Nat West semi-final against us that he could be a little beligerent and he was now on his way to a half-century. Waqar, looking a bit tired and perhaps not firing on all cylinders, was bowling and Ronnie hit him over long-on to bring up his 50. It was a pretty brave stroke against one of the world's fastest bowlers.

'"That's an interesting shot!" said Adrian Dale to me,' recalls Steve.

'"Yeah," I replied, "it's also a bloody good shot for us!"

'After that, the atmosphere in the ground changed. Waqar was fired up. He roared in and bowled Ronnie all ends up. He then gave him a bit of a verbal send-off and received a telling-off for his troubles but that was a turning point in the match, if not the season.'

And so to Taunton for the denouement. Match-winning innings by Matthew Maynard and Tony Cottey had seen off Essex to set up the final act of the season. The mathematics were simple. If Glamorgan won – and picked up every available bonus point – they would beat Kent to the title, regardless of what happened at Canterbury. Everything looked set fair – even the weather.

Suddenly, out of nowhere, Glamorgan had a problem. Waqar was ill. In fact, so ill that he might not be able to play. Having rejected a plea from Majid Khan, the Pakistan Cricket Board's chief executive, to help out with an injury crisis in the Sahara Cup in Canada, Waqar found himself holed up in a hotel room facing the prospect of not playing for anyone. The sharp instrument that had cut a swathe through opposition batting orders throughout the summer was in danger of being blunted.

'I really wasn't feeling well at Taunton,' says Waqar. 'The night before the game, I had a fever and couldn't really sleep. I shouldn't have played against Somerset but I did because we had a chance of winning the championship.'

'I had a call from Waqar at about two o'clock in the morning of the Thursday when the Somerset game was due to start,' recalls Dean Conway. 'He was feverish and cold, so we checked his temperature. He obviously had some sort of bug. At that stage, he was pretty doubtful. I felt he probably would get through the game but he would suffer after giving everything for the best part of a day.

'Forty minutes before the start, Waqar had a little jog around and, although he didn't feel great, he said he wanted to play. The Somerset doctor came down to check him out and revealed that Waqar had quinsy – a nasty throat infection. The doctor said that Waqar needed antibiotics straightaway and, in his view, shouldn't play. But as it was ten to eleven, I wasn't going to tell Waqar that!'

Waqar made light of his illness to take four of the first six wickets to fall as Somerset reached 252, and then left his hotel room to contribute 5 to Glamorgan's reply. The virus meant he was unusually ineffective in Somerset's second innings when Darren Thomas took the honours but, by the time Steve James had hit the championship-winning runs, Waqar was well enough to celebrate! As the party continued on the Taunton balcony, he emerged from the Glamorgan dressing room holding not one mobile phone but two. It's good to talk and he had a lot to talk about.

'When they signed me, Glamorgan had big hopes that they were going to win something. I was pretty sure that we could do well

135

and the boys really did work hard. Everybody put their heart and soul into winning the championship.

'It was basically down to the team spirit. I was very pleased because I played three seasons for Surrey and we never won anything but in my first year with Glamorgan we won the title. It really made me happy because of the faith Glamorgan had put in me and I felt I had really participated in the success.

'I will remember the 1997 season forever because playing for Glamorgan was a great honour. When I think of all the overseas players who have come before me – like Majid Khan, Javed Miandad and Viv Richards – I was so proud to help win the championship in my first season. I have got one more year of my contract to go – let's see what happens after that.'

All Glamorgan supporters will be hoping that Waqar returns to Sophia Gardens in 1999 – along with Duncan Fletcher, perhaps, after his season off? Colleagues and commentators are unanimous in the view that Glamorgan would not have become county champions without Waqar.

'He was the final piece in the jigsaw in the bowling department,' says Hugh Morris, the former Glamorgan opener and now the Technical Director of the England and Wales Cricket Board. 'We needed someone to complement the consistency of Watkin and Croft, and Waqar was the bowler to do that.

'I didn't really know him that well before he came to Glamorgan but I was very impressed by the way he fitted into the whole set-up. He was very relaxed about it all, he got on well very quickly with the lads and really seemed to enjoy being in Cardiff. When you come from another country, it's important that you're made to feel welcome and I think Waqar was and he appreciated that.'

'One of the great sights in cricket always has been a fast bowler running in from the distance,' says Don Shepherd, now a BBC Radio Wales summariser. 'I can go back to Wes Hall, Brian Statham and Fred Trueman. Waqar has a glorious, balanced run-up – a little like Ray Lindwall – and a nice smooth action. He possibly wasn't as quick as he was when he played for Surrey but when the conditions were in his favour, he was unplayable.'

Another member of the 1969 Glamorgan championship-winning side, Roger Davis, believes that Waqar has continued the tradition established by other world-class overseas stars who have come to Wales.

'Players like Waqar Younis and Viv Richards are highly disciplined people. They're very responsible as professionals and they bring that into a changing room. When younger players see how well they behave and look after themselves, how they train, how dedicated they are and how much effort they put in, then it rubs off. They don't allow their standards to drop. The others notice this and follow suit.

'Waqar is one of the great fast bowlers of all time. In 1997, he picked up 68 championship wickets, he always tried – sometimes too hard – and he gave everything, although he didn't always bowl as well as he wanted to. He was popular in the dressing room, people respected him – he's a god to players like Darren Thomas – and I think he'll perform better in his second year.'

'Waqar gave Glamorgan a cutting edge that they'd never had before,' says Peter Walker, another 1969 winner. 'In my playing days, we often struggled to bowl out the tailenders. The job of a world-class fast bowler is to get rid of the best batsman at the top end and then come back and blast out the tail. I thought Waqar would do that and he did so – if not quite as often as I thought he would. But he did give the team an extra dimension.

'What sets him apart from everyone else, apart from sheer pace, is the angle of his bowling arm – it's well short of the traditional upright point of release. He lets go of the ball from close to the stumps and bowls a much fuller length than most fast bowlers. He's also got a lethal in-swinging yorker which he seems to be able to bowl almost at will.'

Within weeks of Glamorgan's success at Taunton, Waqar was celebrating again as Pakistan wrapped up a 3-0 series over the West Indies in Karachi. It had been quite a year for the 27-year-old pace bowler but something wasn't quite right. A firm but polite phone call to Glamorgan secretary Mike Fatkin soon solved the problem.

'We'd promised to send Waqar some photographs of the celebrations at Taunton,' explained Mike, 'and we hadn't got round to it. They were very quickly put in the post!'

Mike Fatkin, like most Test and county batsmen, realised that it is always advisable to have Waqar on your side. With nearly 700 first-class wickets to his name, Waqar Younis is indeed a formidable opponent. Looking back, Robert Croft, having faced his new team mate at international level, felt a certain amount of sympathy for Kent's Nigel Long during Glamorgan's second championship match in 1997.

'Waqar's first ball was the away-swinger to the left-hander and Nigel missed it. Waqar scraped his foot on the floor and returned to his mark. The next one was the in-swinger. Nigel left it and the ball went over the top of middle and off. He then bowled another ball which Nigel couldn't get a bat on. Standing halfway down the wicket, with his hands on his hips, Waqar turned to Nigel and shook his head. Then, in his most cultured Anglo-Pakistani voice, he said: "Nigel, you just haven't got a fucking clue, have you?"'

After sending down such a frustrating set of deliveries, most fast bowlers would be effing and blinding all the way back to the start of their run-up. Not this one. Throughout his first season with Glamorgan, Waqar was always a gentleman – and, of course, a Welshman.

'The people in Wales were really loving and sweet to me. I'm really grateful to them for thinking of me as one of their own. I'll continue to work very hard on the field and if I can give them more happiness in the future, I'll be really glad.'

FRINGE BENEFIT

IT couldn't have happened to a nicer guy. Twelve years after making his debut, nine years after being capped and, most importantly, a year after Glamorgan won the county championship, Steve Watkin has hit the jackpot. 1998 is his benefit season.

With the departure of Hugh Morris, Steve shares with Tony Cottey the distinction of being Glamorgan's longest-serving player. Like Hugh, whose benefit followed the 1993 Sunday League win, Steve is poised to reap his rewards on the back of a rare Glamorgan success – and there can hardly have been a more deserving beneficiary.

After more than 200 matches and nearly 700 wickets, Steve Watkin is a credit to his profession. The likeable seamer has been one of Glamorgan's most hard-working and consistent servants. He won three Test caps for England in 1991 and has taken 50 wickets in a season nine times. Last year, he finished with 61 championship victims at nearly 23 runs each.

'The perfect benefit year is either the season when you're winning the championship or the year after,' says Steve. 'Colin Metson's went very well last year, and after our win, it's been so much easier to approach people. A lot of clubs have got in touch to hold benefit functions and the ones we've had so far have gone very well.

'The fact that cricket's in the limelight at the moment has obviously helped. Early on in the year, we held a few events in the Neath area – like a dinner dance and a sports forum – before having the national launch at the Coal Exchange in Cardiff in the middle of March, where the former England fast bowler Fred Trueman was the guest speaker.'

As the start of the 1997 season approached, all the talk was of Steve's new bowling partner, Waqar Younis. Like most people, Watty was delighted to hear that the Pakistani Test star had put pen to paper.

'I just felt that he was the strike bowler we've needed for the last five years. Robert Croft and I were the two who regularly took

50-plus wickets a season but what we needed was a third bowler to do it. Waqar did brilliantly for us all season but the key to me was Darren Thomas – he was the bonus. To come in after 1996, when he wasn't on top of his game, and work hard in the winter, change his action a little bit and take nearly 50 championship wickets – including five in the last game – was fantastic.

'I didn't feel Waqar's arrival took any pressure off me. I just went about my game as any normal pro does. I tried to bowl in the right areas with the new ball, to keep it tight when necessary and then knock the tail over at the death.'

Waqar was still recovering from a foot injury when Glamorgan opened their campaign against Warwickshire at Cardiff. Steve was quickly among the wickets – taking 3 for 32 from 11 overs – but it was his batting which pleased him most during the first match.

'I went in as night-watchman at the end of the first day after Allan Donald had bowled Steve James. Allan was coming in at top pace and the plan was to see him off in order to make it easier for Adrian Dale to come in. I stayed in for an hour-and-a-half and scored 18 and put on 59 for the second wicket with Hugh Morris. I'd rate it as my best innings ever because Donald is one of the world's finest fast bowlers.'

Steve scored another 18 as he and Waqar both picked up a wicket apiece in the draw with Yorkshire and then during the victory over Kent. But again, his batting stole the show at Canterbury when he recorded a season's best of 39 as the Glamorgan tail wagged and wagged.

'Again, we were facing a good attack – England's Dean Headley, Martin McCague, Mark Ealham and Zimbabwe's Paul Strang – and we were in a spot of trouble at 191 for 8. Waqar with 47 and Darren with 48 also scored runs, and I was pleased that my knock helped us reach 279 and eventually win by 87 runs.

'Everybody who plays professional cricket takes their batting seriously. It's just unfortunate that we tailenders aren't able to practise as much as we'd like to because we're playing all the time.'

The game against Durham at Cardiff in late May was the first in which the two Ws – Waqar and Watty – worked in harness to demolish the opposition. Both took seven wickets in the match as Durham were skittled out twice in an innings victory.

'Seeing Waqar coming in to bowl must have a huge psychological effect on batsmen. He's Waqar Younis and as it put the fear of God into some of them, you might have thought they would relax a little against the bowler at the other end. Or, in other words, they would have a go at me.

'But it didn't actually work out like that – especially during the first half of the season – because Waqar is an attacking bowler. He tried lots of different things and he tended to go for four an over. So while he was taking wickets, there were opposition runs on the board too. If I bowled a nice tidy line, the batsmen tended just to see me off, and by going at only two-and-a-half runs an over, it helped to balance the ship.

'I think we were the ideal combination – I kept it tight at one end and moved it around a little bit, whilst Waqar was the all-out strike bowler. He was always attacking the batsmen – that's why we worked well as a partnership.'

For his part, Waqar was delighted with the new arrangement and very appreciative of the support provided by the Glamorgan warhorse. 'Watty is a very fine bowler and whenever there's a little bit of help in the wicket, he always makes the batsmen work hard against him. I think he's one of the best seam bowlers in English cricket at the moment.

'I probably did take some of the pressure off Steve because he's been bowling for Glamorgan for the last ten years or so – I was able to share the load. Darren Thomas and Crofty also bowled well and as we shared the wickets, there wasn't too much pressure on any one bowler. Darren is a very handy sort of a cricketer – he's sharp and nippy and could become a really good all-rounder.'

'To be honest,' says Steve, 'I don't think my performances in 1997 were any different from previous years. Crofty and I used to have a heavy workload and we would get days when we had to bowl ten or fifteen overs in an afternoon and go for 30, 40 or 50 runs on a flat wicket, and that would be reflected in our figures.

'In 1997, Waqar and I would bowl our six or seven overs to get wickets and that was it. Darren would then come on followed by Crofty and Dean Cosker. We two opening bowlers could go flat out, whereas before, when we didn't have the support around us, we had to bowl defensively and within ourselves quite regularly.'

'Steve and Waqar were ideally suited to bowl in tandem,' says former coach Duncan Fletcher. 'Waqar, because he's so positive and attacking, can be a bit loose and he tends to overpitch. But you have to if you're going to bowl people out with swing through the air. We were fortunate in having Steve at the other end applying relentless pressure. He hardly varied in line and length, so Steve and Waqar complemented each other well.'

'If you look at the figures,' says Steve, 'you'll see that Waqar and I both had more than 60 championship wickets at about 22, with Crofty and Darren either side of 50. With that quartet, you've got a good chance of winning the title or at least finishing in the top three. With Waqar, and Darren and Dean Cosker coming through, I think we were transformed from being an average county into a near Test-quality attack.

Steve lent solid support to Waqar in the defeats of Lancashire and Sussex and they shared fairly equal hauls in the matches against Gloucestershire, Derbyshire, Nottinghamshire and Worcester- shire. After Waqar had taken ten wickets in a match – against Northamptonshire – for the only time in the summer, it was Steve's turn to star at Leicester with 7 for 41.

'That was a game we were looking to win to keep at the top,' he recalls. 'We'd been bowled out for 226 and we knew we'd have to work hard to get rid of them for fewer than that. It was probably the first wicket that we had played on that suited my type of bowling. It was a bit of a green top – giving movement off the pitch – and plenty of pace. We bowled them out for 175 before the rain came.'

After picking up three wickets in the draw with Surrey at the Oval, Watty returned to Wales to play his part in Glamorgan's vital victory over Essex at Cardiff.

'Because of all the rain we'd had, the wicket was very, very slow and low and you just had to grind batsmen out. You had to bowl very straight and tight and just hope they'd make mistakes. I got three wickets in the first innings, when Essex played a bit recklessly, and then five in the second – that gave me a lot of pleasure because it was a game we had to win.'

Perhaps more than anyone else, Steve Watkin relished the prospect of the title being decided at Taunton. The County Ground had been a happy hunting ground for him over the years – 23 wickets in his last three championship games there, including match-winning figures of 7 for 49 in 1995. He wasn't to be disappointed in 1997 either.

Despite feeling under the weather, Waqar removed three of the top four Somerset batsmen while Steve picked up the other. To his first-innings haul of three, he added another three as Darren Thomas blew Somerset away in the second to leave Glamorgan needing just 11 runs to win.

'My memories of Taunton are Waqar's opening spell, Hugh and Matthew batting in the dark, Darren's five wickets and that stand of 95 between Graham Rose and Andy Caddick. It was a great feeling when Steve James hit the winning runs in front of all our Welsh supporters. We've always felt that we represent Wales and not just Glamorgan – we play under the Welsh banner and it's the closest we can get to playing for our country. We play with as much pride as any football or rugby international.'

As one of the more senior members in the Glamorgan squad, Steve admits to being a little sceptical about Duncan Fletcher's arrival at the start of last season. 'After all, we had an experienced side. A lot of the players had been together for five or six years. I wasn't sure about bringing in a coach who would come in and start changing things technically at this stage of these players' careers.

'But once the decision had been made, whoever was appointed was always going to get my hundred per cent support – you had to give him the best possible chance. Duncan's greatest attribute was his organisational skills and his man-management was outstanding – he seemed to get the best out of everybody and always had a very good rapport with the players.

'Duncan didn't do much with my technique, apart from reminding me that I was sometimes a bit lazy about following through. I remember Steve Barwick at mid-off and mid-on telling me off about that in previous seasons!

'Out in the field, we tend to help each other anyway. Duncan could see everything that was going on and if it was needed, he would have a chat during the lunch or tea interval but, at the end of the day, if things weren't going right during the two-hour sessions on the field, there were a lot of experienced players – like Matthew, Hugh and Cotts – to ask if you felt you were doing something wrong.'

Steve welcomed the different training drills introduced by Duncan Fletcher – even though some parts of the new coaching regime weren't to the liking of certain supporters. 'If we had a bad session in the field, some spectators used to criticise us for playing soccer and rugby as part of our warm-ups. They said we should practise our cricket skills instead, but the games were a means of getting loose.

'It's very boring to have to do 40 minutes of cricket practice in the morning – you go bananas – and the games were good fun. During a day, we would spend about six hours batting, fielding and bowling, so we needed a change. We had a few minor injuries as a result but generally it worked well.'

'Steve is just a tremendous bowler who performs at a high level day in day out,' says Duncan Fletcher. 'He believes in his ability, works at his skills and gets stuck in. He deserves to have a substantial benefit on the back of the championship win for all the hours, effort and overs that he's put in down the years.'

Sixteen years ago, Glamorgan's answer to Little and Large made their second XI debuts. At five foot five and six foot three, Tony Cottey and Steve Watkin could hardly be more different in size or temperament. But the long and short of it is that they have made an immense contribution to the Glamorgan cause. As part of the Welsh backbone of the current side, these two senior statesmen personify the spirit of the county. Having endured the bad days, they are now entitled to savour the good times. Their generation have created history by winning two trophies in a decade and, with bat and ball respectively, both stalwarts have played a huge part in Glamorgan's revival.

'We used to have a great time going on second XI trips when Glamorgan were the whipping boys of the county circuit,' recalls Steve. 'We'd do our best on the field and have a few drinks afterwards but now it's changed beyond all recognition. We're at the ground early, do our warm-ups, we have team meetings – things that certainly wouldn't have happened in the mid-Eighties. Everybody trains a lot harder, especially in the winter.'

As well as sharing similar career paths, the pair now have the same employer during the close season. Like Tony Cottey in the former county of Dyfed, Steve is a development officer for the Cricket Board of Wales in the old West and Mid Glamorgan areas.

'Coaching is about 35 per cent of the job,' says Steve. 'I spend a lot of my time trying to get cricket clubs to set up junior sides and create links with schools so we can create more interest in the game. We also teach teachers how to coach and start children off in school.

'Everywhere I went during the winter, everyone wanted to talk about Glamorgan's success. The championship win couldn't have come at a better time for cricket in general and me in particular. It has pushed Glamorgan to the top of Welsh sport – I just hope there's plenty of money left after Colin Metson's benefit!'

'There's only one way to top 1997 – and that's for Glamorgan to retain the title for the first time and win a Lord's final.'

As Steve Watkin prepares for what will be a busy season on and off the field, it's to be hoped that the infamous beneficiary curse doesn't strike. Not every player suffers – Matthew Maynard scored more than 1,600 runs at an average of nearly 62 in his benefit year – but, in the wake of the Sunday League success, Hugh Morris experienced one of his most barren seasons with the bat.

You can rest assured that Watty will be keeping his eye on the ball – and watching his follow-through!

BACK FROM THE BRINK

At the end of the 1996 season, Darren Thomas was a medium-fast bowler going nowhere very quickly. After becoming the youngest Glamorgan player, at 17 years of age, to take five wickets on his debut in 1992, his career had gone into a gentle freefall to the point where he was in danger of being sacked. Nearly a hundred wickets in 35 games may have seemed a creditable return but it included 20 at nearly 60 runs each in his most disappointing season so far.

One of Glamorgan's brightest potential stars appeared to have burnt out prematurely. Rather than being given the key, this 21-year-old was on the verge of being shown the door.

Luckily for Tomo – and for Glamorgan – the cricket committee decided to give him one last chance. A year later, his 44 championship wickets at just over 26 apiece – including a career-best of 5 for 24 against Sussex – helped Glamorgan win the title. The gamble had paid off handsomely.

The former Glamorgan all-rounder Peter Walker is a member of the cricket committee. Furthermore, as Director of Development for the Cricket Board of Wales, he is responsible for nurturing talent – something he knew Darren Thomas had in abundance.

'Eighteen months ago, Darren was on the point of going out of the first-class game. After bursting onto the scene with Glamorgan, he'd proved what a promising international bowler he could become with the England Under 19s. But he had problems – not in a yobbish sense – for Darren had great difficulty in accepting that you need a strong degree of personal discipline to succeed. You have to look after yourself, it's not all about bright lights and glamour – particularly if you're a pace bowler. You mustn't forget about the importance of early nights, resting your body and training hard. On the field, nobody tries harder than Darren and he used to take that enthusiasm with him off the field too. Unfortunately, the two sometimes came into conflict!

146

'In the winter of 1996-97, several of us – including myself and national coach Tom Cartwright – had a word with him about his mental application and some technical flaws which we thought he needed to iron out. Ten out of ten to Darren, he got stuck into it.'

'Tom advised me to stay at home rather than go abroad to play cricket during the winter,' Darren recalls. 'He said I should work on my action with him in the nets at Neath. I was very front-on, really open-chested and I was bowling from very wide of the crease, like Devon Malcolm, to try and generate lots of pace.

'Tom tried to get me in closer to the stumps, with my back foot more parallel to the crease and my front foot pointing in the direction of the batsman rather than point – to get more of a side-on action. It worked well and I got my away-swinger going again, as I had in my first two years. It was a big confidence boost.'

When Duncan Fletcher arrived to take up his post as first team coach, he sat back and watched. Rather than trying to change anything straightaway, he bided his time before eventually suggesting that Darren modify his action – back towards his former style of delivery.

'Duncan thought I was putting so much stress on my back that I might injure myself, so he recommended that I should open up a bit more, like Malcolm Marshall. It was obviously strange but we worked at it in the nets and, instead of having my back foot parallel to the back crease, Duncan got me to turn it round to avoid putting any stress on my back. It worked perfectly. We also got my arms and head in the right position – not too open, not too closed – during pre-season.'

'Duncan was a new voice,' says Peter Walker. 'He was a disciplinarian who insisted on certain behavioural standards. Tom's great maxim for bowlers is "always keep your head still", while Duncan thought Darren's action was too square-on. I would like to think it was a combination of the two that actually worked for the lad.

'With his head flopping away to the off side at delivery, there was no way that Darren could have bowled straight with any sort of consistency. By the end of the season, his head was rock steady and his results improved considerably. You can either bruise or destroy a bowling action – it's like trying to smooth an orchid. Coaching has got some – but limited – value. In Darren's case, it saved a career!'

'I was very pleased to help Darren with his bowling,' says

147

Duncan, 'but a little disappointed because I thought I could have helped him with his batting too. I really think he can become a very good all-rounder. We just didn't have the time to cover all aspects of his game. His fielding and throwing were already top class.

'To me, Darren's improvement as a bowler was very satisfying. In the championship, Steve Watkin went for a miserly two-and-a-half runs an over; Waqar and Darren for three-and-a-half, so he must have bowled incredibly well.'

In a repeat of his debut season, Darren began with a bang. Having been given the nod over rivals Owen Parkin and Gary Butcher for the vacant seamer's spot, behind Waqar and Steve Watkin, he tore into Warwickshire and finished with 4 for 62 from 12 overs.

'I knew Waqar and Watty would be taking the new ball and I would be doing the donkey work. Matthew told me I would have a couple of games to prove myself and I thought I'd rather play with Waqar than watch him from outside the ropes.

'He wasn't back for the first game against Warwickshire, so when they decided to bat on a green surface, I opened the bowling with Steve. The ball was moving around quite a bit. Watty and I took a couple of wickets early on and we eventually bowled them out for 151. It was a perfect start to the season. I was a little expensive but it was great to have a few wickets in the bag – six in the match, as I picked up two in their second innings before the rain came.'

While the weather was ruining Glamorgan's second championship match at Headingley, Darren was collecting useful bowling tips rather than wickets – thanks to his burgeoning friendship with Waqar Younis.

'Waqar is the world's best, but like Duncan, we weren't quite sure how he was going to relate to us,' says Darren. 'He turned out to be one of my best mates in Glamorgan. We worked together on my game and it was brilliant to have that experience.

'While we were up in Yorkshire, Waqar showed me how to get reverse swing – you keep one side of the ball dry and dampen up the other side to get a really good gloss on it. I used it a few times during the season – it was fantastic, especially in Cardiff where the surface scuffs the ball up very very easily. Waqar felt that with my higher action, it would work better for me because I could get the ball to reverse swing both ways.

'Waqar's action is poetry in motion – he's unbelievable. My

first impression was, Oh my God! What's this guy doing running in from the boundary! It seemed so long a run compared with mine and Watty's! Once he gets into his rhythm, he's like Michael Holding at his best. It's amazing that he didn't injure himself more often with all the effort he put into each delivery.'

Darren's three wickets and 46 runs against Kent helped Glamorgan record their first win of the championship and after a fruitless draw against Hampshire in Cardiff, Tomo picked up another three in the defeat of Durham. Afterwards, he remembers discussing the county's title prospects with the youngster of the team, Dean Cosker. Out of the mouths of babes and sucklings . . .

'Dean and I started off reasonably well in the first team and, after four games, we said that we were going to win the title – we were that confident! Even after the defeat by Middlesex – in which I took 4 for 52 – we then beat Lancashire, Sussex and Gloucestershire. Waqar bowled brilliantly at Liverpool and against Sussex down at Swansea, where I chipped in with my career best 5 for 24. It was very difficult for me because Waqar and Watty had done all the bowling at Liverpool and I hadn't held a ball for two weeks! I started worrying about my action and my run-up, so it was very satisfying to come up trumps in that game. It was nice because I've always disliked bowling at St Helen's. Then I picked up four wickets as we stuffed Gloucestershire, again at Swansea. Once you're on a winning roll, then you quickly start believing in yourself.'

But the momentum was checked by the draws with Derbyshire and Nottinghamshire and defeat at Worcester. Darren took just one of the 20 Northamptonshire wickets to fall at Abergavenny as Waqar returned match figures of 10 for 134. Four days later, the roof caved in.

'I was dropped to make way for an extra batsman after Matthew decided to bring back Tony Cottey for the game at Leicester,' says Darren. 'I was very disappointed but I understood why I'd been left out. In the previous three games, I'd been struggling for form, so I wasn't surprised. Dean Cosker had been bowling well, Mike Powell was being given a chance after making runs in the seconds and Matthew felt he needed Tony's experience.

'I feared the worst – another disastrous end to the season – but I worked on my game with Duncan in the indoor nets during the draw at Leicester. We just went back to basics.

'"Don't bowl full pace, Tomo," he said. "Look to your line and length, get your action right and keep your head still."

'There wasn't much room – about 7 or 8 yards for my run-up – but we worked hard and I knew I'd be back in on the quick Oval pitch. Duncan spent hours with me and I can't thank him enough for that because it all came right at Taunton.'

Four wickets and his season's best score of 75 not out against Surrey cemented Darren's place in the Glamorgan team for their last two matches. Another invaluable innings against Essex in Cardiff confirmed his growing reputation as an all-rounder.

'I'm another Brian Lara in the making!' jokes Darren. 'I like to think I can bat a bit. I had good little knocks against Kent, Surrey and Essex and my 39 helped us get another bonus point at a crucial stage of the Essex game. I'd like to think I could maybe knock Adrian Shaw out of the number seven spot.'

Three more wickets against Essex at Cardiff – including that of the bellicose Ronnie Irani in the first innings – not only helped set up the showdown at Taunton, but also brought Darren his coveted county cap. 'It was a marvellous moment,' he recalls. 'Matthew had awarded Dean Cosker his second XI cap and then, after my innings, he asked me how many first-class wickets I'd taken so far. I said 45 or 46 and when Wayne Law came on as a substitute fielder, Matthew told him to go and get my sweater and county cap which he gave to me at tea. It was a real reward for all the work I'd put in during the winter.

'"Well done, Tomo," said Matthew. "You deserve it. Keep up the good work."'

The timing was perfect. Everything fell into place for the final game as Darren's mid-season doubts disappeared. Once again, Waqar set the tone by blasting out four Somerset batsmen in the first innings before the sorcerer's apprentice took centre stage in the second.

'Winning at Taunton and taking those five wickets on the last day were the highlights of my season,' says Tomo. 'I was the most fired-up I've ever been. It was very emotional because I wanted to win the championship so much.

'My performance in the second innings was very satisfying because Somerset had got off to such a flier and, for once, Waqar and Watty hadn't made an early breakthrough. I remember all five wickets very well – especially bowling Rob Turner for the first and then getting Mark Lathwell for 47 with an away-swinger. The away-swinger had been my stock ball for most of the season but in that game, for some reason, I was bowling nipper-backers off the seam. I decided to pitch one on middle-and-leg and it went the other way and knocked off stump out of the ground! It was my best spell of bowling ever – everything just clicked. I got into a good rhythm and I concentrated hard.

'The scenes down at Taunton were amazing. I ended up with just a sweater and a pair of trousers – everything else was taken off me by our supporters!'

He may have lost most of his kit but, in return, Darren received a cavalcade of compliments after his five-star display: unstinting praise for a bowling stint which clinched the championship for Glamorgan.

'Under pressure, Darren could be wayward in direction and would sometimes go for six an over,' says Peter Walker. 'So for him to come good as he did at Taunton, just when it looked as if Somerset might make the game go into the last day when rain was forecast, was extraordinary. It was an exhibition of sheer will power as well as a combination of talent and stamina. Darren's spell encapsulated everything that quick bowling ought to be.

'I only hope that he doesn't get lost in the memory of it and that he realises he can consistently perform at that level and even higher, providing he retains his new-found self-analysis and discipline.'

'People expected Waqar to take wickets at Taunton,' recalls Glamorgan's director of coaching Alan Jones. 'It was a huge occasion for Darren and he came on when Waqar, still suffering from a virus, was being smacked all over the ground. That afternoon, Darren bowled quicker and more aggressively than Waqar and thoroughly earned his 5 for 38 from 15 overs. He was brilliant!'

As he watched nervously from the Taunton balcony, secretary Mike Fatkin inwardly applauded the cricket committee's decision to back Darren Thomas in his fight to pull himself back from the brink the previous summer. 'Darren's been up and down since he arrived at the age of 17. He started taking five-wicket hauls all over the place and probably thought it was an easy game. It was for a while but he's found it much more difficult since then.

'You don't invest in a 17-year-old and then chuck him out at 21 or 22. Darren's still developing and it was a pleasure to see him win his county cap during the Essex game, because I think it meant more to him than any other player I've seen. He was so proud and that's what you want – people who are going to put on a jumper bearing a daffodil and play their hearts out for it.'

1997 saw Darren Thomas come of age – both as a player and as a person. Fifty-three first-class wickets were testament to his talent on the field. Away from the square, he was an integral member of a Glamorgan team who thrived on Welsh camaraderie and rejoiced in each other's company. Everyone mucked in, everyone took the mickey, and sons of places as far apart as Llanelli, Karachi and Cape Town became brothers and soul mates.

'Waqar is the second overseas superstar I've had the privilege of working with after Viv Richards,' says Darren, 'but he's a different type of person to Viv who wouldn't come out for a drink with the boys. He'd like to be in the background, relaxing a little bit and doing his own thing – as he was entitled to do. But Waqar would come for a meal with me and Gary Butcher and he became a good mate of mine by the end.

'Fletch helped to turn us all into a family – there were no groups of older and younger players – apart from when we were playing football and touch-rugby! We were a side – not a collection of sub-groups. Fletch was the Dad and we were his eleven sons around him.'

Ask any one of the Glamorgan players for their funniest moment of the 1997 season and they will all – to a man – tell the story of Darren Thomas and the French restaurant in Liverpool. Such is the strength of the bond between them that Darren is quite happy to provide a first-hand account of the tale himself. Laugh? They almost died.

'We were in Liverpool for our rain-affected match with Lancashire and I said to Matt that I'd arrange the team meal on the Friday night. So I asked in the hotel reception if they could recommend a nice place for us to eat.

'I came down the next morning and they'd got it all sorted out. In a thick Scouser accent, the hotel doorman explained that the name of the restaurant was the *Maissez Vous*. During the day, I told the boys to be in reception by half-past seven when taxis would arrive to take us all to the meal.

'"Where are we going?" they asked.

'"Oh, it's a French gourmet restaurant," I proudly announced. "It's called the *Maissez Vous* or something like that."

'We all piled into the taxis and, after spending ages looking for this place, we finally arrived at a local Beefeater called *The Pier*! I couldn't believe my eyes! Where was the French gourmet restaurant? It was then that I realised that this Beefeater had a restaurant? It was then that I realised that this Beefeater had a lovely view overlooking the Mersey!

'The boys didn't stop all night and obviously I ended up with the jester's hat and shirt after that! It was the biggest bloomer of the season – I don't think they'll ever let me forget it. I blame the doorman – he can wear the hat and shirt the next time we're up there!

Nice one, Tomo – *bon appetit*!

ROBERT O'R HENDY:
FOR COUNTY AND COUNTRY

ROBERT Croft was on a roller coaster ride during the whole of 1997. From the fairgrounds of Wellington to Sharjah, Edgbaston to Trent Bridge and Cardiff to Taunton, he experienced the highs and lows of professional cricket in almost equal measure. Between January and December, Robert rode them all – the Big Dipper, the Tunnel of Love, the Ghost Train, even the more mundane dodgems. Through alternate thrills and spills, he finally emerged from the Corridor of Uncertainty, shaken but not stirred.

One win does not make a winter tour – especially in view of the Zimbabwean experience – but after the series victory in New Zealand, the Glamorgan off-spinner appeared to have established himself on the international stage. Seven wickets in the third Test in Christchurch were followed by three in the innings defeat of Australia in the first Test at euphoric Edgbaston. The patriotic Welshman, with a passion for playing for England, had arrived. A summer of spin beckoned, with Robert relishing a home series bowling in tandem – or in competition – with Phil Tufnell, the Middlesex slow left-armer. English cricket was in seventh heaven and Crofty was in his element.

When England's hopes of winning the series turned to ashes and Australia went 3-1 up at Trent Bridge in August, Robert Croft's world looked to have spun out of control. His flow of both wickets and runs had dried up and his place was taken by Tufnell who, on a turning Oval wicket, bowled England to victory and some respectability.

'It was a real up and down season for me,' recalls Robert. 'I came back in high spirits from the tour of Zimbabwe and New Zealand and we won the Texaco one-day series against Australia 3-0 at the end of May. It was a dream come true to win the first Test at Edgbaston but unfortunately things didn't continue in that vein.

'I don't think my form with the ball suffered even though I only picked up another five wickets in the next four Tests – it was just that a couple of catches and stumpings were missed, so things didn't go for me. I was still confident, as far as my bowling was concerned, but my batting had taken a bit of a battering – from the Australians – not to mention a few media commentators who homed in on it. My top score in seven innings was only 18 and I struggled with the short-pitched stuff.

'But I just kept telling myself all the time: Hang on – you've been picked to play for England primarily as a bowler and it just hasn't quite worked out with the bat. I was quite happy with the number of chances my bowling was creating but they just weren't being snapped up.'

Disappointment with England was replaced by determination for Glamorgan. The 'Old Enemy' may have been in the process of being soundly beaten by their 'Old Enemy' but it failed to dampen Crofty's enthusiasm for his club and real country. 'I've always said that when I'm with Glamorgan, it's like playing for Wales and when I play for England, I'm representing the British Isles. I don't know if it's an old saying but I honestly feel that way.'

Sympathy and support were not in short supply back at Sophia Gardens. 'Robert is a tremendous bowler and I think England treated him badly,' says coach Duncan Fletcher. 'You make your own luck in life but he was unlucky in that he had catches dropped, stumpings missed and appeals turned down and then, in the one game where the pitch was a real turner, he didn't play. Every other wicket had been prepared for seamers and he had to bowl on those.

'But his attitude was first class in view of the pressures he must have been under. In the dressing room, he was good in the way that he took part in everything and kept going. There were times when he came back to us and he was understandably down. He was frustrated and he showed it. We just had to manage that through but he responded well. He accepted what we were saying in the chats we had with him.'

The scorebook shows that every time Robert returned to the Glamorgan fold, he delivered the goods. After the defeat at Lord's, he took five wickets as Sussex were soundly beaten at Swansea and then six in the draw with Nottinghamshire, soon after the Headingley humiliation. While Australia were clinching the series at Trent Bridge, he chipped in with seven wickets and 60 runs as Glamorgan narrowly failed to win the Worcester run-chase.

'I always felt that every time Robert bowled a ball, we could get a wicket,' says Duncan Fletcher. 'At one stage of the season, he did lose some of that inner confidence and belief in himself. I think any human being would have done so – anyone would have come back with doubts about his ability to play for England.'

Crofty admits that the transition from Test to county cricket was sometimes difficult but he refused to panic. 'Had I been, say, 23, I would have worried about my bowling but having played for a few years, I realised there was nothing wrong. It was just the rub of the green. You can walk out one day and take 5 for 50 when you bowl really well and the next day bowl just as well and end up with 0 for 120. If you do it well enough for long enough, it will even out and the boys knew that.

'The one thing about the Glamorgan dressing room is that it's a great leveller. It works both ways because when you come back from Test-match duty and you've done well, you're never allowed to fly up into the clouds but when the boys see you're on a bit of a downer, they pick you up as well. Nobody's allowed to get carried away or keep their head down. Even though my Test form may have suffered, when I returned to the county circuit, I was in a happy environment.'

Never more so than on the last day of the drawn championship game with Nottinghamshire in Colwyn Bay at the beginning of August. Robert received the ultimate honour for a Welsh-speaking Welshman by being admitted to the Gorsedd of Bards at the National Eisteddfod at Bala.

'I come from a Welsh-speaking area around Llanelli and, to me, becoming a member of the Gorsedd is a form of acceptance by your own people. It's their way of saying: "Crofty's not a bad fellow – he tries to promote Wales in the proper way" and it's some sort of recognition. Only one other cricketer, Alan Jones, has been admitted, along with all the rugby players who have been honoured, and it was superb to follow them.

'The day itself was like something out of Anneka Rice's old programme *Treasure Hunt*! I was picked up at seven o'clock in the morning from the helipad in Colwyn Bay – the first time I'd flown in a helicopter – and it took half-an-hour to get down to Bala. All the press and media were waiting but the officials whisked me through. I was pleased to see Ray Gravell there – he was the guard, the man with the sword that day! During the ceremony, my name was read out as "Robert o'r Hendy" and there was a bit of an extra cheer because everyone wanted Glamorgan to do well.

'It was superb walking up there wearing the green robe and seeing the pleasure on the faces of the people around you – from all walks of life. Sadly, my parents weren't there but I picked out a few faces in the crowd and all my relatives from Hendy were watching the ceremony on the television. It was a very proud moment for me.

'It's hard to compare it with lifting the championship trophy. Being admitted to the Gorsedd was a bonus. I didn't set out at the start of the season to become a bard. It's something you can't set out to try to be. It just happens. But winning the championship is something I've dreamt about since I started playing cricket at the age of nine.

'After the ceremony, we had to rush off because I had to be back by ten o'clock – Fletch wouldn't have let me go if I hadn't been able to make it by then. As we approached Colwyn Bay, the groundsman put out the white Sunday League marking discs in a circle so we could land properly. All the boys were there taking the mickey, cheering and clapping – it was a little embarrassing.'

Robert's flying visit to Bala had little effect on his performance back in Colwyn Bay. With Nottinghamshire still 145 behind in their second innings, he struck with his second ball by bowling Tim Robinson and finished with 3 for 52 from 30 overs as Notts managed to hold out. 'I bowled quite well but we did miss Dean Cosker, our left-arm spinner who was playing for the England Under 19s side, and his replacement Phil North, who could have done the trick but he'd been dropped for oversleeping on the first morning of the match.'

From the skies high above Bala, the roller coaster ride took Robert down to the depths of Chelmsford. After a week off, the storm which had been brewing throughout the summer finally broke.

'At certain times, there seemed to be a lot of pressure on me when I came back after not having done well for England,' recalls Robert. 'I think I was on a bit of a slide towards a blow-up which came in the Nat West Trophy semi-final against Essex. I had been a little bit on tenterhooks for a few weeks. I was snappy and instead of laughing at certain jokes, I just didn't.

'It was mostly my fault and I think Fletch could see it coming –

157

things weren't going well at Test level. As well as being very good technically, he was able to read people well – he was a good man-manager. He kept reminding me to stay focused – which I usually am on a cricket field – and we got things sorted out pretty quickly and concentrated on the run-in to the end of the season. Although the Chelmsford incident was in no way right, it almost had to happen. My volcano was just waiting to explode.'

The flare-up with Robert's close friend Mark Illott erupted towards the end of the Essex innings as they chased 302 to win in deteriorating light. After one ball of the 54th over, the pair traded pushes and shoves during a frank exchange of opinions. Handbags at dusk, broadcast live on BBC television.

'What's the matter with you?' asked Croft.

'The light's gone bad,' Illott replied.

'Hang on a minute!' cried Croft. 'Two overs ago you were smacking Waqar Younis over his head for fourteen in one over!'

'Yeah, but we've just lost two wickets.'

'You just want to have your cake and eat it!'

In retrospect, Robert concedes that both players were at fault. 'It was six of one and half a dozen of the other. I felt that, as they'd won the toss and put us into bat, they should accept that in a 60 over match, they were going to be batting late on. They had just been knocking Waqar around and apparently the light was fine then. I felt they wanted it both ways by going off after losing two wickets. Of course, our best chance of winning was to stay out because it was so dark.

'Mark was well within his rights to point out that they'd lost a couple of wickets. After all, the ball had just missed his off stump and it would have been better for Essex to come back the next morning. But the incident probably wouldn't have happened if we hadn't been such good friends. Had we not have known each other so well, then we wouldn't have been so close to each other exchanging insults!'

Eventually, the players did leave the field. When they returned the following morning, Darren Thomas raised Glamorgan's hopes by taking the ninth Essex wicket before Peter Such broke their hearts when he carted an attempted yorker, which turned out to be a full toss, to the long-off boundary. The dream of a Lord's final was over for another year but Robert Croft's personal nightmare was to continue.

Glamorgan and Essex both moved swiftly by fining Robert and

Mark £1,000 each, even after their very public handshake on the Chelmsford balcony. But the newly-created England and Wales Cricket Board wanted to flex its muscles. A top-level inquiry into the incident implied that the punishment in no way fitted the crime.

'It was a little bit strange,' says Robert, 'because Gerard Elias, Glamorgan's then deputy chairman, who was chairman of the ECB's discipline standing committee, was obviously satisfied with the fines but other people at Lord's weren't. A thousand pounds was pretty steep but I was quite prepared to pay it.

'As a result of the second hearing, we were given a two-match ban, suspended for two years. To be quite honest, I was amazed because I thought the incident had already been dealt with in the correct fashion – quickly and in-house by the two counties. It was a severe penalty because cricketers are not paid as much as footballers. A thousand pounds means a lot more to us than them.'

Although the Chelmsford incident was roundly condemned by some sections of the press and media, there were few recriminations within the Glamorgan camp.

'Duncan and I haven't actually spoken about the incident on the field,' says Robert, 'but he was totally supportive of the team's fight to turn the game around. His wife actually taped the game and Fletch was in my corner because it looked more like Mark pushing me than me doing anything. I was pleased that he was prepared to defend me.'

Skipper Matthew Maynard was disappointed by the Nat West defeat but delighted with the determination shown by his team. 'The Croft-Illot incident wasn't good for the game and you can't condone any behaviour like that on a cricket field but it showed that we were a more aggressive and competitive team than in previous years.

'Crofty overstepped the mark but I was pleased that we were showing total commitment. We believed that if we had stayed out there that night then we would have reached the final, because we were on a big roll. As it happened, we nearly did it the next morning. Nevertheless, I was proud of the fighting spirit shown by the team.

'Earlier, Stuart Law had virtually taken the game away from us with an incredible knock; we were out of it. Pre-Viv Richards's spell with us, that would have been it. We would probably have lain back and surrendered. Viv had given us a new hardness and after our great Nat West wins over Hampshire and Yorkshire, it seemed destined to be our year for Lord's but it wasn't to be.

'I was happy with the way the two players were dealt with. There was talk of banning them but I think that would have been over the top.'

In between the hearings, Robert was left out of the England team for the final Cornhill Test at the Oval. As Phil Tufnell returned match figures of 11 for 93 on a spinner's paradise, Crofty's season was in danger of going pear-shaped.

'Robert accepted his punishment,' says Glamorgan secretary Mike Fatkin, 'and came back fighting – in the figurative sense. Being dropped by England could have knocked a lot of people sideways but he showed a lot of guts coming back, and I think he resolved to throw himself into helping Glamorgan win the championship. He showed a side of him I hadn't seen before.'

'Robert would undoubtedly have taken wickets at the Oval where the ball turned square,' says Don Shepherd, one of his mentors and Glamorgan's record wicket-taker. 'Throughout the series, he always came back to bowl very well for Glamorgan, playing his full part in their success. I like to keep an eye on his action and if he nods at me for my approval, I nod back if I think everything's alright – and it was. I have memorised his action which, in my view, is now complete and grooved – certainly, he's the best off-spinner in the country.'

Five wickets – including that of Kevin Curran for 159 – helped Glamorgan to a comprehensive win over Northamptonshire at Abergavenny and another five enabled Surrey to be squeezed out of the championship race in the acrimonious draw in London.

'The Chelmsford business and being dropped by England was a low point for me,' recalls Robert, 'but the worst moment of the season was the second day at Taunton. After beating Essex at Cardiff, we knew we had to win our last match to lift the championship but it was pouring down with rain! I just couldn't believe that we had come this far, only to be hit by the weather. I remember leaning against the wall outside the Taunton dressing room and not being able to see a break in the clouds. There was nothing. I just thought: It's all come to this.

Crofty had woken that day full of hope and expectation – and not just because Glamorgan were fewer than a hundred behind Somerset's first innings total. The devolution vote, announced so dramatically in the early hours of the morning in Cardiff, heralded the dawn of a new era. By a margin of just 6,721 votes – 0.3 per cent – Wales had slipped the shackles of the English yoke and contrary to public opinion – at least that of the Glamorgan side – Robert was highly delighted.

'It was so hectic during the run-in to the end of the season that I couldn't find time to organise a postal vote. In the devolution run-up, I was aware of the debate but I kept my thoughts close to my chest. Both sides rang me up trying to get me to support them publicly but I thought whoever was going to win the argument should do so on political grounds rather than by using sporting celebrities.

'I think sport gets dragged into politics too much and when sportsmen and women lend their names to political causes, it makes the process easier. They should be kept apart. During the debate, I played the role of Devil's Advocate in the Glamorgan dressing room because there were a few of the boys – like Tony Cottey – who were really up for it. They had come out publicly in support of devolution – adding their names to the "Yes" campaign. I remember winding them up by saying perhaps devolution shouldn't happen! This will probably be the first time they'll know about my views but deep down I was as pleased as they were with the result.

'Once it was known, I didn't mind saying that I thought we had to start running things ourselves. The way it was going, the time had come for Wales to have a bigger say in its own affairs. Decisions were being made a long way east of the Severn Bridge.

'The result may have been very close but people are often scared of too much change. Even though there was a lot of talk about Wales wanting devolution, in the end, people were worried about something so new. I missed all the excitement of the night itself because I was in bed asleep preparing for the second day at Taunton.

'I see the close devolution result a bit like life as a bowler. It doesn't matter how you get your wickets, just look at what's written down in the scorebook and in the papers the next day! I don't care how many voted. Devolution got through and now we'll see if it really can work for the betterment of the Welsh people. It was a great 48 hours for Wales when we delivered a positive result on the cricket field on Saturday evening.'

Once the rain relented soon after lunch, the second day at Taunton was dominated by the match-winning partnership of 235 between Hugh Morris and Matthew Maynard. By the close, Morris and Robert Croft were undefeated on 136 and 18 respectively. Saturday morning saw Crofty and Adrian Shaw finally come good with the bat. The off-spinner achieved a season's best 86 – including three sixes and nine fours – while the wicket-keeper raced to his first fifty of the summer.

Somerset were faced with scoring 275 to avoid an innings defeat. Robert repeated his performance in the first innings by dismissing Marcus Trescothick but it was the old warhorse Steve Watkin and the young Turk Darren Thomas who inflicted the real damage.

'I only fully realised that we'd won the championship when Dean Cosker took the final wicket, with Somerset just 10 runs ahead,' says Robert. 'The way the summer had gone with the weather, who knows where we would have been had they'd have been able to bat out that night and it had poured down the next day? It would almost have been nicer to have bowled them out, so we wouldn't have had to bat again but I'll take what came anytime.

'It was a fitting climax for Steve James, who had missed out on Test selection to the West Indies, to hit the winning runs and then to be carried off at the end. It's a shame all the lads couldn't have been on our supporters' shoulders because each and everyone played a part. In every game, every one of the fourteen players we used did something for the cause.

'Tony Cottey once said to me that we'd done so well because we were a crowd of lads who played Colts cricket together. We'd been very successful juniors and we brought that confidence with us into first-class cricket. It's taken a few years to come through but we did win the Sunday League in 1993 and now the championship, four years later.

'The turning point was the arrival of Viv Richards in the early Nineties. He was a magnificent cricketer who, even if slightly past his best, had an effect on the opposition as well as us. He was a hard taskmaster who wouldn't accept anything less than your best. He said he would be with us for three years and that we'd win something. And we did.

'The key thing about Glamorgan is that everybody is pulling for everybody else – from the chairman to the caterers, from the physiotherapist to the groundsman, from the coach to the most junior player. We're all working in one direction. Everyone is prepared to listen to other people – something that Fletch has instilled in the side.

'Through the help of the coach, Matthew and the senior players, we have found a direction which has been missing since 1993.'

Most spectators who managed to make the trip to Taunton will never be able to forget Robert's rendition of *Alouette* from the dressing room balcony during the celebrations. Having already performed *Calon Lân* as the players collected the championship trophy, Crofty decided to stick with tradition.

'I sang *Alouette* because I did it from the Canterbury balcony in 1993. I thought: Let's keep a good thing going! Hopefully, I'll sing it from the balcony at Lord's next year! But I couldn't understand the stick I received when I got home. People said they couldn't believe how awful it was but I could see what they were getting at after I saw the highlights on television and heard myself singing when Alan Wilkins was interviewing Peter Walker and Don Shepherd, two members of the 1969 side who had been commentating on the closing moments of the match.

'As they spoke, all you could hear was me singing, "Oh, I love your pointy head!" and I then realised how terrible it must have sounded for anyone who was either there or watching on the box!'

Glamorgan's championship win in September marked the end of Robert Croft's personal roller coaster ride. For the rest of 1997, he remained on a glorious high with selection for the West Indies winter tour being coupled with inclusion in the one-day squad which won the four-nation Sharjah tournament in December. England finished the year as they had begun it and Crofty was back in business. The wheel had come full circle.

'We spent a week in Pakistan preparing for the tournament and my first visit to that country was certainly an eye-opener. The squad knitted together well, there was a good team spirit and, during the competition, we beat two of the sides more or less in their own backyard, before we outplayed the West Indies in the final.

'I didn't take too many wickets but my job basically was to keep it nice and tight and, along with Mark Ealham, to create some pressure in the middle of the innings. It was our job to peg sides back after the first 15 overs which are normally a bit hectic.'

The England party left for the West Indies in the New Year with Robert hoping to add to his ten Test caps. Specialist coaching by selector Graham Gooch had identified a flaw in his batting and, as a result, the expected short-ball barrage held fewer fears for Glamorgan's wannabe all-rounder.

'Basically, I was moving too much before the ball was bowled and my weight wasn't in the right place. We used videos to pinpoint the problem and at the end of the sessions, my confidence had been re-built and I was raring to go.

'Every time you play for England you're on trial. The eyes of the world are on you but there seems to be more of a squad system to the England set-up now. Obviously, I was disappointed to be left out against Australia at the Oval but, at the end of the day, Phil Tufnell had been pitching up at four or five matches without getting a game and I knew he would play in the end because England's results hadn't been up to standard.'

For the first three Tests against the West Indies, possession proved to be nine-tenths of the law – Tufnell retained his place as England fought back to level the series at 1-1. But after taking 11 for 101 in the match against Guyana in Georgetown, Crofty was picked, alongside his fellow spinner, for the fourth Test. Although Robert made a successful comeback, England were bowled out for 137 in their second innings in fewer than 63 overs and lost by 242 runs.

'It was a frustrating first eight weeks of the tour for me,' says Robert, 'but I was pleased to be given a chance to show what I could do in a Test.'

After taking 3 for 89 in the West Indies first innings, Crofty second top-scored with 26 as he put on 64 with Mark Ramprakash to help England avoid the follow-on. With a St David's Day daffodil – presented to him by a spectator – tucked into his pad, Robert put his winter net practice to the test out in the middle and passed with flying colours. He then took another three wickets as the West Indies were dismissed for 197 and hit the third highest score of England's innings by making 14 out of 137.

But there was more disappointment for Crofty when he, rather than Tufnell, was dropped for the fifth Test in Bridgetown to make way for the third seamer, Andy Caddick. The selectors surprisingly opted to retain the Middlesex left-arm spinner, despite Robert's return to form with both bat and ball. In the end, England were thwarted by rain on the final day and Robert failed to make the team for the final Test in Antigua.

With another Test and one-day series behind him, Robert Croft has returned to Wales with a new challenge – to help Glamorgan retain their title.

'I'm not in the business of making predictions because there are so many outside factors which can influence the outcome,' says Robert, 'but I certainly think we've got a strong enough squad to win the championship again this season. It may not be a large squad but we've got a group of boys who play with a different spirit and feeling to any other county.

'After our success in 1993 and 1997, I would now like to win a one-day final at Lord's. We've won the equivalent of the FA Carling Premiership, now it's time for the FA Cup. 1977 – when we last got to Lord's – is a long time ago and now we've got the side to go there and win. We've lost Hugh Morris but someone else will take over from him, and I honestly believe that this is the best squad of players Glamorgan will see for possibly the next ten or fifteen years. We must continue to deliver.'

If you're good enough, you're old enough

Like Johnny Clay and Don Shepherd, Dean Cosker will always have a special place in the history of Glamorgan County Cricket Club.

Just after quarter past six on Saturday, 20th September 1997, the left-arm spinner trapped Ben Trott lbw and the Somerset second innings ended on 285 all out. Steve James may have actually scored the last of the eleven runs needed to win the championship but Deano will be remembered as the man who took the decisive wicket.

When Johnny Clay performed the feat in 1948 and Don Shepherd emulated him 21 years later, both men were approaching retirement. At 19, Dean Cosker was just starting out on his Glamorgan career. A championship-winner's medal in his first full season in domestic cricket? It beggars belief.

'I didn't actually think I was going to get another bowl at Taunton,' recalls Dean. 'I'd had 11 overs and picked up one wicket, Darren Thomas was doing very well and Waqar was waiting to come charging in and end it all but, for some reason, Matthew called on me.

'I wasn't nervous because that's not really in my character. I always thought we would get the last wicket that night and I had three chances to get Trott out before I trapped him. The fourth ball was a little bit quicker, it surprised him and hit him on the toe. It pitched middle and hit his pad about middle-and-leg. It was great when the umpire's finger went up – the best feeling I've had in my career so far. I'll never forget the roar from the crowd! I just loved it. I jumped up in the air and then jumped on our keeper Shawsy and legged it off with Darren.

'I've since received a lot of flack from the boys about how, in my first year in the championship team, I'd come on to bowl and taken the last wicket so now I think I've made it – they're good like that! Everything's happened so fast and perhaps some people feel I don't appreciate it but I can assure them I do.

'I'm going to remember it as a great experience and hopefully win a few more championships in my career. My big ambition now is to get to a one-day final at Lord's but the championship must be the pinnacle.'

Although he was born in Dorset and educated in Devon and Somerset, Dean has strong Welsh connections. His grandparents come from Swansea where his father Des was born and brought up. 'My mother Carol is from Stafford, so I consider myself to be at least half-Welsh – especially after last season!

'Somerset and Gloucestershire were interested in signing me early on but it was Glamorgan who snapped me up when I was 16, after Graham Reynolds, their liason officer-cum-scout, had approached me. Darren Thomas, Gary Butcher, Adrian Shaw and I have been together since the county under 17s.'

In his debut season, Dean played in five first-class matches and took 16 wickets at nearly 39 runs apiece. During that summer, he represented England Under 19s against New Zealand and toured Pakistan the following winter. His obvious promise helped persuade Glamorgan to release the experienced left-arm spinner Neil Kendrick and Dean was in the frame when the new season began.

'Matthew told me he was keen to get me involved in the four-day game – to make use of the ball which was likely to start turning on the last two days. I played in the first championship game in 1997 against Warwickshire, but I didn't bowl in either innings and wasn't chosen for the trip to Headingley.'

When Glamorgan moved south to Canterbury, Dean seized his opportunity. After taking two catches but not bowling in Kent's first innings, he removed three of the top four batsmen and finished with 4 for 64 from 25 overs in their second.

'That spell was one of the highlights of the season for me,' he recalls. 'I was still trying to establish my place in the side and it was touch-and-go whether we'd win the game. It was well-contested and evenly-poised and I was really pleased to get Alan Wells in my first over on the final day.

'After a discussion with Duncan and Matthew, I switched from bowling around to over the wicket from the first ball. On the previous evening, I'd seen that Alan wasn't too happy with me coming over, so I bowled one on middle stump – perhaps middle-

and-leg – and the ball turned just enough to get a nick. Alan was well taken at slip by Cotts and that wicket proved to be the turning point. It helped us win the match and me to take two more wickets to finish with my season's best.'

Another two followed in the draw with Hampshire but Dean bowled 20 wicket-less overs in the defeat of Durham. Gary Butcher returned for the Middlesex collapse at Cardiff before the spinner was recalled to play in the two matches staged at St Helen's last summer.

'I didn't bowl against Sussex but picked up seven wickets in the Gloucestershire game – three in the first innings and four in the second. I was very pleased to get the England wicketkeeper Jack Russell out twice. He's a fidgety character who can stick around.

'My main memory of that match was the arm ball I bowled to Monte Lynch in the second innings. It was the first time I'd tried it all season, it was quite quick and swung a little bit. Monte was stuck in the crease and was trapped lbw. Those four wickets did wonders for my confidence and it was a big win for us because Gloucestershire were also up near the top at the time.'

A single wicket in the draw with Derbyshire was Dean's last contribution for a couple of games – initially because of the club versus country debate. With Zimbabwe Under 19s on tour, the young spinner was very much in demand.

'It wasn't really a problem for me,' he recalls. 'I had my heart set on playing for Glamorgan, especially as Zimbabwe weren't the toughest of teams. If it had been Australia or South Africa, that would have been different. But because we were in such a good position in the championship, I felt that I was becoming a key player bowling in tandem with Crofty and I didn't want to let Glamorgan down.'

Although Dean was picked to play in the one-day internationals and the first Test, it was agreed, after discussions between the England and Wales Cricket Board and Glamorgan, that he and a couple of other players would be released from the rest of the series. That meant he missed the rain-affected draw against Nottinghamshire – along with his prospective replacement, Phil North, who overslept on the morning of the first day and was left out of the team as a result. The wicket turned enough for Robert Croft to collect three victims but Glamorgan badly missed the other half of their spin attack.

Dean wasn't picked for the defeat at Worcester and took no

wickets in the innings victory over Northamptonshire at Aber-gavenny and the draw at Leicester. On his return to the side against Surrey, three second-innings wickets took him to seven-teen for the season. But in thirteen overs in the penultimate match against Essex at Cardiff, Dean failed to add to his total and appeared to have gone off the boil.

After taking two wickets in Somerset's first innings at Taunton, he was called upon to bowl what turned out to be Glamorgan's last over of the summer. Although some commentators felt the youngster wasn't used enough during 1997, Dean was more than happy with the way he was treated.

'As a captain, Matthew was a great help. He was always asking me if I wanted the field changing. With his experience of first-class cricket, he knows how people play and, having just come on the scene, I'm quite adventurous. It's not always the right thing to be but Matthew was happy for me to take risks. His belief that he can set a field which I'm going to bowl to gives me great confidence.

'It was good being the baby of the team because I could look around and learn from the experience of other players. Matthew and Steve Watkin are great role models for me. Matt has a good attitude towards the game – on and off the field – and Steve is so reliable and consistent – with a theory for everything. He helped me along the way.

'It was a great privilege to play with a Test bowler like Waqar and it's frightening when you see him running in against county batsmen. I think a lot of his wickets were the result of the aura that he has about him.

'Everybody knows all about the great Glamorgan team spirit. Everyone pulls together. There's a great atmosphere in the chang-ing room, where we're always having a laugh, but we're deadly serious when we get out onto the pitch – and that's what counts. A few of the counties used to think we were a bit soft but we were more aggressive in our approach last year.'

Like the other youngsters in the Glamorgan squad, Dean is grateful for the help he received from new coach Duncan Fletcher. 'Duncan seemed to think that Tomo and I had a good career ahead of us and he wanted to bring out the best in us. He helped me a lot with my batting by encouraging me to be more aggressive.

'Duncan also gave me a few tips about flight and urged me to look at the batsmen's behaviour – is he coming down the wicket or sweeping? – and then try to figure out what they are thinking.

Little things, hard to describe, but, when I look back, I realise he did a lot for me. He was happy with my action and said that if I was bowling well and maintained a good rhythm then I didn't have to change anything.'

Duncan Fletcher was delighted to have Dean Cosker in the Glamorgan squad. His control and variations of flight added balance to the attack. 'Dean could become a real talent but it's too early to say if he is exceptional at this stage because he's still got some work to do on his batting and fielding. But already he's a very good bowler.'

That view was confirmed by Dean's performances on the England A winter tour to Kenya and Sri Lanka. 'I was very happy to be called up by England so early on in my career. I was playing in a benefit six-a-side tournament for Colin Metson at St Fagans near Cardiff when I heard the news on the car radio. Fletch and Steve James were with me and obviously Steve was disappointed not to be going to the West Indies but I was determined to make the most of my chance.'

As expected, Dean was pitched into direct competition with another left-arm spinner, Ashley Giles of Warwickshire. Giles always appeared to have the upper hand but Dean aquitted himself well, taking 11 wickets at just over 24 apiece in the 2-0 unofficial Test series win over Sri Lanka A.

'It was great bowling with Ashley,' says Dean, 'a good learning experience. I didn't get into my rhythm early on in the tour but I was happy with the way I bowled in Sri Lanka, having worked hard on my action with coach Mike Gatting.'

During the tour, Dean celebrated his 20th birthday. His winter performances have marked him down as one for the future but, in the short term, he's confident of helping Glamorgan to build on their success. 'I think we have a good chance of retaining the title. The nucleus of the side is still here and I think there's more to come. I can certainly take ten or fifteen more wickets than I did in 1997.'

'Dean's track record to date has been phenomenal,' says Peter Walker, a former left-arm spinner himself. 'Spinners don't usually mature until their late twenties, so in that respect, Dean is mature beyond his years. Who can say what the future holds for him? If he keeps taking wickets and improves the other aspects of his game, then a full England cap must be a strong possibility.'

Dean Cosker is a bright boy. With ten GCSEs and 3 A levels, he turned down a university place to concentrate on cricket. So far, it has proved a very good career move. A championship winner's medal and an international A debut in his first full season represents a remarkable return.

His team mates in the Glamorgan dressing room are certain to make sure success doesn't go to his head – they won't let him become too big for his cricket boots. The good thing is that Dean Cosker himself is intelligent enough to realise that he must keep his feet on the ground – and not just behind the popping crease.

THE TWELFTH
(AND INVISIBLE) MAN

CHAMPAGNE corks were popping, photographers' bulbs were
flashing and 3,000 Glamorgan supporters were saluting
their heroes on the pavilion balcony at Taunton.

With team photos being disrupted by individual players
disappearing to record media interviews, nobody seemed to notice
at first. In the aftermath of Glamorgan's third championship win,
the mother of all parties was just beginning. Chaos reigned.

Some players were down on the pitch mixing with the masses,
others up in the dressing room. The odd one – like Robert Croft –
was standing in front of a microphone exploding the myth that all
Welshman can sing.

Then someone asked the question: 'Where's Butch?' Amid all
the celebrations, the 22-year-old all-rounder, who figured in just
over half of Glamorgan's seventeen championship games, was
nowhere to be seen. Had he actually arrived in Taunton? Nobody
seemed to know. Where was he? The twelfth man appeared to
have become the Invisible Man.

Gary Butcher was, in fact, at home in Cardiff – the victim of a
misunderstanding with his great mate, Darren Thomas, the hero of
that last day's play at the County Ground.

'I was watching the game on television and fully intended going
down to Taunton on the Saturday afternoon. Once Darren started
taking the wickets, I was all ready to leave. The trouble was I'd
borrowed Darren's car and I couldn't get it started! He'd
forgotten to tell me – or assumed I knew – that it had an
immobiliser. It was very frustrating because I couldn't work out
why it wouldn't start. I was also a bit worried that something had
gone wrong with the car.

'It was a very strange feeling when Steve James scored the
winning runs. I really wanted to be there and it was amazing
watching the scenes on television. I knew that something major was

taking place. I've since been told that I missed out on a good evening – I just hope there are going to be more to come in the future!'

Gary Butcher has an excellent cricketing pedigree. His father Alan played for Surrey, Glamorgan and England and is now coach at Essex, while elder brother Mark made his England debut in the Ashes series last summer. Gary – or the Meatseller as he is sometimes called by his team mates – has been a fringe player since making his Glamorgan debut in 1994.

At the start of the 1997 season, Gary had played 20 first-class games, scored 750 runs and taken 23 wickets at just over 46 apiece. A dependable, late middle-order batsman and right-arm medium bowler, he had yet to make a real impression. More a bits-and-pieces player than a genuine all-rounder, he knew he was likely to be on the periphery during most of 1997 – and so it proved. But with Waqar still recovering from injury, Gary found himself playing in the first match against Warwickshire.

'I didn't bat and took only one wicket and then, partly because of the weather, it took a long time for my season to get started. I'd maybe play a game but not bat and then it would rain for the next game, so I didn't get the chance to do anything. I was in and out of the team for the first seven or eight games in what was a stop-start sort of season for me.

'It was difficult being part of the squad but not in the team. I wanted to be out there playing but the games I missed out on were basically down to the type of pitches we played on. When Matthew Maynard opted for two spinners, Dean Cosker was picked. I probably played most of my games when Robert Croft was away on England duty.'

After being dismissed lbw by Darren Gough for 0 at Headingley, Gary picked up a couple of wickets in the only Yorkshire innings but was left out of the side to face Kent at Canterbury. In came Dean Cosker and his 4 for 64 helped sweep Glamorgan to victory.

When Gary returned to the side in place of Croft for the draw with Hampshire at Cardiff, he scored a season's best of 58 but missed the innings victory over Durham a week later. The Middlesex defeat – he made 21 and 0 – in the middle of June proved to be his last game until the beginning of July. After the convincing wins over Lancashire and Sussex, Gary was recalled for the defeat of Gloucestershire but, batting at number six, made 0 and only bowled one over in the match.

A flicker of form produced 22 runs in the draw at Chesterfield, after conceding 36 from 9 overs in Derbyshire's first innings. The flame burnt brighter in the next game as Gary made 48 not out – second top score – in the rain-affected draw with Nottinghamshire at Colwyn Bay.

It was Butcher the bowler who impressed in the defeat at Worcester. Three wickets for 87 from 20 overs – his best figures of the season – made him the pick of the Glamorgan attack but knocks of 5 and 18 did little to prevent Worcestershire winning by 54 runs. Dean Cosker returned for the draw at Leicester so signalling the end of Gary's on-field involvement with the championship campaign. His season was over, almost before it had begun.

'It was great being in the twelve although not playing was obviously a disappointment,' Gary recalls. 'I just got on with my duties as twelfth man. If anyone in the field needed a drink or piece of equipment, I would take it to them and it was my job to sort out their lunches – basically, I had to make sure all the players were happy. It might sound a bit like being a waiter or dogsbody but everybody's gone through it in their career. I was happier being with the first team than turning out for the seconds, because I went to every game thinking I was going to play. There were a couple of times when I felt I was a bit hard done by but that happens to every cricketer.'

Like Darren Thomas, Gary struck up a good relationship with Waqar Younis who was always available with advice when asked. 'I'd like to think we became pretty good friends, because we spent quite as lot of time together and often travelled to games in the same car. Occasionally, I had to answer one of his two mobile phones – he always got a lot of calls!

'Waqar's one of the best fast bowlers in the world but he's just an ordinary guy off the field. He's a great person to have in your side because you feel you're in the lead even before a ball has been bowled.'

After winning the Swansea Balconiers' Most Improved Player Award in 1996, last season must be considered a disappointment for Gary Butcher. Averaging 22.5 with the bat and nearly 34 with the ball in the championship, fewer runs and wickets hardly represented an improvement. But realistically, Gary considers the season to have been another step along his learning curve.

'I'd liked to have played more but, looking back, it was just great being with Fletch and the guys – just watching and learning. Duncan was an inspiration with all his new ideas. He was a really nice guy who everybody wanted to work for.

'When he introduced the new drills pre-season, everyone just stood there scratching their heads at first but we adjusted to them really quickly and even began to look forward to them! One involved fielding five or six balls at pace and running around cones in between returning the balls. The drills were hard work and I certainly felt my fielding improved – I picked the ball up more cleanly and my throwing was better.

'I used to really enjoy the warm-up football and touch-rugby games. When it was cold and raining, at places like Chesterfield and Colwyn Bay, we used to go and play for an hour or so. It was great fun! Everyone really enjoyed it and the games were also keeping us fit.

'With everyone pulling in the same direction, the team spirit was fantastic. Halfway through the season, when we were at the top of the table, I thought we might be in with a chance of winning the title but nobody mentioned it – until the last four or five games when every point became vital.'

As one of the younger players, Gary benefited directly from Duncan Fletcher's influence. The coach made a slight alteration to his run-up but feels more needs to be done before the all-rounder becomes the finished article.

'It was really a toss-up between Gary and Darren for the third seamer's spot,' says Duncan, 'and Darren beat him to it. He was more focused and took the opportunity to improve his game. Butch is a more flamboyant type of cricketer who's got to work harder at certain aspects of his play. He's a raw talent who's got to realise that plenty of hard work is required to refine his game.'

The message has been received and understood. Taking a leaf out of Darren Thomas' scorebook, Gary turned down the chance to play for Hawkesbury Cricket Club in Sydney over the winter. Instead, he helped out in a new sports shop in London opened by the former Surrey and Glamorgan left-arm spinner, Neil Kendrick.

'I decided not to go away because I wanted to work on both parts of my game. Personally, I think I'm a batsman who can also bowl. I feel I can get a lot better at both but it's going to take a lot of hard work and self-belief. I'm happy with the one-year contract I've been given but I've got a few points to prove – both to myself and other people. But I have to get into the first team to do so.'

A possible route might be via the vacancy created by the departure of Hugh Morris to a desk job at Lord's. Gary is listed in the *Cricketer's Who's Who* as a right-hand opening bat and would love the opportunity to replace the England and Wales Cricket Board's new Technical Director.

'I used to open at school and for youth sides and if I was offered the chance, I'd jump at it. I've batted at three, four, five and six for Glamorgan in the last two years and if I'm given the opportunity, I'll definitely take it up. In an ideal world, I'd like to have a big season in 1998 and then take it from there.'

During his career, comparisons will inevitably be made between Gary, his father and his brother Mark, who played a key role in England's victory in the third Test against the West Indies earlier this year.

'I don't think I've suffered by being in Mark's shadow but his selection ahead of Steve James against Australia and then for the Caribbean tour did cause me a few problems. A lot of people in Wales felt that Steve, rather than Mark, should have played for England. It was quite difficult hearing things like that all the time because Mark is my brother after all! Occasionally, it was a bit tricky.

'I must admit I was surprised to see Mark Ramprakash recalled for the West Indies trip after the number of chances he's had. I thought that decision was worse than Mark going ahead of Steve.'

Having missed out on selection for nearly half Glamorgan's championship games, there was a certain irony about Gary's non-appearance at Taunton – almost as if it had been preordained that, even in the moment of glory, the understudy would be left waiting in the wings.

Glamorgan's bit-part player is now desperate for a crack at a leading role. Every understudy has his day and 1998 might be the year that the twelfth man is transformed from Invisible Man to Action Man.

PART 6

Behind the Stumps

KEEPING ON THE BALL

A DRIAN Shaw is one of the characters in the Glamorgan dressing
room – what Tony Cottey describes as one of the 'louder
voices'.

Along with Cotts and Robert Croft, he likes a bit of banter.
He's one of the lads who enjoys a joke. Keeping wicket and
keeping spirits up are his business and he relishes his role as the
Glamorgan court jester.

In the 1997 *Cricketer's Who's Who*, his family links with the sport
were listed as 'Mum thinks Mark Ramprakash is handsome' and
'Grandad saw a game once'. The 26-year-old wicket-keeper from
Neath, who has also played Premier Division rugby at centre for
his home town, is the player with the most nicknames in the
Glamorgan team. They range from Gloves, Teflon – the non-stick
material – and Cymbals, to the less obvious Dale and Barrymore.
Adrian bears more than a passing resemblance to those two stars of
British light entertainment, Dale Winton and Michael Barrymore.

But throughout the county's 1997 championship campaign,
another comparison was made which Adrian found very difficult to
laugh at. By choosing him ahead of the more experienced Colin
Metson on the strength of his batting, Glamorgan handed him a
double-edged blade. Adrian was given both the opportunity to
establish himself as the county's wicket-keeper batsman and the
biggest headache of his career so far.

The contrast could hardly have been greater: fewer than 20
matches compared with Metson's 200; 33 first-class victims as
opposed to 558; a novice instead of a player who was unfortunate
not to play for England and a general acceptance that, behind the
stumps, there was only one winner, Metson.

Behind the euphoria of Glamorgan's third championship success
lay a tale of triumph over some vindictive and small-minded
prejudice. As well as maintaining his form, Adrian had to deal with
keeping a small section of Glamorgan's supporters off his back.

'In 1996, I played in ten championship games, including the last
five,' recalls Adrian. 'Before last season began, I was told that I

was going to start in the first team. I got the impression that Matthew and Duncan were backing me to give the team a good balance. Five batsmen, five bowlers and a wicket-keeper who could get a few runs.

'But there was no danger of me becoming complacent because I knew there were a lot of people – members, committeemen, supporters and reporters – who wanted Colin in the team. As a result, I didn't feel that I would be in the team – come what may. I always felt that they might go back to Colin because of his track record – I still felt under great pressure.

'There were quite a few times – especially at Cardiff – when comments were passed about me within earshot as I walked off the field. If I'd dropped a catch or made a low score, some supporters would occasionally say things like "Bring back Metson!" to my face.

'I remember warming up before the Essex game at Cardiff – stretching my hamstrings with my foot up on an advertising hoarding. A group of blokes about two yards from me were discussing the wicket-keeping situation and saying how wrong it was that I was in the team rather than Colin. They must have known who I was and that I was standing right next to them! I was aware of a lot of bad feeling against me.'

The former England and Glamorgan all-rounder, Peter Walker, was appalled by the reaction of some supporters to Adrian's selection:

'Very rarely have I come across abuse as personal as that in all my time in the game,' he says. 'I must admit I was always a Metson supporter on the grounds that if you had the world's best fast bowler, you needed the best keeper behind the stumps but Adrian did well. I was one of the sceptics but Adrian is a trier, he was doing his best and that kind of behaviour from so-called supporters is reprehensible and certainly didn't make either Adrian's or Colin's position any easier.

'Adrian may not be one of the top half-dozen wicket-keepers in the country and perhaps he's a shade too tall to ever become one. Most of the best glovemen are short, nimble men but to Adrian's credit, he kept battling on and made some telling contributions with the bat when it mattered – confirming why he was preferred to Colin.'

'It was very disconcerting to have so much opposition to my selection from various sections of the club,' says Adrian. 'Certain members of the press have been hypercritical of my performance over the last two seasons and I would be daft if I said it hadn't got to me, because it did. As a human being, you don't like to be criticised in public but as a sportsman, it comes with the territory. When you fail, you fail in public – the criticism did sometimes sap my confidence.'

But in the Glamorgan dressing room, where it really mattered, there was nothing but support – both from Adrian's fellow professionals and coach Duncan Fletcher. To a man, the team closed ranks behind their young wicket-keeper.

'The players backed me. They wanted me in the side for the sake of balance. Some of them had played second XI cricket with me and they were always in my corner. When I hit a couple of bad patches during the season, they stuck by me and I appreciated that.

'I was hugely disappointed with my batting. I set out at the start of the season aiming to get 750-800 runs – or, if I was very lucky, 1,000. I felt I had the ability to reach four figures but I batted less than any other keeper in the country. The ratio was ridiculous – something like four innings in every three games.'

In the seventeen championship matches, Adrian made 352 runs in 20 innings with a top score of 53 not out and an average of just over 23. He knew he hadn't done himself justice.

'I batted quite well but not as well as I would have liked to. I should have doubled the number of runs I made but, then again, I was also expecting to bat about another eight or nine times.'

'I know Adrian had a disappointing season with the bat,' concedes Duncan Fletcher, 'but he was still far better than Colin. There was never any room for Colin because he wasn't a good enough batsman. We tried him in the second XI and he still couldn't get runs. I'm sorry – but professional sport is a hard taskmaster.'

Adrian's start was less than impressive – successive ducks against Yorkshire and Kent. But 30 as an opener in the second innings at Canterbury set him off on a lucrative mini-run. He made 35 in the draw with Hampshire and 33 as Durham were brushed aside in an innings defeat. One run in two innings against Middlesex was soon forgotten as Adrian returned to familiar figures when Sussex arrived in Swansea.

'I made 34 not out on a poorish wicket which enabled us to reach 172 in a very low-scoring game. In that innings, nobody got over fifty, I made second top score and then in our second innings only two made half-centuries.'

A useful 16 not out helped Matthew Maynard declare at 400 for 5 against Gloucestershire before Adrian justified his selection as a batsman in the draw with Derbyshire.

'My 38 in partnership with Adrian Dale at Chesterfield helped us to avoid the follow-on. I went in at number eight that day because Butch was playing and Darren had gone in first wicket down. We were 222 for 6 and I put on 90 with Daley. In the next game against Nottinghamshire at Colwyn Bay, I made 31 not out as part of a last-wicket stand of 51, before Matt declared. My innings weren't major knocks that jumped out at you but I did make contributions at various times throughout the season.'

It was Adrian's display as a wicket-keeper which caught the eye in the game at Worcester in late July. After only Glamorgan's second defeat of the season, he was hauled before the captain and coach. Everybody's gloves came off.

'They weren't happy with my performance in the game as a whole and I accepted that I hadn't kept very well. There was one specific incident which led to the meeting. Robert Croft was bowling to Phil Weston, a left-hander, and Matthew was at first slip. Phil went forward and edged the ball wide of my left glove between me and Matthew. Phil went on to make 114 and I felt it was a little unfair that I got the blame for the missed catch.'

'Adrian responded very well to criticism,' recalls Duncan Fletcher. 'At the start of the season, I just left him alone at first. Then I offered him some advice but he didn't seem to take it. He seemed to stagnate until eventually he drifted backwards. Matt and I decided to have a chat with him at Worcester.

'We told him he wasn't good enough,' says Duncan Fletcher. 'There were certain areas of his game that he had to work on and we couldn't see any evidence of him doing it. Adrian responded magnificently. From then on in, he worked twice as hard as anyone else.

'We felt that he had a very narrow channel of wicket-keeping – he wasn't diving in front of first slip enough. We noticed that Hugh Morris was taking a lot there instead of Adrian. He wasn't moving well, so we gave him a few routines to get him to dive and move.'

'I felt I was going to be dropped after the Worcester game,' recalls Adrian, 'but they stuck by me – for which I'm very grateful. With the pressure they were under – after two draws and a defeat – it would have been very easy for them to leave me out, but Matthew is a very loyal captain and he stood by me. Duncan did his job by making us gell as a unit. He had this wonderful knack of knowing the right amount to put into team meetings – when to let the captain have his room, when to butt in and when to give someone a bollocking. I obviously accepted their opinions because, at the end of the day, they're the ones that count. I went away to work on what they said and my form returned soon after.'

Five catches in the innings defeat of Northamptonshire, two in the draw at Leicester and then seven victims against Surrey confirmed that Adrian's wicket-keeping crisis was over. His batting, which had settled a close Nat West Trophy tie at Southampton in July, reached a peak in the county's championship decider against Somerset.

In the wake of the Morris-Maynard onslaught, Adrian and Robert Croft made hay while the sun didn't shine. In fading light, they put on 71 for the sixth wicket, with the rejuvenated wicket-keeper finishing on 53 not out – his season's best.

'Looking back on my knock at Taunton, it probably wasn't that important because we won with a day to spare but it did give us the opportunity to win the game that night as we had a lead of 275 on first innings.

'I had felt after our first three games that we would be there or thereabouts at the end of the season but I hadn't been too confident about our chances of winning our last two matches. It was a fabulous performance down at Taunton and I was proud to have played my part in such a collective team effort. Championships aren't won by superstars but by all players contributing. Everything we need for a successful 1998 is there – as long as we can replace Hugh Morris's runs.'

With Colin Metson having left the club, Adrian Shaw now has a new challenger for the role of Glamorgan gloveman. The county's only close-season signing has resulted in Worcestershire's Ismail Dawood joining on a two-year contract. A product of the Yorkshire Academy, Dawood spent a year with Northamptonshire before scoring more than 1,000 second XI runs for Worcestershire in 1996.

The 21-year-old right-handed wicket-keeper-batsman has been an England Under 19s tourist to Sri Lanka and the West Indies and, not surprisingly with a nickname of Hectic, the new boy is in a hurry to oust Adrian from the number-one spot.

'I would have been more than happy to stay at New Road,

where I'd been offered another contract, but I want regular first XI cricket. With Steve Rhodes almost a permanent fixture at Worcester, this was too good an opportunity to pass up. I know I'll have to fight Adrian for the right to play in the first team but I'm confident in my own ability and will relish the challenge.'

'Matthew told me they were about to sign Ismail just before he went to New Zealand,' says Adrian. 'I know he's got a very good batting record but he's only played two first-class games, so we've yet to see what he can do outside the seconds. I haven't seen enough of his keeping to comment on it but he's a very nice lad. I'd be very disappointed if I didn't start the new season as the number-one keeper, but it's up to me to perform and hold my place.'

Skipper Matthew Maynard is delighted to have created competition for the role of all-round rather than specialist stumper. 'There were several wicket-keepers who we could have approached but in terms of age, experience and playing ability, we feel Ismail is the right one for us. Although he's still only 21, he's packed a lot into his career so far and I'm sure there'll be great rivalry between him and Adrian.'

'Adrian will definitely benefit from having Ismail breathing down his neck,' agrees Duncan Fletcher. 'We wanted to put pressure on him. Competition is very healthy whether you're a batsman, bowler or wicket-keeper.

'I think Adrian can improve as a wicket-keeper but there are certain aspects of his play which worry me – like his agility. Keepers have got to be very quick around the stumps to grab balls that have bounced off the pads. He's quite a big man and doesn't seem as agile as a keeper should be but you never know. I have a philosophy for cricket and for life: what you put in, you get out. And Adrian's certainly put a lot in.'

Peter Walker believes Adrian Shaw will respond positively to the competition provided by a second wicket-keeper-batsman – even though history is against the near six-footer.

'The only very tall gloveman I can recall who was out of the top drawer was Johnny Waite of South Africa. He too was a fine batsman but his sort don't surface too often. For Adrian to have a long first-class career, he's going to have to develop his own individual technique to accommodate his size. He's got plenty of determination, an excellent attitude and he's an exceedingly nice guy – ideal team material.'

Last winter was a busy one for Adrian Shaw the coach. As well as looking after under-11 schoolchildren in Cardiff and the Vale of Glamorgan, he passed his Advanced Level coaching award before beginning nets.

'I just tried to work on my game – I'm never going to be "the new Colin Metson" because I'm a totally different animal to him. I just want to be myself and make the best of what I am.'

More than anything, Adrian Shaw is an honest, down-to-earth cricketer. Since being voted Glamorgan's Young Player of the Year in 1995, he has worked hard to establish himself in the county side. Aware of his shortcomings, he's striven to eliminate them from his game and is desperate to retain the wicket-keeper's job as his own.

Adrian will surely rise to the challenge set by the Glamorgan powers that be following the arrival of the younger pretender from New Road. With the disappearance of the pro-Colin Metson lobby, he will once again be able to laugh, unhindered, at life, cricket – and, of course, himself.

'I was moving house when we played Gloucestershire in Swansea in July last year,' recalls Adrian. 'After the Sunday League game, I went out and had a few more beers than I should have with Steve Watkin and then took a taxi to what I thought was my home. I got out of the car, paid the driver and then couldn't get the key in the door! I spent ten minutes trying to force it into the lock – I even rang the doorbell! – before it dawned on me that it was my old house at Cadoxton in Neath! I'd only moved the day before and I was now living about three miles away in Tonna, on the other side of the valley. Having already paid £8 for the taxi, I had to walk all the way home and didn't arrive there until half-past two in the morning! There are always some things I'm not going to get quite right!'

STUMPED ON THE SIDELINES

To bat or not to bat? That is the question which has bedevilled the game of cricket throughout the 1990s. Wicket-keeper-batsman or specialist stumper? Does your gloveman have to be a middle-order batsman?

Colin Metson doesn't think so – but then he would say that wouldn't he? After sixteen years as a professional cricketer, the former Middlesex keeper spent the summer of 1997 on the outside looking in. While not exactly on the scrap heap, Colin found himself on the way to the knacker's yard – at a time when, as Glamorgan's 1997 beneficiary, he was expecting to take advantage of their finest hour for nearly 30 years.

Colin Metson was delighted to have been awarded a benefit after a decade at the club. Since arriving from Middlesex in 1987, he had performed brilliantly behind the stumps to a variety of bowlers and he felt that the recognition of services rendered was fully deserved.

At one stage, Colin's form had propelled him onto the fringes of the England squad but eventually it came down to a dog-fight between specialist Jack Russell and the all-rounder British bulldog, Alec Stewart. Stewart won the initial battle but, after another Ashes failure, Russell's keeping skills and unconventional but effective approach to batting saw him restored to the England team, leaving Stewart free to concentrate on dealing with the West Indies pace attack.

During 1997, as Russell was being neglected by England, Colin Metson knew how he felt. Glamorgan decided to follow England's lead by opting for Adrian Shaw, a promising young batsman who could also keep wicket, rather than the genuine article who made fewer runs.

While Russell put his head down and forced his way back into contention, Colin Metson had other things on his mind – like a benefit year to run. As it turned out for him, there was no way back and his association with Glamorgan was to end on a disappointing but not bitter note.

186

After six years at Middlesex, where he challenged England keeper Paul Downton for a first-team place, Colin made a record 160 consecutive championship appearances for Glamorgan between 1987 and 1994. He played a key part when the county won the Sunday League in 1993 – Glamorgan's first trophy for 24 years – and he holds the county record for first-class catches (seven in an innings and nine in a match). He stumped 51 batsmen in his first-class career but his batting average of just under 17 was to prove his Achilles' heel.

'I'd got a good idea of the selection policy from the previous year,' recalls Colin, 'because in 1996 Adrian played the last five championship games. As captain, Matthew Maynard was keen to encourage him to play and perform, to see if he was up to it.

'At the start of last season, with Waqar coming, Robert Croft having a successful winter tour and with Matthew looking to play Dean Cosker as the other spinner, I was hoping he might prefer the more experienced wicket-keeper.'

But the writing was on the wall for Colin from the opening game against Warwickshire. Adrian Shaw was the preferred choice because of his batting potential. Glamorgan had decided to use six batsmen with their keeper at seven. There was little argument about who was the better gloveman but Colin's track record had become a secondary consideration.

'Matthew decided he was going to give Adrian a long run in the first team, although he did say to me that he'd have another look if I got some runs in the seconds. In my view, he didn't say it in a convincing way.

'Obviously, my benefit took up a lot of my time, which meant it was difficult to work on improving my batting. I probably made a mistake in asking the second XI coach, John Derrick, if I could bat in the top four or five because I ended up opening for a couple of months after the first few games. If I had gone in at say six or seven, I might have got some runs. My highest score was 20 against Surrey at Usk in July.

'There was never a problem between myself and Adrian. I found it difficult to give him advice because we were both fighting for the same spot. He is a fine cricketer and a better batsman than me and he knows I'm a better keeper. If we were the same type of cricketers, then there might be some rivalry. I'm a wicket-keeper who can bat at number eight and he's someone who can bat at number six or seven and who dons the gloves.'

187

As the season wore on, and Glamorgan maintained their championship challenge, Colin continued to play for the seconds and busy himself with his benefit. His solitary first XI appearance in his last season with Glamorgan was against the touring Australians at Cardiff in the middle of July.

'Fletch called me at a quarter past nine on the morning of the match,' recalls Colin. 'He said Shawsy had ricked his neck taking his jumper off, so could I come down to play? I arrived at the ground, got changed and at half past ten it was confirmed that I was playing.

'I just concentrated on my game and I was happy with the way it went. I got three catches in the two Australian innings as well as a good stumping off Dean Cosker, which pleased me. It was my first first-team game for about a year and a completely different atmosphere from the seconds. I was nervous on the first morning and I wanted to do well because I thought it might be my one chance.

'Unfortunately, I didn't get any runs – Paul Reiffel bowled me – and I didn't bat in our second innings as the game ended up as a draw. Matthew and I hardly spoke for the whole three days. I think he found it difficult with me being there and perhaps I'd have felt the same if I'd been in his position.

'As I walked off Sophia Gardens at the end of Australia's second innings, I had a feeling it was going to be my last game for Glamorgan. Even though it was the middle of the summer, barring injuries to Adrian Shaw, I felt that Matthew wasn't looking to pick me whatever happened.

'So I decided to take a little longer to walk off and I had a good look around to take it all in. I didn't feel sad because I'd had eleven good years at Glamorgan. I remember hearing some generous applause and some pleasant comments about my return.'

Colin felt his reappearance in the first team was a one-off and when nothing was said to him afterwards in the dressing room, he assumed that Adrian Shaw would return for the Derbyshire game. But he was disappointed by the way he was treated after the Australia match in particular and throughout the season in general.

'It would have been polite for someone from the management to tell me, after my appearance, that the team would be back to normal for the next match. In fact, I think there was a lack of communication from Matthew and Duncan because neither told me what I needed to do nor was I informed about what was going on.

'I admired Duncan for what he did when he came over but he never actually sat down and looked at any part of my batting technique or offered me any advice. I had very few conversations with Duncan.'

The game against Worcestershire a month after the tourist match might have been a turning point in Colin's season. Glamorgan lost by 54 runs and Adrian Shaw's performance was put under the microscope, first by his captain and coach and then by the press. The calls for his predecessor's return reached a crescendo.

'I thought I might get the nod at that stage,' recalls Colin, 'and there was a lot of talk about changing the side during the second and third week of August. The press gave Adrian a pretty bad time after the Nat West semi-final and the Worcestershire defeat, and suggested to Matthew that he should change the team. I thought I might get a call but I never really expected it.

'I didn't really feel frustrated but I was aware of people telling me that I was. The worst thing was people coming up and saying that I should be playing – they couldn't understand what was going on. But after speaking to Matthew, I realised that he wouldn't change and the more the press went on about it, the more stubborn he became.

'I had committee members saying to me that I should be playing but I knew they weren't going to say it in committee because the side was winning. I'm not daft, I knew that Matthew would just turn round and say that the team was first, second or third in the championship – that was his team, so why change it?'

In the dressing room, Colin received sympathy but, crucially, no support from the members of the team. 'In those sort of situations, you can't really take sides,' says opener Steve James, who shared a room with Colin on away trips. 'You have to back the captain. There was no back-biting. Shawsy was given the job and everybody got behind him. When he got a lot of unfair stick and was under pressure, the boys rallied around and he did a good job.

'It was obviously very disappointing for Colin because he was a very, very fine keeper. There was a certain amount of sympathy for him, the boys respected his cricketing ability and, around 1993-94, he was definitely the best keeper in the country – but life had to go on.

'The fact that it was his benefit year didn't enter the equation. You don't pick someone for sentimental reasons. Matthew made

189

the decision on cricketing grounds – what he thought was best for the side. He was right and we won the championship. Matthew stuck his neck out and made a brave decision and although a lot of people disagreed with him, it worked. You can't really say whether we would have won with Colin rather than Adrian playing.'

'Some people said to me that Glamorgan would have won the championship by the end of August with me in the side,' says Colin, 'but nobody can be that certain. You have to say that Matthew has been a successful captain because he's now up there with Wilf Wooller and Tony Lewis.'

The cloud created by not being selected did have a lucrative silver lining for the 1997 beneficiary. Second XI cricket gave Colin more time to devote to his benefit season which eventually netted him about £125,000.

'It worked both ways,' explains Colin. 'I got a lot of sympathy from spectators who supported me during the season and I had more time to organise the smaller events. But what really makes a successful benefit are the big luncheons and dinners in London when 300 or 400 people attend and spend daft money on cricket memorabilia.

'If you're not in the side, even though you're an established player, I'm not sure whether companies support you as much as they would do if you were playing. I couldn't approach who I wanted to – I no longer had the pulling power because I was out of the team. For instance, I couldn't get a sponsor for a London dinner – either in the Long Room at Lord's or a top hotel.

'I was delighted with the response to my benefit in Wales but I know it would have been easier to raise money had I been playing in the first team. In the end, I think the pros and cons of not being selected balanced themselves out.

'The benefit was successful because of all the hard work everyone put into it. I had mixed contributions from the players. I felt that there was good support from three or four of them – Waqar made himself available for the functions I asked him to attend. But one or two who have had benefits in the past weren't as supportive as they might have been.'

Although he had only played in the tour game against Australia, Colin Metson travelled down to Taunton for Glamorgan's final championship match of the season. Not part of the squad but still on the Glamorgan staff, he thought he should be there.

'I went down to support players who I felt would appreciate my presence – those I'd known through the years. I felt I was part of the building of the team and I was pleased for them. But I didn't think I could really dive in there with the champagne and start spraying it around!

'I was happy to be there but I didn't stand out on the balcony and wave and get all excited. I had a bottle of Budweiser and stayed back, well away from the celebrations in the dressing room. I went out to the balcony area and talked to a committee member or a supporter and then when the cameras arrived, I went back into the dressing room.

'I wasn't part of the squad which had won the championship – as I had been with Middlesex in 1985. I'd played in ten games during that season when Paul Downton was away on Test duty. I wasn't there at the end when Middlesex actually won it but I got a medal and went up to Buckingham Palace with the team. Taunton would have been worse for me if I hadn't have experienced that with Middlesex.

'It was a bit embarrassing when I went out to the side of the balcony at Taunton a couple of times – some supporters started chanting my name! It was nice of them to do that but a little awkward for me.'

The whole summer of 1997 was a little awkward for Colin Metson. At a time when he felt his experience would prove invaluable to Glamorgan, he found himself in the wilderness – unwanted, unused and unaccustomed to the hard-nosed approach which drove Glamorgan on to their third championship title. Team selection reflected an uncompromising policy, where runs counted more than catches and the players displayed an unusual toughness throughout the summer.

'I think Glamorgan have been too friendly on the pitch in the past,' says Colin. 'Perhaps one of my traits is that I wasn't mouthy or aggressive enough as a wicket-keeper towards the batsmen, as seems to be expected these days. There appeared to be a definite policy to be harder during 1997. I remember Steve James grabbing John Stephenson in the Nat West quarter-final against Hampshire and Crofty squaring up to Mark Illot at Chelmsford – something they would not have done three years ago.

'I was delighted when Glamorgan won the championship because it was what we'd been striving for over a number of years. But it was very disappointing to have seen out my last season from the boundary because I felt I could have made a meaningful contribution for another two or three years.

'As a professional in a high-profile sport, you have to be prepared to take some hard knocks but I often found the situation a little bizarre. I accepted that it was the skipper's prerogative to field the team of his choice. I've played long enough to know that these things happen. I've seen it happen to other players – you just have to get on with it.

'I will always remember one or two of my benefit functions when I received standing ovations. They were stirring events and very enjoyable and, as a Glamorgan player for eleven years, they gave me immense pleasure.

'And remember, it was good for my benefit that the boys were winning because it kept people interested through to the end of the year. I had quite a lot of functions in September, October and early November, so I can't complain.'

When his contract ran out, Colin Metson decided it was time to hang up his Glamorgan gloves. After working for five winters as project co-ordinator with the Castle Services Group, he joined the haulage and freight company on a full-time basis and now operates from their offices in Cardiff. A return to the game through club cricket might be on the cards at the turn of the century but, for now, Colin wants a break.

As news of his departure was made public, Glamorgan's secretary Mike Fatkin was quick to pay tribute to the county's former wicket-keeper.

'We feel Colin was extremely unlucky not to have been picked for England. His quality behind the stumps has been recognised throughout the county game. It must have been very difficult for him, having been a regular for such a long time, to be watching the side from the sidelines and, knowing the sort of standards he has always set himself, we can fully understand his decision to retire. But you can't argue with Matthew's decision to pick Adrian Shaw as keeper, because at the end of the day, Glamorgan won the championship.'

It is sad to recall that for much of his last season at Sophia Gardens, Colin Metson was the 'Forgotten Man' who, because of his benefit, couldn't afford to be forgotten. Judging by their response though, the county's loyal supporters appreciated his contribution as they dug deep into their pockets to support the specialist stumper.

Unlike Haydn Davies and Eifion Jones, Colin Metson failed to collect a championship medal with Glamorgan. The King of Catches may have been dismissed – almost out of hand – by the county's selection policy but he will always be fondly remembered as one of the finest exponents of the art of wicket-keeping ever to wear the daffodil. And, of course, he'll have that nice little nest egg – all of it cash in hand – to remind him that his efforts did not go unrewarded.

PART 7

From the Boundary

THIRTEENTH MAN

WHEN Steve James flicked that famous four down to fine leg to win Glamorgan the county championship at Taunton last September, Byron 'Dasher' Denning was, for once, lost for words.

Nearly sixty years after he began his love affair with the club by watching Wally Hammond score 302 for Gloucestershire at Newport, the county's scorer was speechless. He recorded the result in his big blue book and sat in silence for a few moments.

Since Somerset were the home side, Byron could afford just to listen to the public address announcement that Glamorgan had won by 10 wickets and completed a hat-trick of championship wins. Had it been Sophia Gardens, rather than the County Ground, he would have been struggling to keep his composure as master of ceremonies.

'I'm a very emotional man and I just sat there with a feeling of intense relief,' recalls Byron. 'My wife Olwen and one of her friends suddenly appeared behind me in the scorebox and patted me on the back but I couldn't speak. If I had tried to, I would have cried.'

Of course, Byron remembered 1948 and 1969 but this one was special. Thirteen years of painstaking scoring from Durham to Southampton, from Manchester to Canterbury and from Colwyn Bay to Cardiff had been rewarded with the ultimate prize. This was his team, they were his boys and he was so proud of them.

'Eventually, when we'd packed up all the books,' he says, 'I went over to the pavilion to speak to the umpires. There'd been a couple of injuries in Somerset's second innings and I wanted to clear up my timekeeping with them.

'When I got into the Glamorgan dressing room, the celebrations out on the balcony were in full swing but, once again, as everybody was hugging each other, I couldn't talk. I was in a little bit of a daze and gradually it began to dawn on me. I've always been a bit of a pessimist but suddenly I realised that I'd become the most successful Glamorgan scorer ever! We'd won the Sunday League in 1993 and now the championship. What right have I got to be a pessimist anymore! That said, I'll never be an optimist! That would be forsaking the habit of a lifetime.'

Watching Glamorgan has been just that for Dasher who inherited his nickname from a former Somerset player, Peter 'Dasher' Denning. In fact, it is an entirely inappropriate moniker. Two heart attacks mean that Byron's work involves lots of dots but not too much dashing.

'I have always been fascinated by sport but I've never been much good at it,' he admits. 'I played a bit of cricket for Cross Keys, where I was born, but always in the second XI, apart from one match in the first team on FA Cup Final day when nobody else wanted to play!

'My administrative career started when I became secretary of the school rugby and cricket teams – I wasn't playing but at least I was involved.'

Byron trained as a teacher and was a former manager of Ebbw Vale Leisure Centre and warden of adult education centres at Blaina and Ebbw Vale. He also spent 12 years as secretary of Cross Keys Rugby Club.

His active association with Glamorgan began when he became a member soon after the Second World War. He was elected onto the committee in 1970 to represent Monmouthshire but found the experience very frustrating.

'I've always wanted to be doing something but the committee seemed to do nothing,' he recalls. 'I became involved as a scorer for the match manager when the Sunday League started up but when I heard the club needed a new scorer for every game, in 1984, I volunteered for the job. As I was on the committee, they jumped at the chance of appointing somebody who wanted to do it. They were very grateful and the job became salaried in 1986.

'I took over from Frank Culverwell who was coming to the end of his working days. Various people like Phil Clift and Andrew Hignell had also helped out on a match-by-match basis.

'I love scoring because it's the nearest I can get to playing cricket. I wanted something to do because being on the committee then meant attending meetings, sitting up on the balcony and chatting to people. It wasn't very satisfying and I needed some-thing to get my teeth into.'

When public-address system duties were added to Byron's brief, a star was born. As the man on the microphone, the voice of Glamorgan cricket in Wales, his occasional *faux pas* have become legendary. No one – not even one of the game's superstars – has escaped.

'Not long after Waqar arrived,' recalls Byron, 'I introduced him to the Cardiff crowd and thought nothing more of it. At the end of the day, I went up to the dressing room to give the players their bowling figures and Matthew Maynard came up to me.

'"Dasher," he said, "I want to introduce you to Waqar."

'I gave Matthew a rather quizzical look.

'"Yes," he said, "this is Waqar Younis."

'I was still a bit puzzled.

'"Not Waqar Hussein!"

'Apparently, I had announced that the bowler coming on at the Cathedral Road End was a combination of one of the world's fastest bowlers and the Essex and England batsman. The name Nasser Hussein just came into my mind – Waqar thought it was very funny.'

So did the captain, who was also grateful for Byron's unintentional contribution to the cause. 'Waqar had a new nickname for the rest of that spell,' Matthew Maynard recalls. 'We started calling him Saddam and it worked pretty well – he got fired up and picked up a couple of wickets!

'The thing I like about Dasher is that he spends just enough time on the microphone – he doesn't go overboard like some announcers do. He says the right things at the right time and although he does make the odd gaffe – remember, he's getting old! The players don't mind that – we have a bit of a laugh.'

Darren Thomas has seen the funny side on more than one occasion over the last couple of seasons. 'There was the time I introduced Darren Cosker and Dean Thomas – I got their christian names mixed up – and the day when Darren was coming into bat in Cardiff and I announced him as Gary Butcher!

'He was wearing his helmet, it was very dark and I couldn't see anything except his forearm. Like Darren, Gary's a bit swarthy so I opted for him. Darren more or less stopped in mid-stride and gave me a filthy look in the scorebox as all the other players were falling about all over the place!

'From what I gather, everyone in the ground enjoys my gaffes – they're very tolerant of an ageing gentleman! I have a very close relationship with the players and they pull my leg a lot – especially Tony Cottey. I have a love-hate relationship with him. Probably because of my age – I'm 69 – I was particularly prone to calling players by their wrong names last season.'

Thanks to modern technology, the basic business of scoring has changed dramatically since Byron first put pen and pencil to paper in 1984. Unlike some of his colleagues, he decided to tackle computers head-on.

'I saw them as a challenge. I wasn't going to let them beat me and as a result, I have learnt to master mine and have enjoyed using it. Computers were introduced in the early Nineties by the former Test and County Cricket Board and the Press Association so that the up-to-date score would be readily available for evening papers and on Ceefax and Teletext at the touch of a button.

'I use a laptop which is connected via a telephone link to Leeds, where the Press Association is based. We send ball-by-ball details to Leeds and the information is then sent out to whoever wants to buy it.

'I record every ball on my laptop but I still score in a book. The laptop hasn't taken over from the book because if you have a computer breakdown or a telephone-link failure to Leeds, and you're out of action for any period of time, you must have a written record to refer to. The computer supplements the traditional method.

'What usually happens is that the home scorer does the laptop. We both have to make sure we don't show any real enthusiasm for either side. I can't jump up in the air when Glamorgan win because I know very well what it feels like when the other side have won.

'It's become a pressurized job – you've really got to have your eyes peeled! Even scoring with a book requires concentration. With the laptop as well, it's double the concentration. I'm also in touch with the electronic scoreboard by walkie-talkie – we correct each other! – and then there's the PA system to run.'

Mistakes are an inevitable part of scoring – whichever method is used. But whereas a rubber can quickly erase a wrong dismissal or score in a book, it's not so simple to correct information which has been put into the computer wrongly.

'We had a dismissal once at Leicester where we were square-on to the square and not in our usual position behind the bowler's arm,' recalls Byron. 'We were about 80 yards away from the wicket and when the bowler appealed, one of their batsman was given out and walked. We thought it was lbw and put that decision in the book and the laptop. A couple of minutes later, when it went up on the scoreboard, the umpire turned to us to gesture that it was in fact caught. We assumed wicket-keeper Colin Metson had taken the catch but when the corrected version went up on the board, Matthew turned around and made us aware that he'd actually taken the catch at first slip! So there were three separate dismissals but only one of them was right!

'It caused us a fair bit of concern because in trying to alter the decisions we had to get back to the original ball on the laptop! Then we had to come back to the current play and catch up.'

With the modern-day scorer having so many duties, it is perhaps surprising that more mistakes aren't made. As Byron juggles his various and varied tools of communication, every now and then, things do go hilariously wrong.

'I remember once picking up the microphone instead of the walkie-talkie. One of the umpires, Mervyn Kitchen, signalled a wide and I was asked by the scoreboard to confirm it.

'"Yes," I said, thinking I was speaking into the walkie-talkie. In fact, having used the microphone, it sounded as if I was saying to Mervyn: Yes, I agree with you – it's a wide.

'Mervyn turned round to me and gave me a look as if to say, I'm glad you agree!'

Scoring, like cricket, is a team effort in which individual characters can flourish. Byron is quick to acknowledge the support he receives from his band of willing helpers in Cardiff. The scoreboards are connected so that when the main one changes, so does the small board at the Taff End of the ground.

'Gordon Eccles operates the electronic scoreboard with Alan Jones,' says Dasher. 'They squabble like a couple of cats and whenever there's a mistake, one always blames the other! We're all part of a team and I've got to keep an eye on them because we all make mistakes. But I have to say that they make the most!'

Byron's wife Olwen did nothing wrong during the game against Middlesex at Cardiff but it failed to stop her being ribbed about her involvement in the innings defeat. 'During that match, Alan Jones was on holiday so Olwen volunteered to help Gordon,' recalls Byron. 'Our second innings was a complete and utter disaster and when 31 all out went up on the board at the end of the match, Gordon and Olwen were taking down the plates and switching off the lights.

'Every newspaper in the country had a picture of the score with Olwen in the background! All her friends told her she'd made a mess of the game because she'd been operating the board during the collapse!'

201

Byron Denning clearly sees scoring for Glamorgan as a labour of love. For their part, the club obviously value his contribution ever since he marked his first card fourteen years ago.

'I owe an immense debt of gratitude to the administrators here – particularly to secretary Mike Fatkin. They ensure that all my stuff is carried over to the scorebox and brought back, so I've hardly had to lift a finger. Olwen has driven me virtually everywhere and the committee have been very generous with our expenses.'

With Byron's three-score-years-and-ten looming on the horizon, thoughts of retirement are not far from his mind. Dashing about at his age is no longer an option, which meant he missed Glamorgan's 221 run-win in Liverpool last June.

'I went to every away match apart from that one, because reaching the pavilion there is like climbing the north face of the Eiger. My second heart attack has left me a little out of breath, and it's not easy to climb steps. The thought of going back to the pavilion for lunch and tea was simply horrendous, so I stayed at home and Gordon Lewis, the second XI scorer, went in my place. I must admit to being a little bit envious when Waqar won it with his seven wickets but nevertheless I was delighted with the result.

'Whilst the old ticker still goes on, I'm quite happy to continue. I managed quite well last year. Calling it a day will largely depend on my health and whether I'm still doing a good job.

'I think my public-address system gaffes are at the stage of being amusing but, at the same time, they haven't been that frequent. I'm not making mistakes every day or even every match – I don't think I'm an embarrassment to the club, put it that way! I can cope with the job, but my birthday in August might be a good time to sign off – after all, I've had a pretty good innings! I can't say at this stage.'

Glamorgan will be hoping that Byron postpones his retirement for as long as possible. Sophia Gardens just wouldn't be the same without him. 'I think he's irreplaceable,' says Mike Fatkin. 'He has a sense of humour, a sense of tact, he gets on with everyone and he just loves what he does. It'll be a very sad day when he retires – he's a breath of fresh air around the place.'

'Dasher is a great character,' agrees skipper Matthew Maynard. 'We were obviously very upset when we heard about his most recent heart attack a couple of years ago and it's been tremendous the way he's bounced back.

'He's very trustworthy and very helpful to me as captain if I ever have to go to ask him any questions. He's got his scorebook which I dive into every now and then to see how the guys are doing. He's our thirteenth man, really – he's one of the lads. He's always about the place and the players think a helluva lot of him. To me, he's a tremendous person and a good friend to have around the team.'

As Dasher begins what might – or might not – be his last season as scorer, it is perhaps worth recalling one of his intentional announcements which has now passed into Glamorgan folklore. During a championship match against Worcestershire at Abergavenny in 1990, Graeme Hick had just taken the home attack to the cleaners and the results made pretty gruesome reading: Mark Frost 0 for 109, Steve Watkin 1 for 93, Steve Bastien 1 for 90, Robert Croft 1 for 71 and Nigel Cowley 1 for 101.

When Worcestershire declared their first innings on 514 for 4, Byron addressed the crowd:

'For those spectators with small children, I suggest you cover their ears – I am about to read the Glamorgan bowling figures!'

It goes without saying that no such announcement was needed during the summer of 1997.

'Bevs' and 'The Chalker'

Edward Bevan has a job most Glamorgan cricket fans would die for. After a successful club career with Gowerton, during which he led them to the Haig National Village title, he has been paid to follow the county's fortunes for the last sixteen years.

Andrew Hignell is the teacher who, after never quite being chosen for his school or university team, was determined to be involved in the game he loved.

From April to September, with some expert help from Glamorgan's record wicket-taker Don 'Shep' Shepherd, Edward and Andrew travel around the country, courtesy of the BBC. As commentator and scorer, Bevs and the Chalker make up the Radio Wales cricket team – a sort of Welsh version of *Test Match Special*, without eccentrics like Henry Blofeld but still with the odd fruit cake. Edward describes the action, Don provides the analysis and Andrew furnishes them both with endless facts and figures.

Bevs has been the reporting voice of Glamorgan cricket through the good – but mainly the bad – times. Since 1982, he has faithfully reported the county's attempts to re-establish a reputation forged by the Tony Lewis team of the late Sixties and early Seventies. Bevs was there when Glamorgan won the Sunday League in 1993 and when they clinched their third championship win last September.

'It was dreadful in the mid-Eighties,' recalls Edward. 'The club didn't have a ground of their own, the wickets were poor and they kept signing players from other counties and overseas who were past it. The county had no direction, money was going down the drain but in the last five years everything has been turned around. The targeted membership drive, buying Sophia Gardens, the signing of Viv Richards and Waqar, which has been vindicated with trophies, and the youngsters that have come through to the the first eleven – everything has been done professionally by a top-class team on and off the field.'

Edward Bevan is virtually one of that team. He sees the players at close quarters because he shares their living quarters – their

204

hotel is his home-from-home in the summer. As he and Shep pound up and down the motorways, Andrew Hignell lets the train take the strain – and somehow finds time to surf the Internet. As well as scoring for the BBC, he is Glamorgan's honorary archivist with special responsibility for their web site. After last season's championship win, Glamorgan are now on a roll and on line.

Away from cricket, Andrew is head of humanities at Wells Cathedral School in Somerset. Cardiff-born and bred, he began scoring at Glamorgan second XI games in the late 1970s and became the official BBC scorer in 1981 when he joined the late Carwyn James and Alun Williams in the radio commentary box.

'I manage to fit the cricket around my teaching commitments, thanks to a very sympathetic wife and a very understanding headmaster,' Andrew explains. 'I was present, at least for part of the time, at all of last season's championship matches except two of the most exciting ones – against Lancashire and Sussex. On both occasions, I was stranded on a train in transit.

'I was on my way to Liverpool when we stopped at Wolver-hampton because a man had suffered a heart attack. I don't know whether he was a Lancashire supporter listening to the score from Liverpool on the radio or not but I certainly was – pulling my hair out as Waqar took his hat-trick!'

A week later, the same thing happened as the Chalker made his way from Wells to Swansea for the first of two championship matches at St Helen's. 'This time, the train got stuck just outside Cardiff because of some failure. I arrived at St Helen's literally as the last Sussex wicket fell after Waqar had demolished them!

'The commentary team is almost like a mini-family,' says Andrew. 'We're part of the extended Glamorgan family – we just know each other's mannerisms, peccadillos and idiosyncracies. Obviously, there are times when I know not to speak and I always seem to sense when Edward and Don are going to need something.

'Every now and then, Edward does surprise me. I remember once at Leicester, when a Glamorgan supporter and his wife appeared at the back of the box and handed me quite a large slice of a lovely-looking fruit cake. I couldn't resist the temptation to eat it and, of course, it was then that Edward turned to me, saw that my mouth was full and promptly asked for the bowling figures! The cake rapidly appeared on the commentary-box glass as I coughed and spluttered my way through them!'

At the start of last season, Bevs shared the general optimism about Glamorgan's chances of making an impression on the championship, largely because of their varied attack. He was soon to appreciate the importance of Glamorgan's recruitment of Duncan Fletcher as coach.

'Fletch was an unknown quantity,' recalls Edward. 'We didn't know how good he was but he turned out to be terrific. I would compare him with Carwyn James when he was in charge of the British Lions rugby team in New Zealand in 1971. Carwyn would tell people like Barry John, Gerald Davies and David Duckham to go and play football behind the posts because there was nothing he could teach them. In the same way, Duncan didn't used to bother much with the more experienced Glamorgan players but concentrated on helping Darren Thomas, Dean Cosker and Gary Butcher. He would talk to and work with them all the time.

'Duncan was also an astute tactician. In the game at Canterbury, Kent wanted 319 to win and at the start of the final day were 156 for 3 with Alan Wells 84 not out. The left-arm spinner generally goes around the wicket but Fletch had a word with Dean Cosker the night before and suggested he go over the wicket from the moment play started. The second ball Wells faced that morning he nicked to Tony Cottey at slip and Glamorgan went on to win.'

Statistics rather than tactics were on Andrew Hignell's mind as Glamorgan played their second successive match at Sophia Gardens. After drawing with Hampshire, they were in the runs against Durham and the Chalker was licking his lips. As James, Morris and Maynard all made hundreds, history was about to be made in front of his very eyes!

'I've always wanted to see Glamorgan score 600 in an innings,' says Andrew, 'and I was very disappointed when they fell three runs short in this match. Strangely, having reached the highest-ever Glamorgan total of 586, Matthew went and declared on 597.

'I had a word with him afterwards and all he said to me was: "There's more to cricket than bloody statistics!" which is fair comment and typical Matthew. I'm sure it will happen and if I'm there – great! It's always nice, in the words of Max Boyce, to say "I was there".'

The euphoria of the innings victory over Durham quickly evaporated when Middlesex gave Glamorgan a dose of their own medicine in their next match at Cardiff. Having taught a few lessons in the morning, Andrew arrived from Somerset just before lunch to find England spinner Phil Tufnell still at the crease on his way to his season's best score of 21.

'I thought the wicket must be flat if that was happening, and then, in the space of just 14 overs, Glamorgan were bowled out for 31! It was like a bad dream. All the things you never thought could happen were happening. It was even worse than the bad old days of the 1980s when Rag, Tag and Bobtail were playing for Glamorgan. It was unreal.

'For once, we were nearly speechless in the scorebox until Matthew came over to say it was just one of those things. After that defeat, I did some homework on shortest-ever innings and when, a week later, Lancashire were bowled out for 51, I was stuck on Wolverhampton station! But I did ring Edward up to give him the information.'

During the rain-affected win over Lancashire at Liverpool, Edward Bevan witnessed the two sides of Waqar Younis from close range – world-class international fast bowler and first-class chap.

'Waqar was a very friendly man who would never turn down any autograph-hunter. When it was raining at Liverpool, Don and I looked out onto the outfield and saw him playing football with half a dozen kids. That was typical of Waqar. He would never refuse to go to a dinner, he was always polite and never lost his temper. Whilst playing for cosmopolitan Surrey in London, he'd never experienced anything like the warmth and generosity of the Welsh people.'

Waqar displayed a more hostile side of his character when Matthew Maynard's men took to the field after two days of rain. For the first time in the season, he showed just why Glamorgan wanted him on board by taking 7 for 25 from 7 overs. 'For some reason,' recalls Bevs, 'Lancashire had prepared a green pitch. They thought Wasim Akram was going to play but he failed a fitness test. Peter Martin was in their side, along with medium-paced Ian Austin. The Glamorgan players couldn't believe it.

'Waqar was unplayable in the Lancashire innings and the umpires, Vanburn Holder and Jack Hampshire, told us that no international side in the world would have survived against him that day. He was devastating! The wicket was green, they'd left a little grass on it and it was a misty, dampish sort of day with some cloud cover, so the ball swung everywhere. He just created havoc and let's not forget that Steve Watkin bowled beautifully as well.'

Edward and Don were two of the lucky ones. The supporters

group, the Swansea Balconiers, had travelled up by coach for the match but had barely seen a ball bowled because of rain. Play was possible only until lunch on the first day, there was none on the second or third days or the morning of the final day but then it brightened up.

'The Balconiers were staying about ten miles away,' says Edward, 'and after being told by Lancashire that there would be no play on the last day, they decided to do some sightseeing. Some went off to the Coronation Street set, the rest to Aintree. Nobody bothered with the cricket. When they got back to ther hotel and switched on Ceefax, they thought it had gone beserk! Lancashire all out for 51, with Waqar taking seven wickets! They rang the ground and I confirmed the news. They weren't really angry – just surprised and delighted that Glamorgan had won. But the poor devils had paid to come up all that way and hadn't seen any cricket at all!'

After a hat-trick of wins over Lancashire, Sussex and Gloucester-shire, the Glamorgan bandwagon ground to a halt at Chesterfield. The team picked up nine points in the rain-affected draw with Derbyshire as skipper Matthew Maynard picked up chicken pox. His reaction in the county's next match summed up the fighting spirit which helped Glamorgan to win the championship.

'I remember Matthew deciding to play against Yorkshire in the Nat West quarter-final in Cardiff,' recalls Edward, 'and having to give his team talk from outside the dressing room! He'd been put in quarantine and wasn't allowed near any of the players. He felt like death but went out and top scored with 62 – incredible stuff!'

The annual trip to Colwyn Bay proved one of the most eventful ever undertaken by a Glamorgan side. Dean Cosker was away playing for the England Under 19s, so the former Glamorgan spinner, Phil North, was drafted into the squad to play Nottinghamshire.

'Phil was sharing with Hugh Morris,' says Bevs, 'and when the alarm in their room went off, Hugh got up and shook Phil. He kept trying to wake him up but there was no response, so eventually Hugh left him and headed for the ground where the start had been delayed by rain. Phil just didn't pitch up in time and when he did, he admitted his mistake, apologised profusely but was sent back to South Wales.'

The sense of loss, of a missed opportunity, wasn't confined to the bowler himself. Having been tipped off about Phil North's

For the Benefit of Mr Metson . . . a fleeting appearance against the Australians.

Dean Conway says goodbye to Hugh Morris . . . 'That's one less old-timer for me to nurse through next season!'

'Bevs' and 'Fletch' . . . 'Just answer the question: are you coming back in 1999?'

A scorer in the Nineties . . . 'Dasher' Denning at work.

Andrew 'The Chalker' Hignell – from blackboard to scoreboard.

(A. Bolton)

Travelling support for Glamorgan's minstrel boy . . . 'Does anyone know the words to *Alouette?*'

Tony Lewis, Peter Walker and Don Shepherd.
Legends in their own lunchtime . . . 'I don't know what you two are laughing about! How are we going to dine out on 1969 anymore?'

Phil Clift and Jim Pleass . . . celebrating a famous half-century in 1998.

The Eagle(stone) has landed . . .
Jimmy is found after fifty years by Pinner's John Spencer.

The moment(s) the championship was won. 'That's out! . . . .'

(Peter Jay/*The Independent*)

(Peter Jay/*The Independent*)

. . . and *now* we've won!'

probable return, Andrew Hignell had done some research and was raring to impart some information to his BBC colleague.

'Over the years, I've learnt how to anticipate events,' says Andrew. 'It stems from something Carwyn James told me when I first started. "The art of commentary," said Carwyn, "is doing your homework and being one step ahead – knowing something, or getting it ready, before it actually happens."

'So my briefcase can be crammed full of seemingly irrelevant statistics and then, when they're needed, I can pull them out of a hat. Unfortunately, Phil overslept and didn't play, so the information I had gleaned on him was of no use to Edward. For the record, Phil would have equalled the record of eight years between separate appearances set by Bertie Perkins. He played in 1925, disappeared to Malaysia before coming back on holiday in 1933 when he was drafted in as Glamorgan found themselves short!'

At Colwyn Bay, Glamorgan were thwarted by the Nottingham-shire tail. 'After that draw,' recalls Edward, 'I thought that Glamorgan had blown their chance. At tea on the final day, Notts were eight runs ahead with two wickets standing and it looked as if Glamorgan were certain to win. But Notts didn't lose another wicket on what was a very flat track. Chris Tolley and Jimmy Hindson put on 80 and Glamorgan just couldn't get them out. As we drove back south, Don and I wondered, if they couldn't get rid of tailenders like that, whether Glamorgan actually had the firepower to win games from then on.'

The gloom deepened after the defeat at Worcester where Matthew Maynard was criticised for making a charge for victory and failing by 54 runs. 'The skipper got some stick for not playing for a draw,' says Edward, 'but in an interview he did with me afterwards, the former England batsman, Tom Graveney, described Matthew's first innings of 161 not out as the best he'd seen at New Road. It had helped Glamorgan to secure maximum batting points by reaching 350 in about 50 overs. When you think that Tom has seen players like Graeme Hick and Glenn Turner, it was a fantastic tribute.'

Another high-scoring batsman was keeping the Chalker busy in the next game against Northamptonshire at Abergavenny. Steve James scored two hundreds in a match for the first time as Glamorgan put their championship challenge back on track with a six-wicket win.

'I've seen Steve battle through the good and bad times and he

209

was really needed that day,' says Andrew. 'Hugh Morris was injured before the game and Matthew dislocated a finger during the match, so Steve was the senior batsman.

'I also happen to love Abergavenny – it's my favourite cricket ground. If there is a cricketing heaven it must be Abergavenny – something always seems to happen there. The Australian Andrew Symonds broke the sixes record there a few years ago and Glamorgan nearly set the record for a second-innings total when they reached 493 chasing 495. It's so quaint with its odd irregular boundary – there's something old-fashioned and very civilised and quintessentially English about Abergavenny – even though it's in Wales.'

When Glamorgan moved north-east to Leicester, rain once again wiped out a chance of victory. Apart from Steve Watkin's seven wickets, the match was largely unforgettable but Andrew Hignell will always remember the visit to Grace Road.

'On the Saturday evening, the three of us – Bev, Don and I – were invited to the team dinner at an Italian restaurant in Leicester. We had a lovely evening and talked a lot of good cricket sense – you could tell the boys just wanted somebody to talk to. The run-in was just starting to build up and some of the national papers were tipping Glamorgan for the championship. The next morning, we all woke up to discover that Diana, Princess of Wales had died.

'To go from the high of the Saturday night to the low captured by those television pictures from Paris was eerie. When I got home, I checked my e-mail and found three messages, including one from a man in Kansas City in America. It said: "To Matthew Maynard and the Glamorgan team. Britain has lost a great lady, Wales has lost a princess. Come on, Matthew, go out and win the championship for Glamorgan in Diana's memory."

'I printed the message and took it to the Oval where I gave it to Duncan Fletcher. Matthew read it out at a team meeting and the boys were really touched by it. For them to realise that there were people in America, and others all over the world, supporting them was a great filip.'

Glamorgan needed all the support they could muster when the Surrey game turned nasty on the last day. Surrey batted first after winning the toss and made 204, with every Glamorgan bowler except Dean Cosker chipping in with wickets. Matthew Maynard then led Glamorgan to a lead of 234 before Graham Thorpe's career-best 222 wrested the game away from them.

'After Thorpe's double hundred, Glamorgan needed 254 to beat Surrey,' recalls Edward Bevan. 'Saqlain Mushtaq and Ian Salisbury were bowling on a pitch turning square and there was absolutely no chance of winning it. Matthew knew Glamorgan would have committed hara-kiri had they lost, but he sent in Adrian Shaw and Crofty to have a belt before deciding prudently to put up the shutters when victory became a remote possibility. A win would have kept Surrey in the championship race themselves.

'For Surrey's coach Dave Gilbert to criticise Matthew for not continuing to go for a win was ridiculous. What did it have to do with him? Why didn't Surrey declare and then set Glamorgan a target of, say, 160 in 20 overs? I think it was frustration more than anything and later he probably regretted making those comments.

'What also disturbed me was the behaviour of Ben Hollioake – it was an absolute disgrace! As Matthew and Adrian Shaw were walking off at the end of the game, Hollioake was encouraging the crowd to give them the slow handclap, to give them a bit of stick. For a young England player to do that was appalling – something I'll never forget.'

The tension of the victory over Essex at Cardiff will live long in the commentary team's memory too – especially the match-winning partnership between Matthew Maynard and Tony Cottey. But even that was to be surpassed by the championship clincher at Taunton. As Bevs and Shep motored across the new Severn Bridge, the Chalker made the forty-minute journey by car from Wells after absenting himself from the classroom.

'I was able to teach first thing on the Thursday morning,' says Andrew, 'and then Sir managed to disappear at morning break to Taunton – with the headmaster's permission, I hasten to add!

'In fact, when they saw me trying to teach and keep an eye on Ceefax at the same time, my colleagues at school realised there was no way I was going to be able to carry on, so they very generously covered for me – I was jumping up and down every time Waqar took a wicket!'

Bevs and Shep were also getting rather excited in the commentary box. They couldn't believe their eyes because Waqar shouldn't really have been playing.

'We saw Duncan Fletcher as we were having breakfast,' recalls Edward. "Waqar's not well," he said. "He's been up all night with a fever and a stomach bug. We've had to get the doctor in to see him and I don't know whether he's going to play or not. But can you keep it quiet? It could well be that we'll bat first."

'We agreed, of course, and noticed that Waqar didn't practise with the team before the game. We then saw what sort of player he was. That first morning, he came in and knocked over three early Somerset wickets even though he was feeling dreadful. He was on antibiotics – he was a sick man but his attitude epitomised the determination in the team.'

Waqar had already turned down a request from the former Glamorgan batsman Majid Khan to play for Pakistan against India in Toronto. As chief executive of the Pakistan Cricket Board, Majid wanted him to help ease an injury crisis but Waqar decided that his place was in Taunton.

'He said that he was staying in Britain because he'd made a commitment,' says Edward. 'If Glamorgan were going for the championship, he would stay and help them – everything else went out of the window. Pakistan weren't happy because they lost to India and Waqar knew he wouldn't be very popular when he got back home.'

By the time the Chalker arrived at the County Ground on the Friday, the weather was threatening to trip up Glamorgan at the final hurdle. Play didn't resume until 3.50 p.m. when Maynard and Morris set about the Somerset attack.

'That was probably the finest display of batting at both ends that I've ever seen from a Glamorgan pair,' says Andrew. 'Javed Miandad, Viv Richards and Matthew have, on occasions, done it from one end but Hugh and Matthew both scored so quickly.

'I was delighted for Hugh because we both joined Glamorgan in 1981 and I've been very close to him ever since. He loved setting himself targets and milestones and, at the end of every innings, he would always rush over to the commentary box to go through the book.

'In the back of my mind, I felt this innings, played in front of his parents and former teachers from Blundell's School, Tiverton, where he'd been educated, would be his last for Glamorgan. I could tell by his body language when he came across to look at the scorebook. At the end, he just patted me on the back and said, "Thanks, Chalker."'

As the third day dawned, Andrew Hignell suddenly meta-morphosed into Mystic Meg. The weather could have turned the game into a lottery but the Chalker was in no doubt.

'When I woke up on the Saturday morning, I said to my wife Debra that today we were going to win the championship! Even though Matthew hadn't declared and the weather was far from settled, something just told me so. Debra said she'd go shopping in Taunton. Did I want anything? I said we could do with a nice bottle of champagne.

'When she arrived at the commentary box with bottle in hand, Edward and Don looked at me as if I was on another planet.

'"We're not going to bloody win today!" they cried.

'"Oh yes we are!" I said.

'So when Dean Cosker took the final Somerset wicket, I knew my premonition would come true, although I was a little worried about the light because it was getting quite late.

'Winning the championship was something I had always dreamt about. In 1969, I can remember listening as a schoolboy to Alun Williams describing the scenes on the radio when Shep took the last Worcestershire wicket. But little did I think, that some 28 years later, I would be working for the BBC in the company of Don, who had switched to television to describe the closing moments of Glamorgan's 1997 championship victory.

'Every hair in my body stood on end when Steve James hit the last four – and the champagne cork flew out of the commentary-box window pretty quickly! It was nice for Steve to hit the winning run and for Hugh to be there at the other end.'

As the crowd swarmed onto the County Ground, Edward Bevan managed to retain his composure as he conveyed the excitment of a long-awaited success to the long-suffering radio audience. Fifteen years of trudging around the county grounds of England and Wales during the lean times suddenly all seemed worthwhile.

'In my view, the real key to Glamorgan's success was their perfectly-balanced bowling attack,' says Edward. 'It was the best in the country – three international bowlers in Steve, Waqar and Crofty, with Dean Cosker, who was about to become an England A player, and Darren Thomas coming through at speed. You couldn't get a better balanced attack because you had your men for all conditions. Horses for courses wherever you went. Counties could prepare whatever wickets they liked – it didn't matter, Glamorgan would perform.

'Matthew had a very slow start to the season but then came into form all of a sudden to add to the runs being scored by Steve James and Hugh Morris. Glamorgan were never out of the top three or four and fully deserved to win the title.'

Bevs and the Chalker have been the BBC Wales radio commentary team for more than a decade. They once survived an interruption from Courtney Walsh when the West Indian fast bowler smashed a six off new coach John Derrick into their box. Together with Don Shepherd, they experienced the whole gamut of emotions as they followed Glamorgan in 1997 – from the despair of defeat by Middlesex to the derilium of destroying Somerset to take the title.

As Edward embarks on another season of broadcasting and reporting for *The Daily Telegraph*, Andrew Hignell has been quietly busying himself with some homework – preparing rather than marking it. Pencil and not red pen. Averages and records rather than marks out of ten. Schoolteacher, honorary archivist, Internet operator and who knows – perhaps, one day, official Glamorgan scorer. At the moment, the Chalker is happy with the delicate balancing act he has to perform.

'During the school holidays, I'm always free to cover the county's games and, even during term time, there are odd days when I don't have much in the way of teaching, so I can always find the time to nip across the bridge to Cardiff.

'My biggest aid at the moment is my laptop computer because I've got every Glamorgan scorecard in the database. When I'm not at a game – I saw about two-thirds of last year's play – I can catch up by using scorer Byron Denning's computer or the Internet. It's not that difficult.

'I would like to get more involved and work for Glamorgan in the future – maybe in about ten years time after I've had a career outside of cricket. Then I might be in a position to devote the rest of my life to the game. I think scoring is really a retired person's job because you couldn't live on the wage alone. I expect the second XI scorer, Gordon Lewis, to take over from Byron when he retires and then we'll see.

'In the meantime, I'll have my mobile phone and Ceefax on once the season starts and, even though I'll be standing in front of a class full of children doing another job, my heart will be somewhere else – wherever Glamorgan are playing.'

Agony Uncle

'H E'S a mixture of physiotherapist, psychoanalyst and agony aunt – and he's not a bad drinking partner either!'

So spake a member of Glamorgan's 1997 championship-winning team who, for fear of retribution on the treatment table, cannot be named. He was describing Dean Conway, the man who has manipulated, cajoled and nursed the county's cricketers into action for nearly a decade.

Dean Conway is indeed a man of many parts. Rotund and robust, he is built like a front-row forward. In fact, he is one – tight-head prop for his native Mountain Ash. The Glamorgan physiotherapist is so highly rated by Lord's that the recent England A tour to Kenya and Sri Lanka was his seventh successive winter away from home. Dean runs general practice and company physiotherapy clinics in Cardiff and is studying for an osteopathy degree. He's also in charge of a pretty unusual group of professional cricketers!

'My role is slightly different to that of most county physios,' says Dean, 'because I've sometimes got to pull people out of our side rather than get them onto the field! The likes of Matthew and Cotts will play with injuries when they shouldn't. I'm happy for them to do that occasionally but if there's a chance of their missing three weeks or a month, I obviously have to make some decisions. They're the type of guys who you really need to keep an eye on to get them off the field for their own and the team's good.'

With a quip for every occasion, Dean has become one of the most popular figures in Sophia Gardens since joining Glamorgan in 1989. A master of the one-liner, he can produce a laugh every thirty seconds rather than a minute.

'Dean knits the off-field and on-field aspects of the club together,' says secretary Mike Fatkin. 'He never allows you to be down in the dumps, and he's a good motivator in terms of keeping people going.

'Fletch summed it up after his first two days when he said that Dean was a real quality operator who knows what he's doing, is a good mixer and realises when it's time for a laugh and when to be serious. He's a top bloke.'

The former Glamorgan opening bat, Hugh Morris, has been a close friend of Dean's ever since he arrived at the club – in fact, the new Technical Director of the England and Wales Cricket Board was best man at his wedding.

'Today's physiotherapist is very much part of the management team,' explains Hugh, 'and it's important to have someone in the changing room who understands mood swings, when to talk to people and when to leave them alone. He likes a laugh but he takes his work extremely seriously, he's very professional about it and, to my knowledge, he hasn't got anything wrong in the time he's been with Glamorgan.'

Part of Dean Conway is a cross between a practical joker and a stand-up comedian. He loves pulling people's legs – and not just when they're on his physiotherapist's couch. The new coach had to see the funny side of South Africa's humiliating defeat by the British Lions last summer just before the Sunday League match against Sussex at Swansea at the end of June.

'Duncan works for Western Province in South Africa,' says Mike Fatkin, 'and is a big supporter of Springbok rugby. The players were warming up on the day after the Lions had clinched the series by winning the Second Test. In honour of Fletch, Dean got the boys to line up for a minute's silence in memory of South African rugby.'

Joking apart, Dean Conway is a highly-valued member of the Glamorgan set-up. In fact, he's become so much a part of the Sophia Gardens furniture that he's just signed a new five-year contract.

'I look after a lot of the fitness testing, preventative medicine and training techniques,' explains Dean, 'as well as the more day-to-day stuff – niggles involving hamstrings, calf strains and lower back problems among the bowlers.

'At some big rugby clubs, they have people looking after weights, aerobics, diet and nutrition as well as the coaching staff to take care of the playing side, whereas here, we tend to oversee all of those areas in conjunction with the senior coach. I'm not an expert in all those fields so I'm keen to use outside specialists in, say, gymnastics, psychology and technical cricket skills. Some players respond to them, others don't – you have to have a varied approach.

'We've got a great medical back-up team which means I can sort out scans with a quick telephone call, rather than have to go through all the paperwork. We encourage the players to tell us about something they're not happy about and we investigate early. Obviously a negative scan is a positive result.

'We were very lucky as far as injuries were concerned in 1997. You do your best to prevent them in the first place – from sorting out general levels of fitness to checking the efficiency of the covering on the players' batting gloves – but a lot of it is down to chance. 1993 was good too. In general, the boys are very fit and they work hard so they're less at risk and don't get injured too often.

'I generally leave it to the boys to decide if they are fit to play or not, unless I think they're likely to break down during the game. You usually find that bowlers and all-rounders carry one or two long-standing minor injuries during a season – you just hope they don't flare up at crucial times in a match.'

The first scare of the summer, Waqar's apparent stress fracture of his left foot, was potentially a season-wrecker. In the event, he was fit and raring to go for the second championship game against Yorkshire at Headingley.

For much of the 1997 season, Dean only travelled away to one-day games but as the championship race reached its climax during the last month of the season, he accompanied the players to every match. A run of awkward injuries began when Hugh Morris became the first high-profile casualty of the season before a ball had been bowled in the Northants game at Abergavenny in late August. He'd already missed the Sunday League match against Kent because of the same problem but this time championship points were at stake.

'As we were starting to warm up with a game of touch-rugby,' recalls Dean, 'Hugh bumped into Darren Thomas and turned his ankle. We had just started jogging and the boys were flicking the ball about. There's a bit of a slope at Abergavenny and they were down by the hospitality tents when it happened.

'Hugh has got weak ankles from his rugby-playing days – they're a bit like poppadums. The ligaments stretch a little and the joint becomes more mobile, so that Hugh is even prone to turning on his ankle as he climbs steps. At the start of a four-day game, like the Northants one, it wouldn't normally be a problem for Hugh – we would strap it up – but after the incident at Abergavenny, we did a couple of tests to check the ankle's stability and it proved more painful than usual. There was also evidence of new tearing.

217

'As we had cover and there was still a way to go in the season, there was no real point in risking it. It was actually a pretty straightforward decision as Hugh was struggling to walk. The squad of 14 meant that Matt and Fletch could put in one of the youngsters. Alun Evans was given a chance and shared in a stand of 84 for the first wicket with Steve James.

'After that game, Hugh started wearing an ankle brace to stop it happening again. At that stage of the season, we felt it was better to be safe than sorry. My only concern was that a brace takes a lot of the control out of the ankle. As it happened, Hugh probably could have played by the end of the Northants game but he wouldn't have been comfortable or able to field on the first two days.'

Glamorgan were in the wars during the game at Abergavenny as well as before it. Just after reducing Northamptonshire to 53 for 4 in their second innings on the third day, Matthew Maynard dislocated his right index finger while fielding at second slip. He couldn't hold Alan Fordham's push forward to Steve Watkin and was taken to nearby Nevill Hall Hospital. Dean was worried because the captain had broken the same finger five years earlier.

'With dislocations, you have to be careful when you put the joint back in. If somebody of my size can't reduce it by giving it a tug, it's not going to reduce spontaneously, so you'll need an injection and an X-ray. You must be careful because if it's a fracture dislocation, you might end up pulling the fracture apart.

'Luckily, I knew one of the consultants who was on duty at the hospital that day. The finger was X-rayed to check that there was no fracture and then Matthew was given a pain-killing injection to numb the finger and reduce muscle spasm. Given the history of that finger, I felt it could have been a long-term problem. Matthew didn't bat in the second innings against Northants but was back for the next game at Leicester. He recovered really well.'

The injury jinx struck again in the rain-affected draw at Grace Road. Left-arm spinner Dean Cosker ricked his neck badly during training on one of the rain days.

'He dived and fell awkwardly,' says Dean Conway. 'He was in real agony. At first, I thought he had no chance of playing but I put him in a collar for 48 hours and then saw him three or four times a day and worked hard on keeping his soft tissue supple. It was very much 50-50 on the first day and if the problem had recurred during the game, we would have been in trouble. My being there did make a difference.'

Next stop was the Oval and two more injuries – but neither as serious as the Leicester problem. This time, Steve James dislocated his little finger while fielding during Graham Thorpe's career-best knock of 222 but was able to bat in Glamorgan's second innings, before the run-chase was called off. Then Adrian Shaw had to be promoted to first wicket down after Adrian Dale's back started playing up by going into spasm.

'Adrian's got a congenital spinal problem,' explains Dean. 'He's not the biggest of guys but he's got a big range of movement in his spine. But because it's hypermobile, it can can cause problems and you need to strengthen it throughout the range.

'He manages it pretty well but it flared up two or three times last season. We couldn't put it down to any one factor. After a three- or four-hour drive to Kent, his back was stiff and the next morning he had a spasm. But it would also go during fielding practice and occasionally when he was batting too. I'd normally be able to manipulate the spasms free – especially higher up in the spine but I'm always a bit wary about disturbing discs.'

Apart from soaring blood pressure all round, the penultimate championship game against Essex at Cardiff passed off without incident – the calm before the storm as Waqar fell ill on the eve of the first day at Taunton. Again, Dean's presence proved vital as he helped Waqar shake off a bout of flu to administer the first knock-out blow to Somerset by taking four wickets in their first innings.

'Given that I was looking at Waqar at the beginning and end of the season,' says Dean, 'you might think that he was a physio's nightmare but he wasn't. He was the complete opposite. To make sure an overseas player appears in nearly every game is a huge challenge in anybody's season. With the amount of work he put into one ball, I'd have been happy if he'd played in seventy per cent of the games but, in fact, he played in every one bar the first and bowled himself into the ground at times. He really slotted into the Glamorgan ethos of everybody mucking in and having a crack. He was given some flexibility over timekeeping but when you look at the way he responded on the field, nobody was complaining.'

That couldn't be said about all members of the Glamorgan team who love nothing better than a session on the treatment table where they can unload their troubles on their agony uncle. 'The moans and groans are quite seasonal,' says Dean. 'It often depends on the way individuals and the side are doing. All our players are good patients but if had £25 for every time I have treated Robert

Croft, I wouldn't be here today! Not a day goes by without me having to do something with him but most of it is tender loving care. I'm not saying he's a bit of a hypochondriac – he's a big one, a huge hypo. If you look at the statistics, he's barely missed a game for Glamorgan in his career but I would guess that he's never ever taken the field without some sort of niggle – mainly it's in his mind! What I say to him is this: "Clinically, Rob, there's nothing to worry about." That's the phrase for the season, he's OK then and he goes back out and plays without a murmur!'

'Dean's always been a good listener,' says Hugh Morris. 'He works out the players that are genuinely injured and those, like Robert, who need a bit of pampering. He never used to see me – apart from when I was moaning! I needed surgery five times during my career and Dean was very good and very supportive through all the operations.'

'I've lain on Dean's table receiving treatment for a little niggle many times in the past when I was in the middle of a bad spell,' admits Steve James. 'I'd have a moan about what was going wrong with my game and Dean just reassured me and tried to build up my confidence a bit. It's nice to be able to talk to someone about your problems but, luckily, I didn't need too much attention last season and now I've got my very own physio in my wife Jane. I can confide in her instead of him – and she's a lot prettier!'

Along with Dean Cosker, Steve James was on tour with Dean Conway last winter. Once again, the Big Man was a big help when it came to bonding the England A squad together as they ran into civil unrest in Sri Lanka. But the attraction of touring, even exotic spots, is starting to pall a little.

'I've been away with the the A side for three winters,' explains Dean, 'to Pakistan, Australia and now Kenya and Sri Lanka. Although it would be nice to be asked to become physio to the full England team, if Yorkshire's Wayne Morton decided to finish, I'm not particularly ambitious that way. I've had seven winters away and it's a case of balancing work with family commitments. My children, Sophie who's 4 and Josef aged 2, are getting to an age when they're starting to miss me a lot. I've not got any concrete plans but the main thing over the next couple of years is to get through my osteopathy degree which I'm doing at weekends in Oxford. When I finish, I'll probably combine the two – physiotherapy and osteopathy – and then, clinically, I'll be pretty well covered to deal with whatever's thrown at me.

'I enjoy my England involvement but some of my best mates are down with Glamorgan, which is more of a family than a club. If I had a bunch of prima donnas to deal with, then I probably wouldn't have got the same satisfaction from watching them celebrate on the balcony at Taunton – it was brilliant.'

Certainly, everyone at the club sees Dean as one of the family. They're delighted that he's staying for another five years, if only to ensure that the huge reservoir of stories about him won't be drying up.

'Some of them are unprintable, so I'd better be discreet,' says Mike Fatkin. 'When we were at Colwyn Bay for the Nottinghamshire game, Dean decided that the two of us, plus Andrew Jenkins and Andrew Walker, the shop and catering managers, would go out for a meal and the word "cricket" would be banned. But Matthew Maynard decided to come along too and within thirty seconds he was talking about declaring the following morning, so bang went our resolution. But we did manage to go for a few hours without mentioning cricket.

'Later that evening, Paul Johnson, the Nottinghamshire captain, turned up, so we had an amnesty for about ten minutes. When he got up and left, Dean said to me:

'"Weren't we going to sign him at one point?"

'Matthew looked a bit puzzled.

'"Yes, I think we were," I replied.

'"I certainly don't remember that!" cried Matthew.

'"Well, it was when you were threatening to leave Glamorgan a couple of seasons ago – he was going to replace you!" said Dean.

'Towards the end of the year, when Hugh Morris got the job at the ECB, Dean had just sorted out his contract with us. Hugh came into the room and passed on his good news. Dean then said, deadpan, that if he'd known that, he would have signed for ten years rather than just five!

'When he helped organise the players' stag-night for Steve James on August Bank Holiday, Dean bought a collection of Groucho Marx glasses and noses, and Adrian Dale turned up with a load of black masking tape for eyebrows. Everybody had to wear them all evening and he had Steve dressed up in an England shirt with "The Lydney Love Machine" on the front and "England's Number 1" on the back!'

Apart from cricket and his family, the other big passion in Dean's life is rugby. During his career, he has played for Cardiff and Pontypridd and, whenever he can, he likes to turn out for his home town club of Mountain Ash. Last September, Dean was faced with a physiotherapist's dilemma. The Glamorgan boys were struggling against Essex, in their penultimate championship game, on the same day that Mountain Ash kicked off their new season. What should he do? Desert what looked like a sinking ship or let the lads down against Tredegar?

'I decided to play rugby and organised some cover at Sophia Gardens,' recalls Dean. 'When I left late on the Saturday morning, Matthew and Tony were in, chasing 149 to win. As I got out of my car at the rugby ground, they were up to about 50 for 3. There was a big crowd up there but nobody was too keen on the rugby – everybody was listening to the radio for the score from Cardiff!

'In our game, Tredegar got lots of points – it was an absolute drubbing! During the second half, spectators were shouting out the Glamorgan score to me. My wife Sue was also letting me know what was going on – I remember being told we were up to 70 and then past 100. It was only then that I thought we were probably going to win it. Even my rugby team-mates were wanting to know the score!

'In fact, a couple of us were listening on the touch-line when a Tredegar forward went straight past us and scored a try! In the re-match, the boys did a lot better without me, so that might be it. I've been trying to retire for the last couple of years but studying for an osteopathy degree now takes up a lot of my time. When I've got a free Saturday, I'd love to continue playing but my schedule won't really allow it.

'So far, I've played about half a dozen games in the 1997-98 season and although it's probably not advisable for me to dip in and out of the game as I do, I just love it. I'll have finished the degree at the end of 1999 and, although I'll be 35, I might start playing again then – nothing too competitive, maybe second or third team.'

Like all committed Welsh rugby fans, Dean Conway will go to great lengths to keep in touch with the national team's fortunes when he's out of the country. As the England A tour drew to a close in Sri Lanka, he realised he would miss the clash with the 'Old Enemy' at Twickenham if special arrangements weren't made. After the 3-0 defeat in the one-day series, the squad had to travel from Matare in the south of the country to their hotel in Colombo, just as the game was about to get underway in the UK.

'We were leaving the hotel at five on Sunday morning to fly home. So, on the Saturday night, we drove three hours back to

222

Colombo – the only place which had Star Sports, the satellite TV channel. The England-Wales match kicked off at eight o'clock in the evening our time, so I organised for it to be videoed and ferried by taxi to our hotel, where it arrived at about 11.30 p.m.

'I remember Steve James had rung his wife Jane, the Cardiff Rugby Club physio, before we watched the match, and asked her not to tell him the score. All Jane would say was that Nigel Walker had been taken off injured after four minutes and that she had to go and lie down at the end of the game. So we knew it was either a hammering or Wales had won!

'All the squad had stayed up to watch it and within fifteen minutes I was jumping around like an idiot as Wales went into the lead. Just over an hour later, they had to put me to bed in a haze of Jack Daniels after England had won by a record 60-26! I organised the tape and had paid for the taxi because I had a hunch we were going to do well but we ended up getting slaughtered – what a waste of £20!'

Mike Fatkin considers himself very fortunate to have secured the services of one of England's top physiotherapists well into the next Millennium. A love of life – especially cricket and rugby – makes him an ideal member of the Glamorgan family. There's always one complete all-rounder – and Dean Conway is that one. Physiotherapist, acupuncturist, trainee osteopath, all-round good egg – even if, by his own admission, he's not the greatest of props ever to step onto a rugby pitch.

'I remember watching Dean playing for Mountain Ash in a cup game against Llanharan, four or five years ago,' recalls Mike. 'For some reason, he was very slow in getting from one side of the field to the other and when the ball winged its way back, Dean found himself in between a centre and a wing. They were about two yards from the line. The centre had a quick look at him, saw it was Dean and then flicked the ball over his head to the wing who caught it and fell over the line. Dean was very upset and annoyed – real hands on hips stuff – because, at that distance, he reckoned even he would have scored. All he had to do was catch it!'

Their reluctance to trust him to do even the simplest thing with the ball would seem to suggest that his team-mates have little or no faith in Dean Conway the rugby player. But the cricketers who rely on Dean Conway the physiotherapist for their well-being are only too aware that the future of Glamorgan's health service is safe in his hands.

BACK FROM THE DEAD
(Heaven on Earth)

'It's a fabulous feeling. My wife and I have missed only two games in four years of following Glamorgan – home and away.'

'I just feel excited – that's all!'

'Wonderful – over the moon!'

'Fantastic! A marvellous performance by all the players – they deserve to be knighted for it.'

'It's the biggest occasion of my life.'

'It's the third championship win I've seen – 1948, 1969 and now 1997 – it's a wonderful occasion.'

A POST-MATCH snapshot of opinion of Glamorgan's triumph over Somerset on Saturday, September 20th summed it up. They had come from all over Wales – and parts of England too. So many of them, in fact, that there was no room at the inn. Taunton – and the surrounding area – had been taken over and the town's tourist information office had known nothing like it. Hotels and boarding houses were full, so campsite owners and enterprising farmers had a field day. Any available space was used to accommodate the Welsh invasion for the climax to the 1997 season.

More supporters were planning to cross the Severn Bridge on the Sunday but the players spoiled it for them by winning the championship a day early. How inconsiderate! How selfish! How wonderful!

Having bowled Somerset out for 252, Glamorgan set about establishing an enormous first-innings lead of 275 as Morris, Maynard, Croft and Shaw all excelled with the bat. It was then simply a question of time and the elements. Would Somerset be dismissed on the third or fourth day? Would the weather ruin everything? An air of expectancy descended upon the County Ground.

Jittery fielding – three catches were put down – ultimately

proved irrelevant as a jitterbug of a bowler danced in to destroy Somerset. Having made the breakthrough, Darren Thomas was unstoppable. Five times he was engulfed by his team mates; Adrian Shaw finally lost his Teflon tag as three catches stuck and an eighth-wicket stand of 95 only postponed the Glamorgan party.

It was left to the youngest member of the team, Dean Cosker, to administer the *coup de grace*. The Somerset tailender Ben Trott would not forget his championship debut in a hurry: three wickets in the Glamorgan innings and then the last man standing in the way of history. Number eleven bowling to number eleven, Cosker to Trott, a rap on the pads and an upraised finger. Glamorgan were almost there.

Eleven runs later, it really was all over as Steve James and Hugh Morris applied the finishing touches. Glamorgan had won by 10 wickets. It was a comprehensive victory to round off a memorable season.

The years of waiting were over for about 3,000 supporters at the County Ground – and thousands more throughout Wales and the world. Glamorgan had done it! The no-hopers, the under-achievers, the most unfashionable team on the county circuit had confounded their critics and won cricket's top tournament. It was time for everyone to celebrate and for the club to pay tribute to the special people who had played their part in the team's success.

'Our supporters are great,' says skipper Matthew Maynard. 'They're a bit noisier than those who follow other counties but we players love them – they come with us everywhere. The Swansea Balconiers are tremendous and then there are the individuals and groups of supporters who the players stop and chat to – we thrive on it, we really enjoy their company.'

'They're just brilliant', agrees secretary Mike Fatkin. 'They've watched Glamorgan through thick and thin – mostly thin – and they deserve moments like Taunton. It's nice for the players to be performing for a public that actually wants to see them. They've had and they'll have their difficult times, and supporters are entitled to have a go when things aren't going too well but when you are successful, it's as much for them as for the players and the club.'

Brendan Rauwerda doesn't normally travel to away matches. Ever since he discovered that he had leukaemia, four years ago, the 38-year-old former charity worker from Llanbradach, near Caerphilly, has had to scale down his support for his adopted county but Taunton was special. He had to be there.

'I saw all the cricket at Cardiff last season and the last day of the Gloucestershire match at Swansea when Steve James hit a six – and a spectator on the head – to win the game. Somerset was the only away game I went to in 1997. I travelled down with a friend on the Saturday because I hoped Glamorgan wouldn't be thwarted by the weather.

'My feelings when Glamorgan won were disbelief and utter elation – it was just marvellous, one of those days that couldn't be repeated. It was absolutely fantastic. Like most people who were at Taunton, I was on a high for weeks afterwards.

'It was unbelievable to see people crying and the scenes on the balcony certainly added to the whole occasion. I didn't want to leave the ground. I just wanted to stay there and soak up the atmosphere.'

Brendan Rauwerda's love affair with Glamorgan began when he was living in Belfast soon after the county's second championship win. Through his father, who was always very keen on most sports, he had developed an interest in the game and, for some reason, Glamorgan became his team.

'I was 10 in 1969 when Glamorgan won the championship and probably that's what triggered it for me. I remember sitting at home in Belfast listening to the BBC Radio Wales cricket commentaries in the 1970s and 1980s.'

In 1984, Brendan married his wife Ingrid after they had met at Queen's University, Belfast, and the couple moved to Wales. They have three children – 11-year-old Katie, Barry, who's 8 and 4-year-old Niall. Kate and Barry both belong to the Glamorgan Short Legs, a special membership club for supporters aged 17 and under. Brendan was working for the mental health charity MIND in Newport when he found out he was suffering from leukaemia.

'It came completely out of the blue because I felt very fit and healthy,' he recalls. 'It didn't look good for a while and in September 1994 I had a bone-marrow transplant. Since then, touch wood, I've been fairly OK.

'When I was diagnosed as being ill, I sat down and drew up a list of things which I wanted to do and see before I passed away. I'd been given a forty per cent chance of survival, so the odds weren't particularly good. The list included the children's birthdays, seeing them finishing school and growing up, and Glamorgan winning the championship! That was one of my goals – albeit a long-term one. I thought I would have to stick around for quite a while, maybe for as many as 30 years, to achieve it.

'But four years later, they go and win the championship, so maybe my time has come – I don't know! If I do go, at least I'll die happy, although obviously there are lots of other things I would like to see and do. It's just one of those ironies but now the championship wish has gone by the wayside, I'll have to stick a few more on my list.'

Brendan is officially registered as being partially sighted because, after the bone-marrow operation, his eyesight was damaged. Watching cricket is now, literally, a different ball game.

'It has hindered me but I get by. I can't see the detail of what's happening out on the pitch but I've developed other senses to compensate – I think my hearing has improved. I hear the little nicks and edges louder than I might have done before.

'I never really understood the phrase "taking one day at a time" until I became ill. Then, all of a sudden, it became very clear – you treat every day as your last. One of the fortunate spin-offs of my illness is that I've been able to watch a lot more sport and, most of all, a lot more cricket.

'I'm not officially rid of the disease yet – I won't get the all-clear for another 18 months. I'm on disability living allowance but hopefully I'll be able to get back to work.'

Apart from Taunton, Brendan's main memories of the 1997 season involve two of the early championship games at Cardiff. 'At the start of the Warwickshire match, I remember saying, jokingly, to a friend that Glamorgan would bowl them out before lunch! I wasn't that confident then because Waqar wasn't playing and the side wasn't much different to 1996 but, with eight wickets down in the morning session, I started to think that maybe the team could do something in 1997.

'Another high point was the Durham game when Glamorgan nearly reached 600 for the first time. They had achieved their highest-ever score of 597 but that milestone was followed by the disappointment of not getting those extra three runs. Every other county, including Durham, have made 600 in an innings. It was such a pity – it would have been nice to have joined them.'

At the age of 12, Alun Chivers is one of Glamorgan's youngest supporters. He won't forget the 1997 season in a hurry – thanks to the kindness of coach Duncan Fletcher. Alun has been supporting Glamorgan since he was 4 years old and travels to games with his father Gareth from their home in Sketty in Swansea. The pair – Premier Club member and Short Leg – made a day trip to Taunton on the Saturday.

'It was great to see Glamorgan successful for a change,' says Alun. 'The celebrations were brilliant. I remember seeing the players on the balcony and hearing Robert Croft singing – he was terrible. I think he should stick to playing cricket! Still, when I went into the bar afterwards, he did let me have a blow on his bugle!'

After the post-match celebrations, Alun and Gareth were chatting to Edward Bevan and Don Shepherd when Duncan Fletcher came over. The coach had already given Alun a Western Province sun hat during the Essex game at Cardiff.

'This lad has always got a smile on his face,' Duncan said as he recognised Alun. 'Where's that hat I gave you?' he demanded. 'I thought I told you to wear it with pride!'

'After their victory,' says Gareth, a teacher in Aberdare, 'Alun was understandably wearing a Glamorgan hat. Suddenly, Duncan took off his blue Glamorgan sun hat sporting the daffodil and handed it to Alun. It was a lovely gesture and Alun ended up with two hats from the man who had coached Glamorgan to the title!'

Gareth Chivers is a relatively new convert to the county, having become a member in 1994. He first saw Glamorgan play in 1968 when Alan Jones scored 99 against the Australians at St Helen's. He watched part of all the home championship games in 1997 as well as the defeat at Worcester.

'It was nice to see Glamorgan turn their potential into success,' he says. 'They were a good side who weren't achieving anything. Although they won the Sunday League in 1993, it was all promises and no delivery in the championship. Then, all of a sudden, everything came together.

'Taunton was tremendous. You could see the fulfilment of a lot of the players like Steve Watkin and Tony Cottey who had been through the bad times in the 1980s. It was so pleasing to see their joy. I think we played a part and the boys were pleased to have won something for us.

'The following morning, Alun and I came across Cottey and Crofty in a nearby motorway service station. They had obviously missed breakfast at their hotel in Taunton and were a little worse for wear from the night before. It must have been almost midday when they came in – I remember Crofty was wearing dark glasses. They said a few words to Alun but I don't think they were looking for conversation at that stage!'

Beryl Dummett has just completed her half-century as a Glamorgan supporter. A retired civil servant who worked at the

Inland Revenue in Cardiff, she now lives in Creigiau just outside the capital. Beryl played cricket from 1949 to 1982 for Cardiff, Glamorgan, the West of England and the Civil Service. She saw all of the 1997 championship matches, travelling either by herself or with the Swansea Balconiers to away games.

'According to the players, we've been a big help,' says Beryl, 'but really that's for them to say. I think Glamorgan have got the best following in the country. We're different from the other 17 counties – we're representing a country as well as a county. It's quite unique.

'Although we're members of the England and Wales Cricket Board, invariably they call it the ECB rather than the EWCB. The Test and County Cricket Board was abbreviated to TCCB – that's four letters, so I can't see the difference. I've occasionaly seen it referred to as the EWCB but it's not standard and it should be – especially after what Glamorgan have achieved.'

As a Premier Club member, Beryl has noticed the improvement in facilities at Sophia Gardens over the last three years – especially the quality of food served up to the players.

'The caterers have provided the necessary sustinance which it seems the team hadn't been receiving up until 1995. Before that, they had to go out and buy Mars Bars to give them a bit of strength to get on with things. They just couldn't put up with the food – now it's made a difference.'

Inevitably, Taunton provided Beryl with most of her highlights from the 1997 season as a hard six-month campaign culminated in the county's third championship title.

'Everybody was numb,' she recalls. 'It was a job to speak to anybody, the emotion was so terrific. I can remember seeing Adrian Dale, standing just a couple of inches away from me and he said to someone else, "This is the best day of my life." I wanted to say something to him but I just couldn't.

'Since then, I've watched the video of the day and thought how marvellous it was. For a number of years, we've been regarded as the underdogs and now we've really shown the rest of the counties that we're no fools.

'If I had to choose just one shot from a Glamorgan bat during 1997, it would be the cover drive played by Matthew Maynard on bended knee at Taunton. It reminded me of Denis Compton. One of the television commentators remarked that that shot can't be coached!'

229

Amid all the celebrations at Taunton, Beryl was aware of impending sadness. The rumour that Hugh Morris was on the short list for the post of Technical Director with the ECB had been confirmed and Beryl feared the worst.

'When Hugh threw his batting gloves into the crowd, my heart sank. A few minutes later, I came across his parents, Roger and Anne, and told them I had a feeling Hugh wouldn't be coming back.

' "Oh," said Anne, "they were probably his old smelly gloves – he'll be back!"

'But lo and behold, a few days later, we heard he was off. I think he's made the right decision but I just wish that Micky Stewart had been two years younger and had hung on to his job for a couple of years. I feel that Hugh had reached his peak and another two seasons would have been great for him and great for Glamorgan. He said this was the only job that would persuade him to give up playing and nobody can blame him. It's a terrific opportunity and one that he's always wanted. And what a way to finish his career! As Mike Fatkin, the Glamorgan secretary, asked: "Who's writing Hugh's script?"

'My abiding memory of the season will be the moment when Hugh was felled by Allan Donald in the opening game against Warwickshire. He'd made his career-best score of 233 at the time the ball hit him on the side of his head. The atmosphere at Sophia Gardens was exactly the same as it was when Roger Davis was hit and nearly died while fielding at short leg in 1971. There was complete and utter silence – an eerie feeling really.

'Although it was the first match of the season, there must have been some dried leaves about – it was so quiet that you could hear them moving around, rustling on the ground, as people were waiting to see whether Hugh was alright. As he was taken off on the stretcher, he did lift an arm and I thought: Thank God for that!

'After a few disappointing seasons, I was pleased that Darren Thomas really made it in 1997. There were fewer no balls and less bowling wide of the sticks. Instead, he was putting it right up in the blockhole and on target. I think Darren grew up during the season, he underwent quite a transformation – as did the team.

'The way they came back after that innings defeat against Middlesex at Cardiff showed a terrific amount of character. We've always had the talent but we just didn't seem to be able to finish it off and believe in ourselves. Now the boys believe they can win.'

Dave and Coral Beck make no bones about it. Their whole summer revolves around following Glamorgan. They've supported the county since 1980 and, from their home in Cwmbrân, they set out to watch most of the championship games in 1997. Dave used to be one of the men from the Pru – he's a 55-year-old retired financial consultant – and now that their two daughters have grown up, they can indulge their passion. They mainly travel to games by car, occasionally in the company of the Swansea Balconiers when Glamorgan are playing in London. They admit that, during the dark days of the 1980s, they were tempted to switch allegiances.

'We've been through some very bad times with Glamorgan,' says Coral, 'and we think we deserve a medal for sticking with them this long! On occasions, we have thought about going over to Bristol to watch Gloucestershire but as we're Welsh – I'm from Nantyglo and Dave's from Pontypool – we felt we had to support Welsh cricket.'

'Supporting Gloucestershire was only one of those things you think about doing when you get really down,' says Dave. 'But we always came back to Glamorgan because of our roots.'

Dave and Coral Beck were feeling very down when Glamorgan's championship train ran into the buffers after three successive wins in June and July. First, they salvaged a draw in a rain-affected match with Derbyshire at Chesterfield and then the irresistable force met the immoveable object at Colwyn Bay – and Nottinghamshire won. Their eighth wicket pair put on an unbeaten 80 and the match ended in another weather-hit draw.

'Colwyn Bay was unbelievable,' recalls Dave. 'We let two tailenders rule the roost. I don't think there's any point in getting on the players' backs because they're professionals and they know what they've got to do but I feel that Waqar let us down a little bit there. He was in the side to get rid of tailenders, as well as spearheading the breakthrough when the openers were in.

'Although Waqar had mopped up the tail against Lancashire and Sussex, the sparkle didn't seem to be there at Colwyn Bay. There seemed to be a resigned feeling in the field: Oh, these two are going to last, so we'll just plod on! But I didn't say anything to Waqar or any of the players about pulling their fingers out.'

'My worst moment,' says Coral, 'was up at Leicester in the rain when they didn't put the covers on part of the outfield and the game was abandoned. It was awful and all I could think was that

231

we were going to be beaten by the rain again – as we had been earlier in the season against Kent and Yorkshire. Our championship chances seemed to be going down the drain – quite literally!'

The next match saw Surrey's chances of lifting the title disappearing in that direction when Glamorgan declined to continue chasing an improbable victory target at the Oval. Surrey had been bowled out for 487 and Glamorgan needed 254 to win. A draw put paid to Surrey's chances of staying in the championship race. Dave Beck recalls a particular incident during Surrey's second innings.

'There were 7 or 8 wickets down and Martin Bicknell, who eventually made 53, came to the bottom of the pavilion steps and held his hands out to the captain as if to say: Are we going to declare now and have a go at them? It would have been an ideal opportunity and would have given Glamorgan something to aim for.

'As it was, Surrey decided to bat on, leaving Glamorgan a limited time to go for it. The light then became very poor, although to be fair to Matthew Maynard, Glamorgan did take up the challenge in the first few overs. But when they lost a few wickets, I think Matthew was quite right to shut up shop because he hadn't been given a fair deal in the first place. During that match, my hopes started to rise again – we started to see some real grit coming back into it and the finale was absolutely magnificent.

'During the Essex game at Cardiff, I was holding my breath. I thought we had come so far but now we were going to lose it – probably a throwback to the number of times it's happened in the past. But then everything changed when Maynard and Cottey saw Glamorgan home. It was good to see Tony score runs after the poor season he'd had.'

Having kept their nerve against Essex, Glamorgan moved down to Taunton for the championship decider against Somerset. Dave and Coral Beck went with them.

'It was the best feeling I've ever had, as far as cricket is concerned,' admits Dave. 'I have seen England win Test matches but for our own boys to take the title was something extra special. I'd been waiting for it for 17 years – it's a long time but, by damn, it was worth it! It was a dream come true.'

'I just couldn't believe Glamorgan were going to win something,' recalls Coral. 'I was cheering like mad – yelling and shouting and hugging everyone. It was brilliant!'

Dilwyn Pritchard would have loved to have been able to join in the celebrations but, sitting in front of the television at his home in the village of Rachub near Bethesda, he was kicking himself. Having supported Glamorgan for more than three decades, the 48-year-old civil servant at the valuation agency in Bangor had decided not to go to Taunton.

'I was in two minds about going – I had an offer of a lift down with some friends on the Friday but I was working and there were family commitments with my 11-year-old triplets at the weekend. I was very tempted and I now wish that I'd taken the day off and gone!

'To make matters worse, I got home from work on the Friday just as Matthew Maynard was going up the balcony stairs! I later met three of the lads who'd gone down and they were absolutely thrilled – they said it had been a fantastic feeling after the match, which made me regret not going even more.'

Dilwyn is a typical North Wales Glamorgan supporter. He makes the occasional trip down south – he saw the Hampshire game at Cardiff in 1997 – and attends any matches at Colwyn Bay and Liverpool.

'I arrived at the Lancashire game just after play had started on the Saturday morning and it was all over by half-past four! Waqar was going through a purple patch at that stage and he was completely unplayable against Lancashire.

'It was very frustrating being a Glamorgan supporter at Colwyn Bay when Nottinghamshire's ninth wicket pair couldn't be removed. They played very well but I felt Glamorgan bowled too short, especially Waqar. Darren Thomas got a quick wicket after lunch and everybody thought it would be over by half-past three but they were still there at half-past five! I doubted at that stage whether Glamorgan were going to win the championship.'

As a Welsh-speaking Welshman, Dilwyn is delighted by the number of home-grown players in the championship side. 'Everybody looks upon Glamorgan as a Welsh team and although they're based down in the south, people up here do identify themselves with Glamorgan as the national team. There is a lot of support across the whole of North Wales – and, remember, Matthew Maynard was brought up in Menai Bridge.'

Welsh exiles make up a substantial part of Glamorgan's travelling support. Lyn Thomas saw his first county match against Surrey at St Helen's in 1956 and became hooked two years later.

233

The 50-year-old director of an insurance company lives with his wife Anthea in Chipstead, a small village just outside Croydon in Surrey. Originally from Landore in Swansea, Lyn has lived in the London area on and off since 1972 and for the last seven years, has been accompanied to matches by Anthea. They saw twelve of Glamorgan's 1997 championship games.

'One of my unfortunate memories of the season,' says Lyn, 'is arriving at Leicester half an hour before the scheduled start on the Saturday and finding the umpires walking off, having abandoned play for the day! That was a shock because it was such a lovely morning but overnight rain had affected the uncovered cover-point area of the ground. Like everyone at Grace Road – including the Leicester players – I felt utterly frustrated.

'My other memory must be Matthew Maynard's innings of 161 not out at Worcester. I've never seen anything quite like it. Glamorgan were 78 for 3 when he came in and they needed 276 to avoid the follow-on. They ended up with 398 as Matthew played an immaculate innings. Nothing went off the floor, not a chance – he was absolutely fantastic. He scored a duck in the second innings and we lost the match but it was a great solo performance nevertheless.

'I didn't see Matthew's knock in Taunton because we only went for the Saturday. I remember twelfth man Alun Evans running on all the time to give some tablets to Waqar, who wasn't feeling well after his stomach upset, as well as the part I played in Darren Thomas's five-wicket haul in Somerset's second innings.

'He'd already taken two of them when he came over to field on the boundary near us and I told him that his rugby team, Llanelli, were easily beating their French opponents in the European Cup. He punched the air and went on to blast out three more Somerset batsmen!

'After the game, I remember hugging Hugh Morris as he went to talk to a few supporters. I think it shocked him a little because he wasn't expecting it but he just laughed! I felt elated at Taunton. I was at Canterbury when Glamorgan won the Sunday League in 1993 but this was much better – it was the big one.'

One of Glamorgan's most devoted supporters-in-exile, Laurence Parry, had also been at Canterbury. He was in the crowd at Taunton too, having flown over from his home in Florida to watch about half of Glamorgan's 1997 championship games.

Laurence was born in Llandrindod Wells, went to school in

Colwyn Bay and has spent his working life in hotel management in Britain, France, South Africa and America. He now owns two hotels and six restaurants in Sarasota, not far from Tampa in Florida. Every year, he organises the Sarasota International Cricket six-a-side tournament which features a team from Glamorgan. Having become a member in 1986, Laurence takes every opportunity to watch the county play.

'I took my wife Valerie to Taunton,' recalls Laurence. 'She hates cricket but I drag her to matches whenever we come to Britain. I'm a bit sensitive and I must admit I had tears in my eyes and a beer in my hand at Taunton.

'It was such a great feeling to come back and see Glamorgan win in front of a crowd made up almost completely of people from Wales. It was one of the highlights of my life. My only regret was that I missed the Morris-Maynard stand on the Friday. We were staying in Bristol but we went to Taunton to find it pouring with rain early in the afternoon. Any play looked hopelessly out of the question and because Valerie was getting a little impatient, we went back to Bristol and heard what had happened later when the weather cleared up.

'I was in the member's enclosure on the Saturday but Valerie found herself in the middle of the Glamorgan supporters with a friend of her's who'd never been to a cricket match in her life! They had an absolute ball – they fell in love with the game! They had no idea that cricket could be so much fun. Taunton was a very special day which I'll treasure for as long as I live.'

Not far away from the ecstatic scenes at the County Ground, a life-and-death drama was being played out in the intensive-care unit of Taunton's Musgrove Hospital. Sid Morgan, a retired watch repairer from Glanrhyd near Ystradgynlais, thought his time was up after suffering a massive heart attack.

Sid had arrived in Taunton on the Friday morning with a group of friends from Ystradgynlais. They'd met up with Hugh Thomas, a retired civil engineer from Meidrim near St Clears, who was already in town.

'We decided that we would stop in a local supermarket for a cup of coffee on the way to the ground,' recalls Hugh. 'Sid suffers from a shortage of breath and as we walked along, he said he had to stop for a bit.'

'I've got chronic emphysema,' says 65-year-old Sid, a Glamorgan supporter for more than fifty years, 'and I didn't feel very well.'

235

'I told the other boys to walk on and I stayed with Sid,' recalls Hugh. 'We made our way slowly towards the ground while the boys went to the supermarket. Sid had to stop about three or four times and each time he looked progressively worse. It was obvious that he wasn't too clever, so I asked a girl who was passing if she could call an ambulance.

'Eventually, it turned up and luckily so did Sid's nephew Phil Morgan. They carried Sid into the ambulance – he couldn't get his breath at all. They put him on oxygen, asked us a few questions and Sid told them that he didn't have any heart pains. I packed Phil off with Sid to the hospital and, after I'd collected the other boys, we followed on.

'We made our way to the cardiology unit where we found Phil with his head in his hands. The doctors had said that Sid's heart had stopped beating for about five minutes but they'd managed to recusitate him and he was now in intensive care. They'd thought he was a goner and they weren't holding out much hope of him recovering.

'There was nothing we could do, so we went back to the ground. Rain meant play hadn't started until 3.50 p.m. and the first ball we saw was the one which ended Matthew Maynard's marvellous knock! He was out for 142, caught behind.

'The nicest part of it all,' says Hugh, 'was that after Glamorgan won the championship on the Saturday, we went to see Sid in hospital on the Sunday morning. He was sitting up in bed, surrounded by newspapers and his immediate family. He knew before we arrived that Glamorgan had won!'

'I think I can just about recall getting into the ambulance,' says Sid, 'but the next thing I remember was waking up in hospital the following day. I had all these tubes coming out of me and the staff told me what had happened.

'It was fantastic when I heard Glamorgan had won – even though I hadn't seen a ball bowled. I was in a bit of daze when I heard the result.'

The postscript to this heart-stopping story illustrates the close relationship between Glamorgan's players and their supporters. After spending a fortnight in hospital in Taunton, Sid underwent a successful by-pass operation at Morriston Hospital. As he recuperated at home, the boys from Ystradgynlais rang Sophia Gardens to explain what had happened to their friend.

'I received a lovely card signed by all the team, apart from

Waqar who'd gone back to Pakistan by that time,' says Sid. 'It was much appreciated. I'm glad I'm alive and on the mend now – I feel a lot better, thanks to the win over Somerset!'

When his heart stopped beating at Taunton, Sid Morgan almost died and went to heaven. When he arrived at the pearly gates, did St Peter tell him the news from the County Ground or was it an angel who let slip on the way up that Glamorgan had won the county championship? Whatever happened, Sid obviously decided that heaven could wait. Back from the dead he came, safe in the knowledge that, after a lifetime of supporting Glamorgan, Saturday, September 20th was the day heaven arrived on earth.

PART 8

Those were the Days

TAKE THREE BOYS
(Thirty years on)

Tony Lewis, Don Shepherd and Peter Walker. Three Glamorgan County Cricket Club legends.

As captain, Tony led the county to their second championship; he was chairman when they won their first trophy for nearly a quarter of a century, and as trustee he helped broker the deal which led to his side of 1969 finally taking their place in the history books.

Don dismissed the last Worcestershire batsman to clinch the title for Glamorgan three decades ago and is the only bowler to have taken 2,000 wickets for the county.

Peter holds the record for the number of career catches for a Glamorgan fielder and achieved the best 'treble' ever recorded in nearly 150 years of first-class professional cricket: 1,500 runs, 103 wickets and 73 catches in 1961.

All three played key roles in ending Glamorgan's 21 years in the wilderness after Wilf Wooller's side won the Welsh club's first championship in 1948. Tony was the leader, Don and Peter his trusty lieutenants. All three are still involved in the game: Tony Lewis is a BBC television presenter and writer, Don Shepherd works as a commentator for BBC Radio Wales and Peter Walker is Director of Development for the Cricket Board of Wales, a broadcaster and a member of Glamorgan's cricket committee.

Last season provided the trio with a unique opportunity to make a final, fading trip down memory lane. No longer would they be members of the last Glamorgan side to win the championship. For 1969 read 1997. The county had new heroes – and the old ones couldn't have been more pleased.

'I have to be honest,' says Tony Lewis, 'I didn't see much of Glamorgan during the summer – apart from at the beginning of the season and then towards the end.

'Because I was a captain too, my main memory is of the way that Matthew Maynard batted when it was imperative that Glamorgan played well. In the last three games, having tried Mike Powell as the extra batsman, they reverted back to the five specialists with Croft at six, which meant that Matthew really had to apply himself.

'It was great to see a captain who can separate his own speciality from the job of being captain. You do need the Hugh Morrises of this world, the pillars of any team, but you also need the players who can get runs quickly.

'I remember Matthew playing to his true capabilities at the time, in the month when it was required. It's difficult to combine both roles but he's got the antennae to do it.'

The view from the commentary box was formed over the whole season as Don Shepherd followed Glamorgan around the country for Radio Wales. He had been encouraged by the improvement in 1996 and felt that the county could be a force to be reckoned with – given a reasonable start to the season.

'I recognised that Glamorgan were a pretty good, well-balanced side,' recalls Don. 'We didn't quite know how Waqar was going to perform; Duncan Fletcher was an almost unknown coach but he came with this reputation of being able to bind sides together and the immediate signs were that he gelled well with Matthew and they made a very good team.

'After the frustration of being foiled by the weather against Warwickshire and Yorkshire, Glamorgan showed they were a good side by beating Kent at Canterbury. Left-arm spinner Dean Cosker picked up four wickets in Kent's second innings and I felt that if he could play regularly and thereby balance up the spin attack with Robert Croft, then Glamorgan would be able to cope with all conditions.

'The defeat by Middlesex caused some despondency but when they decisively beat Lancashire at Liverpool and we really saw the best of Waqar, you began to feel that something was meant to happen. After he did it again against Sussex at St Helen's and then Glamorgan beat Gloucestershire, it was a question of them maintaining their form when people were expecting them to win.'

From his office in Glamorgan's portakabin at Sophia Gardens, Peter Walker has a front-row view of the county's matches in Cardiff. As well as fielding phone calls rather than catches, the one-man band of the Cricket Board of Wales normally had his head down working at his computer during 1997. But Peter had a vested interest in keeping in touch with the drama unfolding on the other side of the boundary fence.

'My first memory of the season is going out to lunch with Mike Fatkin,' says Peter, 'who, in my view, is comfortably the best secretary Glamorgan have ever had. He has vision, energy, humour and he's very methodical.

'As we went along Cowbridge Road to the restaurant in late April, I said to Mike that I fancied a bet on Glamorgan winning something. We stopped off at the bookies and I put a tenner on them to take the championship at 14-1. At the end of the season, I felt it only right to share my good fortune, so I bought some champagne for all the office staff to have a party!'

Tony Lewis was out of the country when the glasses were being raised at Taunton and all points west. The former captain and chairman was deep in the heart of enemy territory – playing golf in Kent, the county pipped at the post by Glamorgan after one of the closest championship races for years.

'*The Sunday Telegraph* rang up at ten past seven on the Saturday night wanting a thousand words from me by eight o'clock. I couldn't believe it because I wasn't expecting it to happen so soon – I thought Glamorgan might win the next day. Anyway, I got my computer out of the car and wrote the first 870 words that came out of my fingertips. I met the deadline but missed the Welsh edition.

'My dream has always been for Glamorgan to be a top side, as we were in my day. It was disappointing after that to see everything fall apart, to see Glamorgan scuttling along the bottom for so long and the county become a laughing stock – that's really why I took on the chairmanship.

'I was fed up sitting in press boxes around the world as Glamorgan became the butt of so many lousy jokes. The first thing I did as chairman was put a new press box in both Swansea and Cardiff. The then Glamorgan secretary, Philip Carling, and I decided to concentrate on improving the flow of service to the media, the opinion-formers.

'When they won at Taunton, I felt relieved for the players who'd always been reminded of 1969 by almost everyone. But not by my team, because all players want their successors to succeed.'

'Wherever I go to speak at cricket-related lunches or dinners,' says Peter Walker, 'the 1969 win is always used when I'm introduced – now they'll have to think of something different! I'm happy to share my part of Glamorgan's fame. It's like being asked for autographs – you start to worry when people don't want yours!

'Taunton was particularly poignant for me because the BBC Wales television producer, Gareth Mainwaring, showing a deft touch, decided to let Don and I describe the closing moments – me as commentator and Don as summariser – before Alan Wilkins, another former Glamorgan player, came in to wrap it all up.

'It's said – often correctly in my view – that when you've retired, the game is never as good as it was in your playing days and that no side is as good as yours. So when you see another team about to emulate what you've done, there are inevitably some negative as well as positive vibrations.

'Don and I looked at each other in the commentary box and realised that we were about to lose our mantle of invincibility, but alongside this we discovered a huge kick in sharing, albeit from a distance of 75 yards, the way in which Glamorgan won that game. It was an immensely emotional moment because I didn't think I'd ever see it again in my lifetime – Shep certainly didn't either!

'We sat and watched our successors produce some brilliant stuff. It was a two-day win over Somerset because one day had been washed out by rain – it was a fantastic performance. They simply demolished the opposition. There was a growing realisation that this side was fit to be ranked with anything we played for or against.'

As in 1969, comparisons between Glamorgan's championship-winning sides have inevitably been made. How does the present team match up to the side led by Tony Lewis? Would Matthew Maynard's men have given Wilf Wooller's 1948 winners a run for their money?

'The great similarity between 1969 and 1997 was that we only used thirteen players and they used fourteen,' says Tony Lewis. 'But the great difference is that we only played three-day cricket. I had an overseas player in Majid who was a batsman who could bowl a bit, whereas with the extra day, you need a strike bowler. Within the space of three days, a batsman was fine because we'd squeeze people into tight corners and they'd take chances against decent bowling, but over four days they have to be bowled out.'

Don Shepherd remembers the late run which took Glamorgan to their second title after a dreadful start to the season. 'We were bottom of the championship at the end of the first month and Gloucestershire were something like 50 or 60 points in front. But then we got on a roll and we weren't under as much pressure in coming from behind. In 1997, Glamorgan were at or around the top all season.

'It's difficult to compare the two because, as well as the extra day now, we had no restrictions on short bowling. Both were good sides and all you can say is that you are the best team at the time. We were undefeated while the 1997 side lost two matches – one was a freak result and in the other, they were going for a win.'

Peter Walker believes the two teams shared a sense of collective responsibility forged from a unique Welsh team spirit. 'When someone went through a bad patch, either with bat or ball, another member of the team did the business. All you have to do is to swap 1997 for 1969.

'Everyone of our players could point to a game which they won or helped to win – as can the present squad. We had fine players like Tony Lewis, Alan Jones and, of course, Majid Khan, a genius with the bat on the day when the moon was in the right quarter. Then there was Bryan Davis, an unsung hero at number five who didn't get a hundred until the last game of the season at the Oval, when the championship had already been won in the previous game. We wanted to become the first side since Lancashire in 1930 to go through a season unbeaten in the championship and Bryan helped to do that. He also often made scores in the 50s, 60s and 70s when the top four had failed.'

Another difficulty in comparing the two sides is the type of pitches used in the respective county championship campaigns. Open to the elements in 1969 and therefore erratic in behaviour, the pitches in the Nineties are fully covered under regulations introduced by the Test and County Cricket Board in 1980. The wickets are now more bland and predictable.

'In our day, if you averaged 33 with the bat,' recalls Tony Lewis, 'you'd had an immense season. If you average 45 nowadays, you've had a good season. I believe covered pitches account for a lot of the bad batting you see today. When we were playing, every wicket had a bit of green in it and it spun and seamed a bit too.

'Another important difference was that in 1969, there was no limit to the number of batting points we could pick up. We would aim to score as many runs as we could as fast as possible to get another bonus point. So we had a lot of people down the order wacking away in search of that extra point.

'We nearly always got a good solid start from Alan Jones, a class player and Roger Davis, a good county batsman. The sum total of Roger's talents added up to a lot. In pure and simple batting, he was a very good foil for Alan. Majid was probably the best batsman

in both the sides – 1969 and 1997 – and his match-winning
potential persuaded others that we could win from any position. I
batted at four, Bryan Davis went in after me because his West
Indian technique was a little too loose and adventurous for an
opening batsman. At first, he didn't want to bat at five but he
turned out to be a fine player in that position.

'Peter Walker, a wonderful all-rounder, went in at six and then
in Eifion Jones, we had a keeper who could really bat. He was
followed by Malcolm Nash and Tony Cordle, both of whom could
get quick runs. Everyone chipped in and even a natural hitter like
Don Shepherd learned how to block for the first time, so that
someone could slog at the other end if necessary. Personally, I
tried to play the sort of innings that the team wanted – it often
worked but sometimes didn't. I'd either run out of luck or play a
bad shot.

'We had a great quartet of close fielders – Bryan Davis at first
slip, Majid at second and Roger Davis and Peter Walker on the leg
side. They were breathtaking, outstanding. Matthew wasn't that
well-blessed but he usually managed to get people in the right
place at the right time.'

Twenty-nine years ago, a similar debate to the one concerning
Colin Metson and Adrian Shaw took place in the Glamorgan camp.
Who was to be the team's gloveman? Like Metson, David Evans,
the purist keeper, only played once all summer as Lewis opted for
the wicket-keeper-batsman Eifion Jones.

'We had some excellent bowlers, particularly Don Shepherd
who was a class above everybody else. And in pure wicket-taking
terms, there was Malcolm Nash who, without Waqar's pace, was
just as effective.

'It's impossible to say which of the two teams was the better.
You can only be as good as you need to be in the era during which
you play. 1948 was the same. You can get over simplistic about it –
I've been in the past, as too was Wilf – but what I would say is that
it's now a different game playing on covered wickets.'

The former captain is full of praise for the man who led
Glamorgan to their third county championship. 'Matthew made
brave decisions, he knew what he wanted and where to put certain
fielders and he followed the maxim: Always do to the opposition
what they want you to do least. For example, if you're batting on a
slowish pitch, it's annoying having a fielder standing there on the
drive because if you mistime it, the ball might go to him.

246

'The running of Steve James and Hugh Morris between the wickets was fantastic. They played at a similar tempo to us. Matthew was exceptional but they all contributed – even Tony Cottey who lost confidence during the season but, come the big match towards the end, proved to be a real pro. He made bricks without straw – even when he wasn't playing well. When it mattered, he got runs.

'The balance of the side was very important. We knew from previous years that the batting was strong, the fielding was as good as anyone else in the championship and, as well as Waqar, Steve Watkin and Darren Thomas, there was Robert Croft, the best off-spinner in the country. Bowling in tandem with a promising slow left-arm spinner, Dean Cosker, they were a formidable combination.

'Although no daily whirlwind like, say, Gloucestershire's Mike Procter was in our era, Waqar was still able on most days to blow away the tail. With players like that, you've got all known situations catered for.

'When you're playing for Glamorgan, you automatically have a tremendous team spirit and great public interest. Our former skipper, Alan Butcher, told me that he'd played for Surrey at the Oval for years and had never seen a camera crew on the ground but when he came to Wales, he couldn't move for them! There's always a lot of local Welsh media attention which does help you to bind together.'

According to Peter Walker, the 1997 Glamorgan team was unique – and not just because of the high proportion of home-grown Welsh players. 'In any side, there's usually someone who's a bit of an irritant, particularly if he's one of the better players. It increases the competitive spirit, which is no bad thing, because other players may be rubbed up the wrong way and want to do better than him. There is no such individual in the Glamorgan side. Instead, there are a lot of very solid citizens like Steve Watkin, an absolutely model professional and human being, and Adrian Dale who's a super bloke. However, we mustn't forget that it's easy to be pleasant when you're winning. You can also go the other way and become arrogant but if you've got any sensibility at all – and this is a very sensible bunch of blokes – there's no gloating in winning, just a quiet satisfaction in succeeding.'

The decision to expose the team's almost incestuous Welshness to the overseas influence of coach Duncan Fletcher has been widely applauded but Tony Lewis doubts if such a move would have been made in 1969.

'Obviously, the present committee and the players were keen to go outside and, like Waqar's signing, the decision to appoint Duncan Fletcher has been vindicated. My generation would never have wanted a coach like Duncan because they believed that you didn't win matches from the balcony. You had to go out into the middle and do it yourself. If you relied on a coach, then you'd have tended to use him as a crutch and an excuse for your own failure. We felt you should face your own failings and remedy them – it toughened you up as a player and a person.

'At the same time, the 1997 committee felt there was a need for an outside motivator and perhaps the players did need somebody new. The truth is they were very talented but Duncan seemed to help them deliver the goods. The modern game seems to require such a person, whereas our era didn't.

'I would concede that Duncan had an effect on the way the players performed because they all accepted him and his methods – and that's good. It's just that the concept is difficult for my generation to understand – perhaps you really can't teach an old dog new tricks!'

As the dust settles on a remarkable season for Glamorgan, another old dog is now charged with the responsibility of helping to produce the next generation of championship-winning Welsh cricketers.

For the last two years, Peter Walker has been Director of Cricket Development for the Cricket Board of Wales, the umbrella organisation for the game in the Principality with special responsibility for junior cricket – the 11 to 17 age group. The CBW encourages the creation of vital links between school-children and adult clubs.

'The win couldn't have come at a better time for Welsh sport, let alone Welsh cricket,' says Peter. 'We've had a decade of failure from Welsh rugby and football – no other team game has done anything in that time.

'I've noticed a perceptible increase in optimism, bouyancy and enthusiasm for cricket. There's a huge number of volunteers and kids throughout Wales who are obsessed with the game and there's now a new confidence which will last, whether Glamorgan successfully defend their title or not.

'The win has transformed Glamorgan's viability. There are

sponsors coming on board whereas before it would have been a hard sell to get them interested. Big companies and organisations want to be associated with success. At present, Sophia Gardens compares unfavourably with the Test match grounds but with the kind of impetus winning the championship has given the place, the selling of the club will be easier. By the year 2003-04, the money now coming in will enable the ground to develop facilities to rival anything, other than the six Test match venues.'

Like many former players, however, Peter Walker is anxious to ensure that the county doesn't lose its provincial, homely quality as a result of the Cardiff expansion plans. He welcomes the decision to retain St Helen's as a county venue, thanks to the efforts of the Swansea Balconiers over the winter.

'Ex-players will tell you that, until recently, Swansea had the best atmosphere of the lot – most of the great games involving tourists and championship wins were played at St Helen's where there's a very strong core of support. It would be a terrible shame to lose that altogether if Glamorgan were to decide not to play in Swansea and other parts of Wales because of the exciting and essential developments in Cardiff.

'Glamorgan recognise the unique position they hold in English cricket. They are a national team playing as a county and I don't think that the club will lose sight of that by putting all their eggs in the Cardiff basket.'

The knock-on effects of the championship win are already being felt at the Cricket Board of Wales. Junior cricket is very difficult to sell but progress is being made.

'For most sponsors,' explains Peter, 'there's little mileage in that age group. You've got to attract an organisation with a community spirit or a wealthy businessman who perhaps wants to put something back into his home area. But we have managed to land a couple of sponsorship deals purely on the back of Glamorgan's championship win.

'The former football referee Clive Thomas, now managing director of Caxton Facilities Management, has agreed to donate £2,000 over the next three years for a project in the Rhondda valley, and Carnaud Metal Box Food Ltd, a Neath-based company, came on side just before the championship was won, having seen that Glamorgan had had a very good season, thanks to some home-grown players. They're now owned by an American parent company with headquarters in Worcester. Metal Box's factory at

Baglan, near Port Talbot, is still an important part of their jigsaw and when I spoke at a retirement dinner for one of their senior executives, two of the head-office staff were in the audience. They heard me tell the story of 12-year-old lad who came to the Rhondda Fach leisure centre in Ferndale for coaching.

'Alongside his mother, I watched him play from the balcony. I was told that she brought him to the coaching session whenever she could from their home in Penrhys, the notorious housing estate overlooking the two Rhondda valleys.

'As I drove back to Cardiff in the pouring rain, I passed them on their way home. The boy was still in his whites and he had one of those little airport trollies with his cricket bag on it. He and his mother were bent double going up the hill without a coat or an umbrella. I wound down the window and offered them a lift.

'"No thanks," she said. "It's very kind of you but we're used to this walk. It won't take us long." And off they went. I found out later that she could only afford the bus fare one-way but wanted her son to have a chance to develop his talent.'

When Peter sat down after telling the story, the two directors asked him how they could help children to receive coaching.

'I suggested a scheme called the Dragon Awards which tutors kids in the basic skills and had been underwritten by SWALEC for three years. When they withdrew, the scheme had nose-dived for a year but Metal Box agreed to put in £7,000 a year for three years. It was later doubled by Sportsmatch to bring it up to £14,000 for junior cricket development, which was a bit like winning the lottery! That was as a result of my story falling on receptive ears and Glamorgan's achievements during the summer of 1997 giving it the necessary focus.'

'The timing of the championship win was perfect,' agrees Tony Lewis. 'We're looking for money, we want to develop, we want to create interest and we're no longer the laughing stock of the first-class circuit. Glamorgan cricket has been through some rough patches over the years but now we do have a chance to develop from the grass-roots.'

In the short term, the current Glamorgan team will be striving to retain their championship – something neither the 1948 nor 1969 side managed to do. Even without Hugh Morris and Duncan Fletcher, confidence must be high. How do the three men who masterminded the last-but-one championship win by the county think their successors will fare in the coming season?

'We finished second in 1970,' recalls Tony Lewis, 'but we were limping home – never ever going as well as the year before. I think Kent won their last ten matches. We had good hours and bad hours – but not enough of the good ones.

'Losing Hugh Morris gives another batsman an opportunity to come in but what people mustn't expect is normal service at the start of the season. There are quite a few things to be done before you can presume that you're the same team. I think they've got the talent to retain the title – Robert Croft's presence will be vital but he might be required for six Tests during the 1998 season.'

'We should remember that, besides his batting contribution, Hugh Morris was also a very good slip catcher,' says Don Shepherd. 'His departure does open the gate for a young batsman like Alun Evans, Wayne Law or Mike Powell who've been waiting for their chance. I also think Tony Cottey will return to form to make up for Hugh, at least in part.'

'If you look at the top order of the batting,' says Peter Walker, 'they're all just the wrong side of thirty. Bowlers may win matches but batsman have got to give you the platform against which you can bowl. For all its experience, the batting in 1997 was a bit erratic. Hugh Morris's departure is a huge loss and it would be unreasonable to expect his natural successor, Alun Evans, to turn in 1,800 runs in a season at the first attempt.

'I wonder, too, whether Waqar has got one more fiery season left in him? He played in 36 one-day internationals in 1997 and the strain and wear and tear is bound to tell. He's not a spent force but he's certainly not the bowler he was in, say, 1993 or 1994. He produced two or three electrifying bursts for Glamorgan in 1997, along with some pretty ordinary spells.

'As well as Robert Croft, it depends, too, on whether Dean Cosker makes the breakthrough for England and whether Matthew Maynard wins a recall. Winning the championship in back-to-back seasons would be like winning the Grand National with 20 stone on your back. You might win a one-day competition when all your best players are available, but not the championship.

'After finishing third in 1968, we won the title the following year and then came second in 1970. It was quite some achievement but I don't think this side can repeat that because the strains and stresses in the modern game are too great – but I wish them well and hope I'm proved wrong!'

'THAT'S OUT . . .
AND WE'VE WON!'

WHEN Wilf Wooller's last innings ended with his death in March 1997, there were thought to be only four survivors of the side which won the county championship for Glamorgan for the first time in 1948.

Allan Watkins, Jim Pleass, Phil Clift and Gilbert Parkhouse all played a significant part in lifting the trophy 27 years after Glamorgan had become a first-class club. The rest – Johnny Clay, Emrys and Haydn Davies, Len Muncer and Willie Jones amongst them – had all passed away, their place in the county's hall of fame secure.

But when he formed the Glamorgan Former Players Association ten years ago, a thought kept niggling away in the back of Jim Pleass's mind. Every summer, the association's members would meet at Sophia Gardens to discuss the good old days and every summer, Jim would ask himself: Whatever happened to Jimmy Eaglestone?

Like Pleass, Eaglestone was a middle-order batsman and first-rate fielder who patrolled the deep like an over-zealous traffic warden. After arriving from Middlesex in 1948, he disappeared back to London a year later – never to be heard of again. Could he, Jim often wondered, still be alive? With all attempts to trace him having failed, Jimmy Eaglestone was declared 'missing, presumed dead'.

A half-century on, the mystery has been solved, thanks to Glamorgan's Honorary Librarian, David Irving, who helps Jim Pleass organise the reunions. David's persistence paid off and, health permitting, Jimmy Eaglestone will appear – phoenix-like from the ashes of 1948 – at the association's special meeting in June to celebrate the fiftieth anniversary of Glamorgan's first championship win.

'It all began with the gala dinner Glamorgan held in Cardiff City

Hall last November to mark the county's most recent success,' explains David. 'I decided then that I'd have another go at tracking Jimmy down, so I contacted Middlesex at Lord's. They said they hadn't a clue where he was. I then rang Directory Enquiries and was given three J. Eaglestones in the London area. The first was Jimmy's cousin, who hadn't kept in touch with him, and the other two couldn't help either. So far – not so good.'

The breakthrough came when David appealed for help through the letters column in *The Cricketer* and *Wisden Cricket Monthly* under the headline 'Have You Seen This Man?'. The secretary of Pinner Cricket Club in Middlesex, John Spencer, got in touch. He had seen the man in question and contact with Jimmy Eaglestone was re-establshed by telephone.

'I was absolutely delighted,' says David who established Glamorgan's library in 1988, the county's centenary year. 'I had almost despaired of finding Jimmy and the first thing I did was to let Jim Pleass know he had an extra member of the Glamorgan Former Players Association!'

Jimmy Eaglestone was one of three players to travel west to join Glamorgan's seven full-time professionals after helping Middlesex win the championship in 1947. 'Len Muncer was a brilliant off-spinner,' recalls Jim Pleass, 'Norman Hever a great strike in-swing bowler and Jimmy was a forcing left-hand batsman who batted number six. He was a very pleasant fellow, fair-haired, nice-looking, very quiet and modest.'

Jimmy Eaglestone played 50 games in two seasons with the county. He made his highest score of 72 against Sussex at Swansea in 1948 when he appeared in 24 of the championship games.

Jimmy himself doesn't remember too much about his career-best knock for Glamorgan in their six-wicket win. The records show that his innings took 50 minutes and included a six and fourteen fours. The Sussex match was notable for two other milestones: Len Muncer's haul of 15 for 201 meant he was the first bowler to reach a 100 wickets for the season, and Gilbert Parkhouse scored his maiden century on the ground where he had learned to play the game

'I was very proud to play for Glamorgan,' recalls Jimmy. 'They were very good to me and pretty fair to everybody all round – it was a bit different from being at Lord's! In 1949, I was offered a new contract by Glamorgan but I had the chance to go into business by myself – there wasn't the money about in cricket then.

So I opened a confectionery and tobacconist's shop in Paddington and gave up the game completely. If I wasn't playing at the top level, I didn't want to play at all.'

After six years as a shopkeeper, Jimmy then worked for National Cash Registers for twenty years before becoming a clerical officer with the Gas Board. He retired in 1984 and now lives in Pinner with his wife Doris.

'I'm really pleased that I've been tracked down after all these years,' says Jimmy, who'll be 75 in July. 'Rightly or wrongly, I didn't think Glamorgan would want to know about me once I'd finished playing for them. It's nice to think that they take so much interest. I must admit I was very surprised to receive David Irving's letter. My health's a bit up and down at the moment but I hope to be at the reunion. I'm really looking forward to meeting my old team-mates again – those who're still around.

'All my memories of Glamorgan are good. Wilf was a great bloke and skipper and we were all pals together. I remember being pushed all over the place in the outfield, mainly because I was a bit swift around the boundary. We were a very happy band together and I think that's why it all worked out. We didn't have anybody playing for England then – apart from Allan Watkins who made his debut in the last Test against the Australians – and we all helped each other. There was a tremendous team spirit – it must have been the same in 1969 and 1997.'

Indeed, nearly 50 years later, a similar sense of solidarity helped Glamorgan win the title again with only off-spinner Robert Croft appearing for England.

'Things were so different then,' says Jim Pleass, 'but I think there's a comparison to be made betwen the two sides because the 1997 side was an excellent, well-balanced team. They had batsmen who could get runs quickly, they had strike and spin bowlers and, above all, the fielding was absolutely superb. And a lot of that goes back to 1948 because the same thing applied.

'We had people like Emrys Davies, Arnold Dyson and Phil Clift, who would give us a tremendous start, and then the stroke players would come in – Gilbert Parkhouse, Willie Jones, Allan Watkins and Wilf Wooller. We also had about six or seven all-rounders in the side. Willie and Emrys were pretty good slow left-arm bowlers too and then we had Johnny Clay, the great off-spinner who played a few matches.

'The batting highlight of 1948 was when Willie Jones hit two double centuries in the space of a fortnight – 207 against Kent at Gravesend and 212 against Essex at Brentwood.'

Jim Pleass left the Army after the war and returned to his old job of testing road materials in a laboratory. In 1947, whilst playing amateur cricket for Cardiff, he received the call from Glamorgan. After a train ride to Derby, Jim found himself in the team and, having played a handful of matches, was offered a contract for what turned out to be the championship-winning season.

'I got £6 a week for 22 weeks in the summer when I started playing for Glamorgan,' says Jim. 'In the winter, I did some clerical work with the then Contributions Agency, writing out benefit cheques, and I later went to work for Wilf in his insurance business.

'Glamorgan tried various people in 1948, as they had done with me the previous year. David James, another quick bowler like Hugh Griffiths, played just one championship game. Hugh was an amateur working in the legal profession, so his opportunities were limited. He appeared only four times before making the law his full-time career. It was a good choice because he's now Lord Griffiths, a High Court judge and a former President of MCC. Both he and David hope to come to our special 50th anniversary reunion. Personally, I played in about half our championship matches in 1948.'

Fifty years ago, pitches were covered only at the bowling ends and Glamorgan found themselves playing on wickets which were either wet or drying, particularly in Wales. 'Our bastsmen had to learn a new technique,' says Jim. 'We had to play balls that turned square and although *we* learned how to deal with the spinning ball, the opposition couldn't and very often didn't get more than 200 – with our spinners taking most of the wickets.'

Jim Pleass's abiding memory of the 1948 side is the quality of the fielding, not only around the bat but out in the deep as well. 'The spinners were helped by the short-leg fielders in particular. Phil Clift used to stand at short square leg, no more than two yards from the bat. Allan Watkins was at leg slip and any glance off the bat he or Wilf at forward short leg would probably swallow.

'We also had players who could run like deer, pick up in the outfield and throw over the stumps to Haydn Davies – people like Willie Jones and Jimmy Eaglestone. I myself made a speciality of fielding in the covers and that's an art in itself because of the mind battle between you and the batsman. You've got to try to get him to think that if he pushes the ball, he could probably get a single. So you give him one to start but the next time he tries it, you're in that ten yards a bit quicker and you'll very often run him out.

'Norman Hever was our main strike bowler, who produced very accurate in-swingers. He was also a peculiar character who loved life and who could wine and dine until the early hours and then come back at eleven o'clock the next morning and knock out four or five wickets in the first hour. At medium-fast, right-arm over the wicket, he was supported more often than not, by Wilf Wooller and Allan Watkins. Once they had softened up the top order and taken three or four wickets, it was the turn of Len Muncer and Johnny Clay. When we played at Swansea, we had a special bowler for that ground, Stan Trick, a slow left-armer from Neath who spun the ball yards.'

Phil Clift joined Glamorgan in 1936 on a wage of £2 10s a week in the summer and £1 during the winter. After nearly 200 matches and more than 6,000 runs, he retired in 1955 to become the club's coach for the next 20 years. He also took eleven wickets for the county, including three which won a championship match in 1948. Now nearly 80, Phil remembers the 1948 season as his first as an opening batsman.

'Arnold Dyson was coming towards the end of his career and I did reasonably well, scoring just short of a thousand runs. My highest knock was 73 against Kent at Swansea out of a total of about 170. I was caught behind when I got a thin edge to a full toss. I was always a bit of a dasher, really. I used to try to get on with it, often getting out in the 30s, 40s and 50s while Emrys Davies would be there at the end of the day with a hundred to his name.

'I also fancied myself as a bit of an off-spinner but I hardly ever got a bowl because we had Len Muncer. But in the game against Sussex at Llanelli, everybody else had been tried and, in the end, Wilf said I could have a go. I bowled the last three men out for six runs in six overs to win the game.'

The legendary Wilf Wooller led the side from the front. The county had finished ninth in his first season at the helm in 1947. A self-made cricketer, he often wasn't considered good enough for the St Fagans first team in the days before the Second World War but, by sheer hard work and application, he became a fine county all-rounder. Wilf was a self-opinionated autocrat whose decision was final and, even if it were proved to be wrong, he would rarely admit that he had made a mistake.

'Wilf would listen to you,' recalls Jim Pleass, 'but he would always make his own mind up – very often, before the match started. He would go and look at the wicket at Cardiff Arms Park and then say it would suit the seamers, so Glamorgan would play an extra bowler – I'd be twelfth man. We accepted the fact that we had a squad of 13 and we took our turn to play, depending on Wilf's whims. In his view, the best team would be taking the field for that particular day.

'Even if we found that it wasn't a seamer's wicket and the ball turned square, Wilf stuck by his opinion. He was a martinet on the field – if you spilled a catch or fumbled a ball, you would get the Wilf Wooller glare. You had to do what he wanted, when he wanted it done. But he led by example – as Matthew Maynard does. Whatever Wilf said to you on the field, it was forgotten when you were away from the ground.

'I remember we were playing Warwickshire at Edgbaston and quite a few runs were scored on a placid wicket during a dry period. On the last day, with about three hours for Warwickshire to bat, they were 70 or 80 for 1 but we kept on attacking them. With fifteen minutes to go, we'd actually got nine wickets down. It was a tremendous achievement but we couldn't get the last man out. Back in the dressing room, we were commiserating with each other when Wilf stormed in.

'"You're a bloody shower!" he shouted. "Fancy not getting them out!"

'That was Wilf the competitor, but, off the field, he was marvellous company. He would play chess with me in the dressing room and he would mix with the lads even though he came out of a separate dressing room and gate, for in those days there were different rules for amateurs and professionals.'

'Wilf was a great captain,' says Phil Clift, 'a hard, brave man who would never ask anybody to do anything he wouldn't do himself. He was also one of the finest catchers I ever saw. We were playing Somerset at Weston-Super-Mare and Arthur Wellard had already hit Len Muncer out of the ground twice. Wilf was fielding at forward short leg, I was square and Allan Watkins was the one behind. Arthur picked Len Muncer up again with a full-blooded blow. I looked for another six but Wilf had caught the ball in his left hand, just in front of his face!'

Phil Clift felt the full force of Wilf's tongue when injury forced him to miss the run-in to the 1948 season. Fifty years ago, each county played four teams once and the rest twice, making a total of 26 championship matches. By the beginning of August, Glamorgan had won eleven games but then drew four of the next five before beating Somerset by 8 runs. In the middle of the 22nd game against Northamptonshire, Phil finished on 28 not out on the Saturday night.

'On the Sunday, I played in a benefit match at Newport for Arnold Dyson and turned over and broke a bone in my ankle while going for a quick run. I was all bandaged up but Wilf made me go out to finish my innings on the Monday! I didn't last very long after that and then missed the last three games, against Surrey, Hampshire and our defeat by Leicestershire. I was at home in Cardiff when I heard on the radio that we'd won the championship by beating Hampshire.'

'We had to win two of our last three if we were to finish on top,' recalls Jim Pleass. 'We beat Surrey by an innings at Cardiff, thanks mainly to Johnny Clay, who'd just turned 50, taking 10 for 66 in the match – despite Jim Laker picking up five cheap wickets.

'The crunch game was at Bournemouth against Hampshire. Only ten minutes play was possible on the first day because of rain and a result looked very doubtful. Fortunately, we had a full second day and we batted and fielded like champions. We made more than 300 and took six Hampshire wickets.

'The third day dawned bright and clear, the Hampshire innings folded and they followed on – needing 231 to avoid an innings defeat. By mid-afternoon, nine wickets were down for just over a hundred runs and we were crowding around the last pair like vultures intent on their prey. Johnny Clay was bowling and standing as umpire at his end was, of all people, Dai Davies. As a batsman, Dai had given Glamorgan great service during the years before the war. Charlie Knott played and missed, the ball hit his pad and a huge "Howzat!" went up.

'"That's out . . . and we've won!" said Dai Davies, raising his finger.'

In scenes to be repeated at Taunton nearly half a century later, Welsh supporters invaded the Bournemouth ground before the team caught the train back to Cardiff. Thousands of people turned out to greet them and the celebrations at Cardiff Athletic Club went on long into the night.

'The 1997 team's support didn't compare with ours,' says Jim. 'We often played in front of crowds of between ten and fifteen thousand. The war had just finished, there was still rationing, there was no television and there were no motorways – life was very different. The public had been starved of cricket.

'We had a number of Welshmen in the side – not as many as the present team but in those days there was no alternative to bringing in players from outside. There wasn't a glut of cricketers in Wales, men were coming back from the war and I, for one, lost six years of my career. But a couple of years later, we did field an all-Welsh-born side.

'We used to take our cricket out and about. Apart from Cardiff and Swansea, we played at Newport, Pontypridd, Neath and Llanelli but I think it's nice to have a base in Cardiff as they do now.'

Jim Pleass and Phil Clift were still involved with Glamorgan cricket when Tony Lewis's team emulated the 1948 side twenty-one years later. Jim was a member of the county's selection committee while Phil, as coach, had been responsible for bringing through the majority of the team.

'Nearly all the players used in the 1969 side were our own lads,' recalls Phil. 'Virtually everyone, apart from Majid Khan and Bryan Davis. We were doing then what they're doing now – using home-grown players. Many of them like Jeff Jones, Malcolm Nash, Alan and Eifion Jones and Peter Walker had all passed through my hands.

'Eifion, Alan's younger brother, came to us as a specialist batsman. We didn't have a wicket-keeper at the time but I'd seen Eifion in the slips. So one day I asked him if he'd like to have a go at keeping wicket. He never looked back. In 1969, there was a great feeling of elation and I was proud to have had something to do with it.'

Both men watched the 1997 team clinch the title at Taunton on television. They had managed to attend the occasional game at Sophia Gardens during the summer, including the Durham victory in May when the Former Players Association annual reunion was held. Memories of the two previous championship wins came flooding back but the game has changed a great deal since their team created history fifty years ago.

'There is more pressure nowadays,' says Jim Pleass, 'and money is more important than it was. We used to enjoy our cricket. When a wicket falls these days, the players do all this high-fives business and then they lounge around. We used to congratulate the bowler or fielder and then six of us would get in a circle to practise our close catching until the next batsman came in!'

And what about the advent of the modern-day coach? Both Jim and Phil acknowledge the contribution made by Duncan Fletcher to the 1997 side's success but, like Tony Lewis, they question whether such a role would have been needed in their day.

'I don't think it would have gone down very well then, although it seems to be working up to a point now,' says Jim. 'One of the half-dozen all-rounders in our side, George Lavis, was the coach and his job was primarily to build up the second XI players to first team standard. He tended not to coach us because, as first XI professionals, it was thought we should have known all there was to know.

'We always used to say,' recalls Phil Clift, who succeeded George Lavis as Glamorgan coach, 'that if the captain and the senior professional couldn't manage the first team players, then they didn't deserve to be there.'

'Man-management plays an important part in modern cricket,' says Jim. 'You have to treat today's players very differently, depending on how they react to what you say. That's one lesson I don't think Wilf learned. He tended to be the same with everybody – he'd bawl players out when necessary, whereas today they're counselled! Wilf was a great leader but perhaps not a very good man-manager, certainly not for everyone's temperament. You could say we won the championship despite his approach or because we accepted that he was the boss – what he said went.'

The survivors of the 1948 Glamorgan side are a little like the green bottles standing on the wall. Of the four regular members of the side who are left, Gilbert Parkhouse is in poor health at his home at Penygroes near Llanelli, while Allan Watkins lives at Oundle near Peterborough in Northamptonshire and has difficulty travelling.

Phil Clift, one of the two Cardiff boys, has only one regret: 'I wish I was fifty years younger – I'd like to play cricket now because of the limited over game!' The other, Jim Pleass, is simply happy simply to rejoice in the reappearance of Jimmy Eaglestone. This year's former players' reunion promises to be a very special occasion – celebrating not only the 50th anniversary of the Wooller side's initial success but Glamorgan's hat-trick of title wins.

'Winning the championship three times is some achievement,'

says Jim. 'There's a difference of 49 years between the first and third, with one stuck in the middle, but it's something a lot of counties haven't done.'

'Up to a couple of years ago, I didn't think Glamorgan would win the championship again in my lifetime,' admits Phil, 'but now they have, I think it's wonderful. I know what Wilf would have said had he still been with us – "About bloody time!" But he would have said it with a broad smile!'

PART 9

Back in the Pavilion

More Tales from Taunton

'Matthew's innings at Taunton was a joy to watch. It filled the team with so much confidence. It was if he was saying: I'm out here and I'm going to win the championship for Glamorgan! From the first ball, he looked as though he was going to murder them and against some pretty good opposition bowling, he played the knock that every young schoolboy dreams of playing.'

Adrian Dale

'I couldn't see Matthew too clearly but I knew he was playing well. It was pitch black and there were five lights on the scoreboard – in fact, it was so bright you half-expected to find a German sentry on the top patrolling it! I was flitting around the ground while Matthew was at the crease. If you see someone in that sort of form, you have to watch it – that sort of innings only comes around once in a blue moon.'

Mike Fatkin

'My abiding memory of Taunton is never quite believing that we were going to do it and wanting so hard for us to finish it on the Saturday. There was always the chance that it would go on to the Sunday and the weather forecast was so uncertain.'

Tony Dilloway

'When Dean Cosker took the final Somerset wicket, I thought to myself: What a relief! I ran about 70 yards to hug Deano because we're really close and we went off together arm-in-arm. Once we got into the dressing room, I had to go into the corner and just think to myself about what we had done. I must admit, I got a bit emotional and had a bit of a weep. Fletch came in and put his arms around me. I thanked him for everything he'd done for me but he told me not to be so soft.'

Darren Thomas

'I wanted a stump as a souvenir so I had a word with Steve James before he went out to bat with Hugh Morris.
"Look, Jamo, whatever you do, you've got to get me a stump!" – and he did, even though he lost it on the way back to the pavilion!'

Adrian Dale

265

'When I actually hit the ball, I thought we would get one run, maybe two if I ran quickly. But when I got down the other end, I saw Hugh picking up the stumps and running off! The ball had gone for four, but I still thought we needed one more to win! I realised I'd miscounted so I grabbed a couple of stumps but in the melee, as the crowd came on, I lost my bat and one of the stumps.'

Steve James

'My brother Gary, who's a policeman in London, was down for the game and he saw this guy running off with one of Steve's stumps. He went up to him, tapped him on the shoulder and showed him his police identity card.

"Give me that stump or you're nicked!" he said.

So the guy handed it over and Gary gave it to me.'

Adrian Dale

'A couple of supporters put me on their shoulders, then one of them slumped to the ground and I suddenly hit the deck with a bump – it was quite frightening! I had my helmet on and everyone was banging me on the head.'

Steve James

'At this stage, Steve was still being mobbed out in the middle and I saw this other guy running off with another stump. He agreed to swap it for my shirt, so I stood on the boundary waiting for Steve to come off – with two stumps of my own! I felt like telling him not to bother! In the end, Steve kept his and I gave one of mine to Matthew.'

Adrian Dale

'When I got to the dressing room, the celebrations were in full swing and I felt like a bit of a gatecrasher. You always dream about hitting the championship-winning run but I made such a cock-up of it. I could have been out twice for 0 and then I didn't even realise they were the winning runs when I'd scored them!'

Steve James

'When Steve hit the winning runs, I was on the balcony without a pint in my hand for the first time that day – I was absolutely thrilled! I'm a great supporter of Glamorgan cricket, whether I'm on the committee or not. Since 1993, the club has had superb support and I felt so good for them. I looked around the County Ground and saw all those people so happy.'

Roger Davis

'The celebrations were brilliant – I picked up a couple of cracked teeth from being in the dentist's chair with Waqar shoving bottles of champagne down my throat!'

Darren Thomas

'In 1993, Mike Fatkin and I were both in the crowd downstairs, waiting beneath the balcony. But this time we had both decided we wanted to be part of the dressing room – you don't win the championship every year! The players made us feel very welcome, which was great because if we'd felt uncomfortable we wouldn't have stayed. They appreciated what it meant to us as well.'

Tony Dilloway

'I remember pulling all the players into the dressing room and locking the door. I told them to enjoy it for as long as they wanted – even up until Christmas. I then presented Fletch with a Welsh rugby jersey. He was delighted and touched by it. It really showed. Duncan really fitted into our unit well and the shirt was something a bit special from the players that I know he'll remember for a long, long time.'

Matthew Maynard

'Obviously, it was a very proud moment for me. I had worked with the guys and it was like an acceptance that I was now part of this very proud country. It was an indication from the players that I was part of their community.'

Duncan Fletcher

'When we were up on the balcony at Taunton, I just wanted the guys to enjoy it after working so hard for it all summer. All the tension had gone. I hadn't slept too well for the last fortnight. The adrenalin had been pumping so hard – thinking about the games and the weather – I really just wanted to get out there and play all the time.

'My son Tom managed to find his way into the dressing room and Waqar put a bottle of Budweiser in his hand and told him to enjoy it!'

Matthew Maynard

'The relief we felt as members of staff was for the boys rather than ourselves. They had worked their nuts off all summer and they deserved their success. They've been so close in one-day semi-finals before but this was the big one – like climbing Everest.'

Dean Conway

'It was good for me to go back to Taunton because I was coached by Somerset when I was in school at Millfield. It was nice to show people there what I could actually do. It was a big occasion for me because, in a way, I was the local boy made good. The Somerset coach, Peter Robinson, who's also a left-arm spinner, used to come down to the school for a look but he didn't seem to rate me at all. But he did come into the dressing room to say well done. It was sweet for me to take the final wicket to win the championship against the side who didn't rate me but I don't bear any grudges.'

Dean Cosker

'Taunton is one of those days that will live with me for ever. It was like winning the Welsh Cup in rugby or the Premiership in football. It might seem strange but once it was all over and the realisation that we'd actually won the championship had set in in-the dressing room, I felt a certain sense of anti-climax. We'd done it. What were we going to do now?'

Adrian Shaw

'My memory will be the dressing room at Taunton. Everyone was there – Mike Fatkin, Tony Dilloway and most of the committee and we were just all hugging each other. It was the sheer exhilaration, the overflowing of emotion and the controlled delirium that I'll never forget. To see Duncan Fletcher, a great supporter of South African rugby, standing there, knocking back a can of beer and proudly wearing a Welsh rugby jersey like an honorary Welshman was really something! I did a double-take at first. Then I suddenly realised it was Duncan who had the biggest smile on his face.'

Andrew Hignell

'When Waqar and I were in the Somerset clubhouse celebrating with the boys, we said to each other how nice it was to come over to Wales and perform well and, in the process, make everyone happy. We had both participated in our different ways to create this success for these people who had been looking for it for so long. People mustn't forget that the supporters are part of that success – because of them, the players perform better. Hopefully, they'll think of me – and not just Waqar – as an honorary Welshman!'

Duncan Fletcher

'On the Saturday night, I went out with Steve Watkin and his sister Lynda. We were trying to get a taxi back to the team hotel. There were about fifty people waiting at the rank but there was no sign of any taxis. Eventually, we managed to flag a passing cab down. The driver agreed to take us to the hotel as long as we didn't mind if he picked up a fare on the way. We piled into the back of the cab and his customer turned out to be a Glamorgan supporter who'd been at the game. He'd had quite a bit to drink and he proceeded to tell the taxi-driver what a great team Glamorgan were. Every now and then, he kept turning round and looking Steve straight in the face without recognising him. It didn't click at all – he went on and on for about ten minutes. The driver explained to us that he was taking this supporter all the way back to Cardiff that night for about £70, because he couldn't find anywhere to stay in Taunton. As we got out of the cab and paid the driver, Steve gave the supporter a tenner towards his fare – and he still didn't know who he was!

'"Thanks, mate," he said and the taxi drove off into the night.'

Caryl Lloyd Jones

'My abiding memory of the summer will be the morning after the night before. I remember waking up in my hotel room in Taunton which I was sharing with Tony Cottey – not the same bed, I might add – and seeing seven Hendy boys splattered all around the room! The fridge had been drunk dry and everything was everywhere. Thankfully, we didn't have to clear it all up! That's what summed it up for me – the fact that people from the Hendy area were prepared to travel all the way down to Taunton to support us, seeing Waqar Younis and the rest of the lads mixing with the crowd, hearing Waqar singing "Waqar is a Welshman!" and watching him blow the bugle that one of the Hendy boys took down to Taunton – marvellous!'

Robert Croft

'I remember coming down from the changing room about five minutes after we'd won the championship and being greeted by one of our supporters:
'"It'll be difficult to follow that next year!"
'I just thought how ephemeral this game is. So many people have waited nearly 30 years for this moment and suddenly it was gone – we had moved on. Maybe that's sport, I don't know.'

Mike Fatkin

'I was absolutely delighted because I'd watched Glamorgan just about every day throughout the season and I would have hated for them to have got so close and just missed out. It was a long campaign and when you see it culminating in a great win, then you're bound to feel emotional.'

Don Shepherd

'I wasn't at Taunton and, sadly, neither was Wilf, but he was always bullish when we'd won, so he'd probably have told Somerset how awful they'd been! But Wilf was also hugely critical when we didn't win – that was his way. It's just nice to know that they can win – that's the great thing. There's nothing quite like beating seventeen other teams to win the title – it's the professional's prize, they value it because winning a league means so much more to pros.'

Tony Lewis

'At Taunton, you saw a very good side play in an extremely professional way. They had to go there and, in the space of four days, get maximum points against a useful side – even without the injured Mushtaq Ahmed – in uncertain weather. They did the job in three. That summed it all up for me. To see a coach and a captain get it right after we as a committee had put our trust in them was very satisfying.'

Roger Davis

269

'Glamorgan winning the championship in such style at Taunton will have an effect which will last for ten years or more. Young players have now got tangible heroes to relate to instead of misty legends. From this inspirational season will emerge players who, in the next Millennium, will have the same motivation to win the championship as the outstanding team of 1997.'

Peter Walker

'Afterwards, my main concern was to make sure that I didn't leave a trophy worth £30,000 with the players as they started a night of celebrations, so I took it back to South Wales with me. As I drove home, I just couldn't believe we had won the championship! I heard it on the car radio and then I saw it on the television when I got home but I still found it hard to take in – I still do, even today.'

Mike Fatkin

'Winning the championship was unreal – they can't take it away from you. I can still watch videos of 1993 and Taunton and they bring tears to my eyes – it moves me. You don't work here for 13 years and not become part of the emotion of it all.'

Tony Dilloway

'The moment when I lifted the championship trophy and showed it to our fans at Taunton was just terrific – something I had always dreamed about and something I will never forget.'

Matthew Maynard

SOMERSET v GLAMORGAN
The County Ground, Taunton 18th, 19th & 20th September

SOMERSET	1st innings	
RJ Turner	c Thomas b Watkin	40
PCL Holloway	b Waqar Younis	0
SC Ecclestone	c Morris b Waqar Younis	0
MN Lathwell	b Waqar Younis	62
ME Trescothick	c Maynard b Croft	20
M Burns	b Waqar Younis	28
PD Bowler	c Morris b Watkin	63
GD Rose	lbw b Cosker	13
AR Caddick	c Croft b Cosker	11
KJ Shine	c Morris b Watkin	6
BJ Trott	not out	1
Extras	(lb 6, nb 2)	8
TOTAL	(all out, 68.4 overs)	252

FoW: 1-17, 2-17, 3-72, 4-113, 5-155, 6-156, 7-197, 8-217, 9-251.
Bowling: Waqar Younis 12-3-41-4; Watkin 13.4-2-61-3; Thomas 16-2-53-0; Cosker 14-3-42-2; Croft 13-1-49-1.

SOMERSET	2nd innings	
RJ Turner	b Thomas	38
PCL Holloway	c Shaw b Thomas	25
SC Ecclestone	c Morris b Watkin	10
MN Lathwell	b Thomas	47
ME Trecothick	c James b Croft	16
M Burns	c Shaw b Thomas	18
PD Bowler	lbw b Thomas	3
GD Rose	c Shaw b Watkin	67
AR Caddick	not out	56
KJ Shine	c James b Watkin	0
BJ Trott	lbw b Cosker	0
Extras	(lb 3, nb 2)	5
TOTAL	(all out, 70.4 overs)	285

FoW: 1-60, 2-67, 3-88, 4-133, 5-145, 6-153, 7-166, 8-261; 9-273.
Bowling: Waqar Younis 11-0-84-0; Watkin 15-1-75-3; Thomas 15-2-38-5; Cosker 11.4-3-34-1; Croft 18-5-51-1.

GLAMORGAN	1st innings	
SP James	lbw Caddick	8
H Morris	b Caddick	165
A Dale	c Bowler b Caddick	8
MP Maynard	c Bowler b Shine	142
PA Cottey	c Bowler b Shine	13
RDB Croft	lbw b Rose	86
AD Shaw	not out	53
SD Thomas	c Ecclestone b Trott	0
Waqar Younis	c Ecclestone b Trott	5
SL Watkin	c Shine b Trott	5
DA Cosker	b Caddick	7
Extras	(lb 7, w 12, nb 16)	35
TOTAL	(all out, 99.4 overs)	527

FoW: 1-12, 2-42, 3-277, 4-293, 5-404, 6-475, 7-478, 8-482, 9-495.
Bowling: Caddick 34.4-5-132-4; Shine 17-3-88-2; Rose 29-3-152-1; Trott 11-0-74-3; Burns 7-0-65-0; Bowler 1-0-9-0.

GLAMORGAN	2nd innings	
SP James	not out	9
H Morris	not out	1
Extras	(lb 1)	1
TOTAL	(0 wicket, 1.2 overs)	11

DNB: A Dale, MP Maynard, PA Cottey, RDB Croft, AD Shaw, SD Thomas, Waqar Younis, SL Watkin, DA Cosker.
Bowling: Caddick 1-0-5-0; Rose 0.2-0-5-0.

Glamorgan won by 10 wickets

1997 Britannic Assurance Championship

			P	W	L	D	Bt	Bl	Pts
1	(10)	Glamorgan	17	8	2	7	50	57	256
2	(4)	Kent	17	8	4	5	44	60	252
3	(7)	Worcestershire	17	6	3	8	49	54	228
4	(9)	Middlesex	17	7	4	6	33	56	219
	(8)	Warwickshire	17	7	2	8	32	51	219
6	(6)	Yorkshire	17	6	3	8	41	54	215
7	(13)	Gloucestershire	17	6	6	5	35	60	206
8	(5)	Essex	17	5	6	6	39	55	192
	(3)	Surrey	17	5	5	7	39	52	192
10	(1)	Leicestershire	17	4	1	12	37	54	191
11	(15)	Lancashire	17	5	6	6	34	54	186
12	(11)	Somerset	17	3	3	11	38	64	183
13	(17)	Nottinghamshire	17	4	3	10	26	55	175
14	(14)	Hampshire	17	3	5	9	42	41	158
15	(16)	Northamptonshire	17	3	5	9	33	48	156
16	(2)	Derbyshire	17	2	9	6	32	59	141
17	(18)	Durham	17	2	8	7	22	56	131
18	(12)	Sussex	17	1	10	6	24	57	115

1997 Glamorgan Britannic Assurance Championship Averages

BATTING	M	I	NO	Runs	HS	Av	100	50
SP James	17	28	4	1605	162	66.88	7	6
MP Maynard	17	23	6	1106	161*	65.06	3	7
H Morris	16	26	4	1207	233*	54.86	4	3
A Dale	17	25	3	840	142*	38.18	2	5
RDB Croft	13	18	1	577	86	33.94	0	4
PA Cottey	15	19	4	370	76*	24.67	0	1
AD Shaw	17	20	5	352	53*	23.47	0	1
SD Thomas	16	16	4	259	75*	21.58	0	1
GP Butcher	9	9	1	172	58	21.50	0	1
Waqar Younis	16	17	1	289	47	18.06	0	0
MJ Powell	3	6	2	62	41*	15.50	0	0
SL Watkin	17	16	3	138	39	10.62	0	0
DA Cosker	13	8	5	14	7	4.67	0	0

Also batted: AW Evans (1 match) 31

BOWLING	O	M	R	W	Av	BB	5w	10w
Waqar Younis	441.4	83	1551	68	22.81	8-17	3	1
SL Watkin	508.2	143	1393	61	22.84	7-41	2	0
RDB Croft	504.2	118	1259	54	23.31	5-33	1	0
SD Thomas	330.3	49	1160	44	26.36	5-24	2	0
GP Butcher	65.4	14	270	8	33.75	3-87	0	0
DA Cosker	255.3	62	736	20	36.80	4-64	0	0

Also bowled: PA Cottey 3.3-1-19-0; A Dale 49.1-11-169-0; MP Maynard 6.5-0-39-0; MJ Powell 1-0-3-0